Rugged Trails

and

Ragged Shoes

*Joys and Heartaches
of Lora Heatwole
in Mountain Missions
1926-1936*

JANIS GOOD

CHRISTIAN LIGHT PUBLICATIONS
Harrisonburg, Virginia 22802

RUGGED TRAILS AND RAGGED SHOES
Christian Light Publications
Harrisonburg, Virginia 22802
©2014 Christian Light Publications, Inc.
All rights reserved.
Printed in the United States of America

ISBN: 978-0-87813-761-9

Third Printing, 2019

Cover and Inside Design: David W. Miller

"This narrow, rough, winding road has been trodden by many footsteps. Some steps have been very light and care-free, while others were weary and worn. I am glad the stones can't talk."
—Lora Heatwole

Table of Contents

List of Characters

Mission Workers

(All names are actual names.)

Lora Heatwole—Main character who served ten summers at the Roaring Creek mission, from 1926 to 1936.

Nellie Coffman—Lora Heatwole's aunt who was a schoolteacher and assisted with mission work in the 1920s and early 1930s.

Rhine Benner family—Rhine (father), Anna (mother), James, Rhoda, Elva, Timothy, Millard, and Evelyn. The Benners served from 1922 to 1929 in the Roaring Creek mission.

S. H. Rhodes—Bishop who had oversight of the West Virginia missions.

Esther Moseman—Young lady from Pennsylvania who helped with the first vacation Bible school in 1927.

Paul and Eula Good—Resident minister in the Roaring Creek mission between 1930 and 1934 and again in later years. They had two sons, Emory and Harley, while in West Virginia.

Lelia Swope—A single woman who worked at the mission and in the community in the early 1930s.

James and Vada Shank—Resident minister in 1934-1935. They had a son, James Leonard.

Mary Huber—Single woman who assisted the mission during the summer of 1935.

Ida Eshleman—Young woman with nurse's training who assisted in the work in 1935-1936 and also used her nursing skills in the community.

Community People

(Fictional names unless otherwise stated.)

Tillie—A fictional character who plays a part central to some actual events.

Bill—Tillie's husband.

Cal and Millie—Husband and wife.

Noah and Polly Vance—Polly was a faithful Christian and loyal church member. They had several children.

Gertie—Girl for whom Lora sewed.

Myrtle—Girl whom Lora visited.

Bertha Morral *(actual name)*—Lady who delivered mail.

Solomon—Known as "Sol," an elderly man who played the fiddle.

Sadie—An unwed mother.

Della *(actual name)*—Widow with several children; one son died in the army.

Gracie—Fictional character true to setting.

Jake— Friend of the Benner family and mission workers.

Bessie—Young lady who attended girls' club.

Jane *(actual name)*—A poor elderly widow.

Guy Arbogast *(actual name)*—Nine-year-old student of Aunt Nellie's.

Wayne—Teen who lived with Abe and Lizzie.

Jerry—Young boy whose father was a moonshiner.

Jason and Mattie (pronounced MAY tee) **Vance** *(actual names)*—Faithful supporters of the Christian faith and mission work. Jason was a schoolteacher and a farmer. Mattie's full name was Emmatie.

Sarah Vance *(actual name)*—Elderly lady with tuberculosis; a loyal Christian.

Warren Hedrick—Widower.

Mrs. Maud Ketterman *(actual name)*—Ailing wife of Oliver. Oliver donated land for a church.

Mary Ketterman *(actual name)*—Faithful Christian and church member, daughter of Oliver and Maud, married to Ralph Swope.

Avis—Unwed mother who became a faithful Christian and married in the faith.

Earl Champ *(actual name)*—Faithful Christian and loyal to the church.

Rosie—Troubled girl whom Lora mentored.

Ralph Swope *(actual name)*—Husband of Mary Ketterman and helper in the churches.

Daisy—Faithful Christian who married in the Lord. She and her husband assisted with the church work.

Jack—Young man shunned by local girls.

Harry—Local boy.

Buddy—Local young man.

Ruby—Young lady who experienced a radical spiritual change and caused her community to take notice.

Denny—Local bachelor.

Abe and Lizzie—Neighbors and friends of the mission workers.

Other Characters

(All names below are actual names)

James (Jim) Shank—Driver who took Lora and Aunt Nellie to West Virginia, and father of James T. Shank who served as resident minister.

John Moseman—Pennsylvania minister who brought his daughter Esther to the mission.

John Mumaw—Young man from Pennsylvania, special friend and future husband of Esther Moseman. He also held revivals in the region.

Ernest Gehman—Talented artist and fellow student of Lora, Aunt Nellie, and Esther.

Russell Mumaw—Talented artist and Lora's Bible school classmate

Ruth Garber—Earl Champ's boyhood Mennonite teacher.

H. B. Keener—long-term mission worker in West Virginia. He has a daughter Mary.

Preface

Years ago, someone said to me, "There's a story behind Lora Heatwole and Nellie Coffman. Don't let it go."

What the story was I didn't know. In 1997 I decided to drop all other writing interests and pursue Lora's story since Lora was getting up in years. Being laid up for a time gave me an opportunity to make many phone calls gathering information, which further fueled my interest.

I made repeated trips to visit Lora and her sister Nancy. What Lora couldn't remember, Nancy filled in with descriptive information. Nancy and others directed me to one person after another. Through much prayer and patience, the memories that many shared about Lora's West Virginia work eventually came together like pieces of a puzzle.

Leaving the comforts of her home in Virginia's Shenandoah Valley, Lora spent ten summers in West Virginia missions. She was unafraid of hard work, willingly sacrificing time and money, finding in exchange deep fulfillment in working in the Kingdom.

James T. Shank, Lora's fellow mission worker at Roaring Creek, said this about her, "Lora was a good worker. People liked her. She knew how to work with people. She knew when to talk and when not to talk."

I was inspired by Lora's ability to work hard and be happy doing it. While I researched this story, I was busy with my own growing family. Lora told me repeatedly, "It's good to be busy." She was cheerful in everything she did.

Her sister Nancy said that Lora would sing one song right after another all day long.

My prayer for this book is that we will each be inspired to sacrifice willingly, serving faithfully to experience the full rewards of Christian service. Even when we cannot see the results of our labors, the Lord sees, and the fruit of the work goes beyond what we could ever see. In addition, I have tried to plainly present the way of salvation that Lora and other mission workers worked so hard to share.

—Janis Good

Chapter One

Rugged Roads

1926

Lora Heatwole peeked past the curtains into the gray morning to see two headlights. "They are here!" She snatched her gingham sunbonnet from the hook by the door and tied it into place. "Right on time," she said to her mother, "and just a few minutes before six."

Her mother scurried from the kitchen where Lora had just finished breakfast, the smell of bacon and eggs still lingering on her apron.

"I hope you have a safe journey, Lora. You will write to us, won't you?"

"I will, Mother."

Lora grasped the handles of her well-stuffed baggage and hustled out the door Mother held open for her. She skimmed down the steps just as the Model T stopped in the driveway.

"All aboard!" Aunt Nellie grinned as Lora slipped into the back seat beside her thirty-year-old aunt.[1]

Lora crammed her bulging luggage into the tight quarters and turned to wave at Mother. There was no need to make a fuss over her departure. That just didn't happen in her household. Besides, she would be gone only a few months.

"Good morning, Jim," Lora spoke to the driver. "I'm all set and ready to go."

"All right, fair ladies, let's be on our way." Jim Shank's eyes crinkled at the corners as he shifted gears. "There's a long trip ahead on this fine June morning."[2]

Lora glanced at Aunt Nellie, a gleam of anticipation in her eye. "Finally, we can go!"

Her scholarly aunt's eyes twinkled. "Oh, comrade, we are off on an adventure."

The Model T puttered past the barn where the soft lowing of cows broke the morning silence. Lora turned for a last glimpse at the familiar, square brick house where a few lights lit the windows. Home—that place nestled in a hollow surrounded by fertile, rolling fields just outside of Dayton, Virginia—warmed her heart.

She smiled. It was a good home. She had grown up in a large family, the oldest of twelve children. At twenty-three, her callused hands knew the virtue of hard work and had

---

1 Patricia H. Hertzler, *The Story of Melvin Jasper Heatwole and Mollie Grace Coffman*, pp. 21, 23, 27. Lora Frances Heatwole, born November 3, 1903, was the daughter of Melvin Jasper Heatwole (1878-1963) and Mollie Grace Coffman Heatwole (1883-1956). Nellie Coffman (1896-1986), Lora's aunt, was the daughter of Joseph Weaver Coffman (1857-1933) and Sarah Heatwole Coffman (1859-1958).

2 James H. Shank was a deacon in Virginia Conference and had come out of the Old Order church a few years before this. He was interested in the mission work of the church.

the skills for many domestic duties. She had received years of Bible training and had learned practical ways to live the Bible daily. She would miss her family, but at last she was headed west for a new and different life.

Lora sang, and Aunt Nellie harmonized with her:

"I'll go where you want me to go, dear Lord,
 Over mountain, or plain, or sea;
 I'll say what you want me to say, dear Lord,
 I'll be what you want me to be." [3]

As morning light diffused the darkness, they passed through the countryside and approached the mountains that loomed in the west. Some miles later the travelers entered the foothills where ferns grew lush along the streams. The flash of a white-tailed deer disappeared into the underbrush beyond the crystal-clear stream. Just ahead the road curved and grew steep, a switchback here and a hairpin turn there, always winding upward. The motor revved a deeper hum.

Lora took a deep breath to ease the nausea that stirred in her stomach. This trip would not be easy. Though she recognized the familiar symptoms of motion sickness, she dared not complain. Today—June 4, 1926—she was finally on the way to her much-anticipated destination. Fresh, cool air filtered through the windows, which helped a great deal to ease her queasy stomach.

Adjusting her glasses, Lora watched the sun-dappled road churn beneath the wheels. By now her head ached with the constant movement. She shivered and buttoned her duster.

---

3 "Consecration," *Church and Sunday School Hymnal,* No. 105.

"Who would have thought you could shiver in June, Aunt Nellie?" Lora murmured.

Aunt Nellie replied, "Well, Lora, we're in the mountains. Remember?"

Lora gave a weak smile while her head throbbed and her stomach churned. The steep incline challenged the Model T, but eventually it crested the peak and rolled downhill toward a sharp bend. Jim hugged the inside of the road to keep away from the unprotected precipices. A stunning view of distant mountains outlined the horizon beyond the valley. The lone automobile seemed but a speck on the long road that twisted through this rugged country, bumping through potholes and huffing up steep, rough roads, leaving a thin trail of dust lingering in the air.

*Miles of narrow, and sometimes dangerous, roads
wound deep into remote mountains.*

Drawing her gaze back to the roadway, Lora gasped and clutched the edge of her seat as another curve loomed directly ahead. All of her life she had heard about these mountain roads. Now she understood what folks had said at her family table. Lora shuddered. A wrong move could mean disaster, perhaps the end of life. *Lord, grant us a safe journey*, she prayed.

Jim shifted into a lower gear and expertly maneuvered through each curve and challenge. Lora breathed a sigh of relief, thankful that the Home Mission Board had asked him to take them to their destination. No woman in her right mind would drive these rugged, remote roads alone, for travelers in these parts could expect flat tires, an over-heated motor, and delays of many kinds.

"Feeling all right?" Aunt Nellie asked.

Lora answered, "I'll be glad when we get there. Riding is never easy for me."

"I know," Aunt Nellie replied sympathetically.

Lora was miserable. She squirmed among the packages and bags. If only she could squelch her misery, if only the journey would soon end. She just might have to ask Jim to stop so she could relieve her ailing stomach.

The Model T rounded a turn and shuddered to a stop.

"Better give the vehicle a rest," Jim said. "This looks like a good place to enjoy a view too."

Lora scrambled out and took deep breaths of pure air. Ah! It helped to stop moving. She stood by Aunt Nellie as the two gazed westward.

The mountains loomed much closer, green and textured with trees at the edge of the deep valley, where dark forests sprawled among the patchwork of meadows, fields, and thin patches of fog. Tiny houses and buildings lay scattered in the lowlands like pieces on a board game. Here and there smoke drifted from chimneys even on this summer day, for in this country temperatures dipped at night, and a fire could be needed to chase away any lingering dampness.

This remote region of West Virginia was deep in the Appalachian Mountains, an immense stretch of multiple

The view of Germany Valley.

ranges that lie sandwiched between the eastern seaboard and the central plains. During the Civil War this mountain land had protected soldiers and dissenters, and in some regions had even furnished a dividing line for loyalties between the Confederates and the Union. To the east, Virginia held fertile farmlands, cities, towns, and seaports up and down the Atlantic coastline. To the west, unseen railroads ran down to Midwestern cities, the Ohio River, or to ports on the Great Lakes. On either side of the Piedmont, industries sought the resources of this rugged highland.[4]

---

4 Charles Ambler and Festus Summer, *West Virginia, The Mountain State,* 2nd edition, pp. 4, 5, 437.

Lora sat on a rock. Underfoot, dew dampened the thick grass that shot up from brown stubble. She picked a white daisy and studied the petals.

Handing the blossom to Aunt Nellie, she asked, "How's that for something more luxurious than Solomon's robes?"

Aunt Nellie grinned. "Think of it. This flower exists here on the mountain's heights in spite of furious winters and vicious winds. Here it lives, enjoying the simple life far from the bustle of the world beyond this place."

Lora studied the flower's center. She wasn't as scholarly as her aunt, but she often reasoned without saying everything she thought. Within each flower a host of seeds waited to bring life again, perhaps somewhere beyond this spot of earth. How far might the seeds go until they lodged in the soil to sprout and grow?

Birds twittered and there was a flutter of wings in the underbrush. In the open sky, a red-tailed hawk soared while a gentle breeze whispered among the leaves.

Lora sensed Aunt Nellie nearby, and both of them gazed westward. Somewhere over there the Rhine Benner family lived among countless mountain folks. Lora's heart stirred. Who would she and Aunt Nellie meet when they arrived? Could they encourage the Christian girls and assist the weary missionary mother? What awaited her and Aunt Nellie in the hill country beyond?

"Well, Lora," Aunt Nellie quipped as she pushed a red wisp of hair off her forehead, "your grandparents never had an ornery 'Tin Lizzie' to buck the trails. Can you imagine how long it took them to travel by horses into those ridges over there?"

Lora nodded, staring at the peaks against the horizon. "About three days. Just think, Aunt Nellie, Grandpa and Grandma Coffman and Grandfather and Grandmother Heatwole spent time in these very mountains spreading the Gospel!"[5]

"And now we get to help too!" Aunt Nellie's eyes glinted with enthusiasm.

Jim said, "I hope the Lord will bless your efforts."

"Thank you," Aunt Nellie responded. "I hope so too."

Jim added earnestly, "I'm interested in what's going on in West Virginia and want to support this work."

Jim poured gasoline into the tank. With a last glance at the valley, the travelers located a shady place to eat lunch, yet they dared not dawdle too long. It would not do to be caught in this wilderness away from shelter. Lora began to sing again, while Aunt Nellie and Jim joined in with harmony.

> *"But if by a still small voice he calls*
> *To paths that I do not know*
> *I'll answer, dear Lord, with my hand in thine,*
> *I'll go where you want me to go."*[6]

Then they were back on the winding road where blossom-filled blackberry brambles sprawled along the banks and patches of sunlight flickered in dark forest shadows. The woodland thinned, giving way to meadows and farms where men worked the fields with horses and women hoed

---

5 Patricia H. Hertzler, *The Story of Melvin Jasper Heatwole and Mollie Grace Coffman*, pp. 16, 17. Lora's grandparents, Joseph and Frances Heatwole and Joseph and Sarah Coffman, served at various times in the West Virginia missions. One summer both couples lived in the mission house at Job, WV.
6 "Consecration"

their gardens. A fragrant scent drifted in through the car windows.

"Ah, honeysuckle! I love that smell," Aunt Nellie said.

"There it is." Lora pointed to the vines rambling up the roadside fences. She breathed in long and deep.

"I'll go where you want me to go, dear Lord,
Over mountain, or plain, or sea . . .[7]

One mountain range followed another. The road wound past rippling brooks and lazy rivers, past pink laurel clustered on shady banks and through rocky fords. Lora's stomach quivered as the vehicle limped up the other side of the river.

Thump, thump, thump.

"What was that?"

Jim stopped and inspected the tires. "It's a flat," he stated. "I'll have to put on a tire patch."

Lora sighed with relief. "Good. I'll get some fresh air."

Then onward they traveled through small villages and hills. Minutes ticked into hours.

"Look, Lora, there is a school." Aunt Nellie spotted the lone schoolhouse sitting along the banks of a river.

Lora pointed out a small church. "People must be living here. I see a house 'way up there on a ledge." More words from the old hymn came to her, and she started to sing again.

"There's surely somewhere a lowly place,
In earth's harvest fields so wide—
Where I may labor thro' life's short day
For Jesus the crucified . . .

---

7 Ibid.

. . . I'll do Thy will with a heart sincere,
I'll be what you want me to be."[8]

Jim guided the Model T into a narrow valley where two ridges rose sharply on either side of the road. A gradual uphill climb crisscrossed a creek at various points and led past a mill where water rolled across a great wheel. Near the building a man on horseback stopped talking to other men and looked up to see who was coming. Jim waved as the curious men watched them pass.

"We're getting close," Jim said. "Can't be much farther."

Lora leaned forward to take in the new environment where she and Aunt Nellie would soon be living. Homes and scattered buildings clung to the banks just yards from the creek. A swinging bridge stretched across rushing water and joined a path that disappeared into the woods. Who lived there? How soon would they meet, and would they be friendly or gruff?

A chorus of dogs alerted the community that strangers approached. Children stopped playing and women peeked from doorways and windows. From mountainside fields, farmers looked down and watched the vehicle sputter to a stop.

"Troubles," Jim said as he pulled the car to the side of the road to check on the vapors that curled from under the hood.

"Adventure, you mean?" Aunt Nellie quipped.

Lora untied the bucket from the running board. "I'll get the water."

Somehow Aunt Nellie's comment did not seem as funny as usual. If only she could get relief from her misery. She

---

8 Ibid.

walked to the stream, splashed cold water on her forehead, and scooped up a bucket of clear water. Suddenly she heard a feminine voice.

"Howdy."

She turned. Just up the opposite bank a teen girl with short, blonde hair grinned shyly at her. The girl held the hand of a chubby toddler. Surprised by their sudden appearance, Lora returned a warm smile.

"Hello. I'm Lora."

The timid teen grinned. "I'm Tillie."

"Glad to meet you, Tillie. I'm coming to stay for a few months with the Benner family. Do you know them?"

"I stop in fer visits sometimes."

"I hope you will come see me sometime," Lora invited.

"I will." The girl hoisted the child onto her hip.

Lora waved. "Good. I'll be expecting you."

Lora carried the bucket back to Jim, her spirits improved. "I guess an auto needs a drink just like a horse sometimes."

In a short while the travelers rounded the last corner, and there stood the mission house. Lora's heart skipped a beat. Jim looked at his watch, stretched, and yawned.

"It's two o'clock," he said. "The journey took us eight hours."[9]

Lora smoothed her wind-blown hair and stepped out of the car. "We're here! Now if I can just get over this nausea, I'll be ready to get to work."

---

9 According to Lora, this was considered a trip made in good time.

Chapter Two

The Mission Home, a Haven

1926

L ora took a deep breath. She heard the loud rush of water. In the distance, the muffled barks of dogs dwindled while the dust settled on the road.

With bulging luggage in each hand, Lora paused beside Aunt Nellie to survey the two-story mission home. An old apple tree, its gnarled limbs clustered with young fruit, leaned over the porch roof. She scanned the upper windows and nudged her aunt.

"Which one will be our room?" She nodded at the upper windows.

"We'll soon find out," Aunt Nellie returned, grinning.

Lora drew another deep breath while a smile turned up the corners of her mouth. "This place is wonderful—fresh air, the song of the creek. I already love it."

When the mission board had asked her to consider serving here, she had not needed weeks to think it over.

The church's mission program was mushrooming with opportunities for personal workers. The work of itinerate circuit preachers in previous years had opened scores of communities where Sunday schools had sprung up. Souls had awakened under exposure to the Gospel, and mission boards and church leaders had become aware of pressing needs for leaders and personal workers in many areas. New believers needed mature Christians and leaders to guide them in daily Christian practice. The call was urgent. Come and help! Now!

Lora's heart had raced when she read the pages of detailed information in the mission supplement of *Gospel Herald* concerning the needs.[1] She helped in Sunday school work at home, but what about the many children in isolated communities who needed Sunday schools? She took in every word of the articles. Women were needed to relate to mothers about home problems and to teach hygiene, sewing, and cooking. But even more urgently needed were personal workers who could concentrate on moral, social, and spiritual issues.

The doors of opportunity were flung wide open, and the church was compelling people to enter and become busy in the Lord's work. Lora's eyes brightened whenever she read these reports, and she often discussed the needs with Aunt Nellie.

Aunt Nellie's eyebrows had lifted above her rimmed glasses. "Teaching young women and children the Bible?" Her eyes blinked with intense interest.

---

1 C. Z. Yoder, "Evangelism Among the Mountaineers of the Allegheny Highlands;" Lelia Heatwole, "Opportunities For Service Among Our Mountain People," *Gospel Herald,* August 6, 1925, p. 389.

"The church is involved in a great work!" Lora exclaimed. "Song services. Visitations. Relating to women and girls. I'm definitely interested."

Her heart had thrilled when the request came. She knew what her answer would be.

The board member had asked to speak to her. "The work in West Virginia is growing, and the Benner family needs dependable help for Sister Benner and her young children. Also, teachers are needed in the Sunday school work. The board felt that since you have taught children's classes, you would fill the need quite well. Would you consider working there this summer?"

She had felt like shouting her answer at the top of her lungs, but restrained herself. Instead, she had answered in calm, measured words even while her heart thumped with wild excitement.

"I would be happy to go."

The board member continued, "Girls and women need the encouragement and fellowship of other Christian women. It will be a big calling."

"I'm sure there will be challenges," Lora had acknowledged. "Yes, I will go."

Lora thought again about the call to service. Her answer had been easy to give in spite of making good wages at the factory. She was so glad she had said yes. And now she was here!

As she moved through the gate, a man of slight build crossed the lawn with long strides, a wide grin on his face.

Brother Rhine Benner clasped the hand of each guest. "Welcome to Roaring Creek Mission."

"Hello," said Lora setting down her luggage to greet him. "I'm Lora Heatwole." She turned to greet the Benner girl lingering on the porch, with hands entwined behind her back.

"My name is Rhoda." The girl smiled shyly.

"Come in," Rhine Benner said, motioning them to the door where his wife waited to welcome them. "You must be weary."

Roaring Creek Mission Home

Lora picked up her belongings and crossed the threshold.

"Looks like you've been painting," Jim Shank noticed.

"The place needed paint so the mission board gave me the job," Rhine responded with a chuckle.

"Welcome," Anna Benner's tired eyes sparkled as she grasped Lora's hand firmly and gave her the kiss of charity. "It's so good to have you come."

Gently Lora tickled the two-year-old's chin. "Hello. My name is Lora. What's yours?"

Little Elva hid her face in her mother's skirts while Anna picked up baby Timothy. A tall, thin boy of thirteen appeared from somewhere and silently observed the newcomers.

"This is our oldest, James," said Anna, smiling.

"My mother sent some things for you," said Lora as she handed her a box.

"And here are items from my mother too," Aunt Nellie added.

"Why, thank you." Anna beamed with delight as she gave the baby to Rhoda and took the gifts while the children clustered close to watch.

"It's been a while since we enjoyed hard cheese," Anna exclaimed. "We will surely enjoy this. We cannot buy some of these things here. I must write and thank your parents. Rhoda, please take the cheese to the springhouse. I'll get you visitors some mint tea."

"Delicious!" Aunt Nellie sighed.

Lora sipped the fresh tea. "Absolutely refreshing."

Anna said, "You must be tired after that long drive over the mountains. Let me show you your rooms."

She led the way up the stairs and directed Jim to his bedroom. Then she took the women to another room.

"There's a bed, but the dresser is being used. Feel free to freshen up." Anna picked up the pitcher and poured water into a large bowl. "There are nails to hang your dresses along the wall. It's the best we can do."

"We will manage fine," said Aunt Nellie as she placed her satchel on the bed beside Lora's bags.

"Just make yourselves at home."

"Thank you. We'll soon be down to give you a hand," Lora said.

"Some helping hands will be welcome," Anna said. She smiled wearily and started toward the sound of the baby's whimper.

Lora pulled a washcloth from her luggage, moistened it, and drew it across her face. Ah, that felt better. She hung her dresses on the wall along with Aunt Nellie's. Under the bed she placed an extra pair of shoes. Since the dresser already was filled, Lora and Aunt Nellie left their belongings in their travel bags and shoved them under the bed. They would manage somehow.

Down in the kitchen, Lora rolled up her sleeves and went to work along with Aunt Nellie. A song leaped from Lora's lips, and soon the others joined her in singing as energetic hands moved quickly and skillfully.

"There's work for the hand and there's work for the heart,
Something to do, something to do;
And each should be busy performing his part,
There's something for all to do.

There's work for the aged and work for the young;
There's work for us all and excuses for none;
There's work for the feeble and work for the strong;
There's something for all to do."[2]

Lora stirred a pudding for the next day's Sunday dinner, Aunt Nellie swept the floor, and Rhoda folded the diapers while Anna cared for the little ones. Late in the afternoon,

---

2 "Something to Do," *Church and Sunday School Hymnal,* No. 520.

Rhine Benner answered a knock on the door.

"Ker fer some fresh groun' hog?" The eyes twinkled beneath a shaggy head of hair and whiskers. "I done skinned it and cleaned it up. Just needs fryin' nup."

"Why don't you take it home and let your wife fry it for you, Cal?" Brother Benner asked.

Cal leaned his gun against the porch wall. "Oh, now, she done throwed me outta the house. Won't you let me have a bite of supper?"

"Sure you can stay," Brother Rhine agreed. "After supper we can take a walk. Maybe I can talk to your wife."

"Won't do no good, sure as I'm livin'." Cal studied the floor. "I'd be most pleased to have fried groundhog though." He grinned, showing some gaps in his teeth.

"Sure," Brother Rhine said. "Come in and join us."

Cal stepped inside and hung his worn hat on a nail.

"Groundhog?" Aunt Nellie questioned when Brother Benner brought the skinned animal to the kitchen.

"Who's making supper?" Brother Rhine asked with a mischievous grin.

"Lora," Aunt Nellie answered.

"Well, I can fry meat. I guess I can fry groundhog too," Lora responded. "Anna, where is your frying pan?"

Lora fried the meat with a sprinkle of salt and pepper and set the platter on the table.

Cal's eyes twinkled as he sat down at the table. He eyed the meat platter with anticipation. Lora slipped into a chair beside Aunt Nellie, her appetite having escalated regardless of wild meat for supper. Cal's bashful eyes ventured to meet her gaze. Lora flashed a warm smile, and knew that any strain would shortly vanish.

Warmth from the kitchen stove soothed the chill of a June evening in the mountains. Lora breathed a soft sigh. The peace and warmth of friendship settled over her like a soft comforter. Nothing seemed much different than at home, except that different people sat at the long table. God dwelt in the hearts of His children in this mission home among the mountain ranges just as He did at home with her family.

After prayer Cal took a generous portion of groundhog along with his beans and potatoes. Lora and Aunt Nellie took ample portions of beans and potatoes but looked for smaller pieces of meat.

After supper, Cal thanked them all for the good meal. He reached for his hat, flopped it onto his shaggy hair, picked up his gun, and wandered up the hollow with Brother Rhine in tow. But Brother Rhine soon returned with a sad countenance.

"His wife won't let him in." He sighed as he sank into a chair.

"You couldn't convince her to change her mind?" Aunt Nellie asked.

Brother Rhine shook his head. "I'm not sure what their troubles are."

"Wonder where he'll sleep tonight," Anna mused.

"Said he had a log to sleep in," Brother Rhine replied. "Said he's done it before."

"Poor man," Lora said as she wiped the dishes. "Perhaps we can go visit his wife sometime, Aunt Nellie."

Brother Rhine nodded. "As you can see, there's plenty of work around here. The spiritual needs are our greatest focus. And speaking of church work, since Anna is busy with our own children, we need your help to lead singing and teach Sunday school."

"That's what we do at home," said Aunt Nellie while Lora nodded in agreement. "Lora is good with singing."

Brother Rhine went on. "I often have a class with new Christians, so you will need to go ahead with the other classes."

Both nodded while Anna smiled her approval.

"There is much to do. Hungry souls are eager to hear the truth. We must make the most of each opportunity."

"When did you move here?" Aunt Nellie asked.

"1922," Anna replied. "We lived up the hollow at the Sheridan Long place at first until the Home Mission Board purchased this place. You can see the house is rather roomy." She smiled as she gestured toward the rooms.

"The mission board paid $1750 for this place," Brother Rhine added.[3] "Now it's a suitable mission home but needs some repairs, as you can see."

Anna smiled at the missionary newcomers. "I hope you will feel at home here with us. There are so many souls to reach, but I seem to be so busy with my family. I wish I could do more."

"We're here to help," Lora said. "Just tell us what to do and we'll do our best."

"How about you help us sing our Roaring song?" Brother Rhine asked with a mischievous twinkle in his eye as he looked from Jim to Lora to Aunt Nellie.

Rhoda Benner clapped her hands over her mouth and snickered.

---

3 Harry A. Brunk, *History of Mennonites in Virginia 1900-1960*, p. 203

Anna joined in the fun. "Let's teach these new missionaries our song."

The Benner family broke into singing, "Bright and roaring where you are, bright and roaring where you are . . ."

Lora looked at Aunt Nellie and began to laugh as she recognized the tune from the familiar song "Brighten the Corner Where You Are." Then she and Aunt Nellie joined in cheerfully, "Bright and roaring where you are . . ."[4]

The group finished the song with a hearty laugh that ended the evening. But Lora didn't know how very real that song would become as she and Aunt Nellie helped to brighten and encourage the lives of people up and down the hollow and high on the mountain ridges. Neither could she know how entwined her life would become with theirs. Tomorrow she would meet them at church.

---

4 This song is a version the Benner family made up and sang frequently in their home.

Chapter Three

Sunday

1926

L ora and Aunt Nellie walked the short distance to church on Sunday morning to the sounds of rushing water, punctuated by faint birdsongs drifting from treetops. The two eased toward the creek bank where dewdrops shimmered like jewels. They stood in silence, savoring the beauty about them while a flutter of blue swooped across the creek and landed on a low branch. The bluebird twitched, his tail flipping this way and that to maintain balance.

Looking upstream, the two women watched as the water splashed along beneath a tunnel of trees. The currents rippled through sunlight and shadows, gurgling past rocks of all sizes, a swirl to the right, a sweep to the left, splashing, tumbling, and bubbling along, then spilling down wide gray rocks in a white spray to spin a moment in a whirlpool of foam and then racing on and on, faster, faster, toward the slow lazy river on a long journey to the wide ocean.

The stream reminded her of a refreshing promise God offered in the Bible: "I will pour water upon him that is thirsty, and floods upon the dry ground: I will pour my spirit upon thy seed, and my blessing upon thine offspring."[1] Lora sighed. God certainly was able to provide everlasting Living Water, but people had to be thirsty and willing to receive Him. God would never force Himself on anyone. Would she and Aunt Nellie and the others be able to convince the listeners of the blessings that awaited them if only they would open their hearts?

The loud rush of water made Roaring Creek a constant presence in the hollows of the community and offered a pleasant place for refreshment.

She already knew the job would not be easy. A great enemy was at work to thwart God's work in people's hearts. Many would not be convinced of their need of the Saviour; however, a number had already responded to the Gospel. Today she and her aunt would meet some of them.

---

1 Isaiah 44:3

Just up the way, a small white church nestled beneath the two mountains that towered on either side of Roaring Creek. The chatter of voices and skipping of feet announced the presence of the Benner children. Lora and Aunt Nellie turned away from their quiet reverie and started toward the church, mindful of the new duties pressing upon them.

Roaring Church, where the mountain people
loved to come and hear the Word taught.

"No one has arrived yet," Lora said as they joined the Benner family.

"They are coming." Anna grinned. "Just listen."

Muffled voices and childish laughter escaped from the surrounding thick foliage. Lora's heart beat faster at the thought of meeting so many strangers.

Some children dribbled into the churchyard. A few youngsters scampered in a lively game of tag. While Brother Rhine unlocked the door, several boys threw rocks into the water. Others waded in a shallow spot.

A young voice spoke. "Hello."

Lora turned and recognized Tillie, the young girl she had seen the day they arrived. The girl wrapped her arms around the same chubby toddler.

"Hello," Lora studied the youthful face framed by short blonde hair and bangs. "I'm glad to meet you. Is this your brother?"

"Nope. He's my boy." Tillie grinned with pride.

"Oh!" Lora looked surprised. The girl appeared much too young to be a mother.

Anna Benner explained. "Tillie is married to Bill. This is their little boy."

The Jason Vance family attended Roaring Church faithfully.
Jason was a schoolteacher, a farmer,
and assisted with church responsibilities.

Lora squeezed the baby's round hand. Another woman stepped forward and thrust out a hand.

"The name's Mattie.[2] Mattie Vance."

Lora nodded warmly at the friendly woman.

---

2   Pronounced MAY tee.

"I'm so glad you've come," Mattie said. "Come on up the holler to visit us anytime you want."

"Thank you," Lora and Aunt Nellie responded in unison.

Mattie pointed out the girls and boys that were hers. "My husband Jason's over ther'," Mattie nodded toward a slim man who limped toward the church.

Lora located the correct man and wondered if an injury had given Mattie's husband an unnatural gait.

"Come along now." A young mother called to her children as her little one tugged at her head covering. "No, no. You mus'n't pull Mama's covering strings." The woman loosened the child's grip from the black ribbons while she attempted to smooth a stray lock of hair under her covering.

Lora extended her hand and looked into the face of a tall slender woman with thick brown hair. "Good morning. I'm Lora. This is my Aunt Nellie."

Faithful mothers loved to attend the mountain churches with their children. Fathers often came too.

"Polly. Polly Vance is the name." The woman batted her eyes, nodded, and gave a wan smile.

"Glad to meet you, Sister Polly," Lora greeted her warmly and shook hands with the little girls who clustered around their mother.

Several children dashed up the creek bank past a cluster of teens talking. A few men visited at the edge of the church grounds. A sudden pounding of feet and a squeal made Lora whirl around to see what was happening. A young girl of about eleven whizzed past, her legs pumping at incredible speed. Behind her a boy chased in hot pursuit. Like a skilled rabbit escapes a hound hot on his trail, the girl leaped out of the way just in time.

"Missed me!" The red-faced girl hollered as the boy lost his balance and crumpled into the grass. Panting, she skipped near Lora and Aunt Nellie.

Lora reached out to shake her hand. "Hello, I'm Lora."

The girl pushed her strawberry-blonde bangs out of her eyes, wrinkled a freckled nose and grinned, deep dimples denting each cheek. "I'm Gracie."

"I'm glad to meet you," Lora said, smiling warmly.

Just as Gracie moved away, the boy crept up behind her and yanked her hair. "Gotcha!"

"Ouch!" The girl spun around, spat some unkind words, and stuck out her tongue. Then she puckered her lips and spit in his direction. "I'll get you back!"

Lora glanced at Aunt Nellie and stifled her amusement. Deliberately the two set out to greet others. Hands met theirs with firm grip while eyes returned bashful glances at the newcomers. Boys loitered on the outskirts of the crowd until the last possible minute.

The bell clanged and children, squealing with joy, pressed through the door with a thunder of feet.

"Easy now. No need to be noisy in the Lord's house," Brother Benner admonished with a smile. An elderly sister spat brown juice into the grass and started for the building, along with mothers and fathers carrying children in their arms.

"You boys simmer down," a dad cautioned.

The damp prints of bare feet on the floor would soon dry. Silently, Lora joined her aunt on the bench and waited for the service to begin.

Brother Benner walked to the front and introduced the new missionary sisters who had come to live among them for the summer. Young and older faces peered at the visitors and bashfully looked away. It was time for the singing to begin.

Lora's brows lifted with surprise as the congregation joined in singing. These people knew how to sing! They sang loudly and with joy.

"Follow the path of Jesus,
Walk where his footsteps lead,
Keep in his beaming presence,
Every counsel heed."[3]

After singing and a Scripture reading, Lora waited for the boys and girls to find seats at the table in the classroom. A row of timid faces looked at her.

"Hello, boys and girls. I'm Lora and I'll be your teacher for a while. I hope we can have a good time learning about God and His plan for us, His people."

---

3 "Follow the Path of Jesus," *Church and Sunday School Hymnal*, No. 305.

Some faces began to brighten as Lora began the lesson. "I don't know where all of you live, but I suppose a path leads up the mountain or across the foot log on the way to your house. You may know the way home, but sometimes we go places in the dark and we need a light to see where we are going."

Lora held up her lesson picture and all eyes fastened on the page. "In life you will need God's Word to show you the best path to take. This verse in the Bible says, 'Thy word is a lamp unto my feet, and a light unto my path.' " [4]

Lora looked into the upturned faces. Could she impress Biblical truth deep into each tender heart? Would they clasp it and claim it as they faced life's experiences?

"Now let's sing about the Bible that we will use to light our way in life." Lora began with a strong soprano and little voices joined with hers.

"Cling to the Bible!
Cling to the Bible!
Cling to the Bible, our Lamp and Guide."[5]

Bright eyes shone with anticipation. "I like Sunday school class," a little boy commented.

Lora beamed a smile in return. "Good. We will learn many stories from God's Book. The stories are true and will guide us in life. Oh, there is the bell and class is over already."

"We want to hear more stories," one little girl lamented.

Lora bent lower and said, "Come again next Sunday and there will be more from God's Holy Word."

After lunch, Jim Shank left for home. While Anna put the little children to bed, Lora, Aunt Nellie, and the

---

4 Psalm 119:105
5 "Cling to the Bible," *Church and Sunday School Hymnal,* No. 500

older children joined Brother Benner for a five-mile hike to another preaching appointment. The mission was supplied with a horse and buggy, but years of walking had conditioned Rhine for the trails up and down the mountains. A good walk through nature would bring them to their destination. The song of the creek followed them most of the way. Near the schoolhouse where the commu-

This waterfall, along with others in the region, displays the marvels of the Creator's hand.

nity met for preaching, they came upon a vast waterfall that descended from far up the side of the mountain.

Lora's mouth dropped open. She stared up past the surrounding foliage to the top of the rocky cliff where fresh water spilled like a fountain, splashing here and there as it fell against the rocks in a magnificent cascade. She stood speechless while mist dampened her face and dress.

Brother Benner broke the silence. "Scripture says, 'He watereth the hills from his chambers.' "[6]

---

6 Psalm 104:13

"It certainly appears that way," Aunt Nellie added with a tone of awe.

Lora continued to gaze, unable to utter a word. Silently the words of Scripture came. "If any man thirst, let him come unto me, and drink. He that believeth on me, as the scripture hath said, out of his belly shall flow rivers of living water."[7]

Lora sighed long and deeply, as the smell of minerals lingered in the air and beads of moisture collected in her hair. The Scripture was so true. The Lord Himself could bring a pure, clean fountain of refreshing life into each person's heart. She had experienced the cleansing of sin and the ongoing living waters rushing up within her own heart every day. She must share that joy with others!

"We have to go," Aunt Nellie murmured, still looking at the falls as Brother Rhine started off.

"I know," Lora said, turning toward the path. "It's just a lovely picture of spiritual life."

Aunt Nellie grinned with deep-felt acknowledgement. "It is. We have a wonderful object lesson to use as we teach here in the mountains."

Upon their arrival at the meeting place, Lora and Aunt Nellie met more people. Curious but bashful, the mountain folk thrust out work-worn hands to receive the newcomers. New faces and new names bombarded Lora. Would she ever know all these people? The old, the young, the middle-aged, the able, and the disabled shuffled into the small schoolhouse with open ears to the Word.

---

7   John 7:37, 38

By the time they returned home, the sun had already dropped behind the ridge, yet the day's work was not yet finished. That evening, lamplight glowed in the Roaring Church windows. People scrambled down the mountainsides or headed up the hollow to the little church once again for the evening preaching service. Lora mingled with the children and mothers.

As dusk deepened, more people came, for the church was the center of social life in the quiet community. Where did they all come from? Would there be room inside for them all? Mountain men loitered on the outskirts of the crowd, chatting with one another while some wives and children began to fill the benches. A few men joined their wives and children, eager to learn the truth of Scripture.

Again the voices lifted in song, this time in greater volume than in the morning, and a sermon by Brother Benner followed. Like the sower in the Bible, preachers and teachers had for years scattered the seed of God's Word in people's hearts. Some had listened and gladly received it. Seedlings thrived within the souls of some, while others endured the gentle hoeing of the heart-soil, as the Master Gardener broke up the caked clods to prepare the soil for the Priceless Seed.

While Brother Benner spoke, the Spirit moved in people's hearts. Lora felt the Spirit comforting her own soul, yet she longed for everyone there to have peace and joy. Near her sat Tillie, the sixteen-year-old wife with her baby on her lap. What a sweet young mother. Did she know Christ in her life? Her eyes drifted to Jason and Mattie Vance. They listened with joy on their faces. Sister Polly was drinking in every word. Some seemed to understand. Others listened with blank expressions. Lora's heart warmed with love. These people mattered to God. *Please Lord, touch each one!* she prayed.

After church Lora learned a few more names. Then Sister Polly came over to chat, and her shyness of the morning had seemed to vanish. "It's good to talk with you women," she said. "Won't you come up the mountain and see us sometime?"

"I hope we can soon," Lora responded.

"We'd love to," Aunt Nellie said.

Polly's face glowed. "I'll be watchin' fer ya. Now don't you fergit, you hear?"

The congregation dispersed, with many carrying lanterns to light their way home. A ring of light from Brother Benner's lantern bobbed on the road and a whip-poor-will sang in the trees.

As Lora walked, her mind turned to the origin of this mission. She had heard about it many times through her growing-up years. "I think I can understand why Potter John loved and cared about these people long ago," she said aloud.

Aunt Nellie glanced at Lora. Both of them knew the story well.

"Who was Potter John?" one of the children asked.

Lora smiled at her scholarly aunt who loved to tell how the Gospel had come to the West Virginia Mountains. "You tell them."

"It began before the Civil War when preachers crossed the mountains on horseback to share the Gospel," Aunt Nellie began. "Can't you just see those weary ministers after a long ride on horseback? The mountain people took the ministers in and gave them food to eat and a place to sleep. The people loved to listen to the Good News the men brought to them."

Overhead the stars shone brightly as the little group neared the mission home.

Aunt Nellie continued, "Then when the Civil War came, a man named Potter John Heatwole escaped from being drafted into the Confederate army."

"Why did he escape?" the child asked.

"He did not want to kill people. He believed what Jesus taught in the Bible—that a Christian could not love an enemy and shoot him at the same time. So Potter John threw scouts off his trail by walking backwards in the snow."

"Why?" the child questioned.

"So the officers could not find him. He came here to the mountains and taught the people about the Bible. They listened and became followers of Jesus too."[8]

"Now there are little congregations dotted across the mountains," Rhine Benner said as he stepped up to the door. "But there's still work to do here."

"There sure is," Lora agreed as the weariness crept into every muscle and bone. "That's the most work I've ever done on the Lord's Day."

"Busiest day of the week," Anna Benner said. "Sunday is not a day of rest on the mission field."

"There isn't much time to loaf around here," said Rhine Benner playfully as he opened the door for them all. "Especially not on Sunday."

---

8 Minnie R. Carr, "'Potter' John Heatwole," *Valley Mennonite Messenger*, Vol. 5, No. 27 (January 5, 1967), No. 28 (January 12, 1967), No. 29 (January 19, 1967). John David Heatwole (1826-1907) was often called "Potter John" since he was a potter by trade and other John Heatwoles lived in the area.

"I reckon it would be miserable to loaf," Lora added.

"I doubt that's something you workers know how to do," Brother Benner chuckled as he blew out the lantern.

Chapter Four

Duties

1926

L ora hummed a tune as she lowered the laundry tub into the garden and allowed the water to seep into the ground at the base of the tomato vines. She eyed the tomatoes, just beginning to ripen, and longed for the first tangy slices to add to the meals she helped prepare. The barking of dogs echoed through the hollow, which meant that Bertha Morral must be bringing the mail. Lora hurried past the long lines of laundry flapping in the breeze and hung the tub on a nail on the back porch wall. Then she sped to the front gate for the mail.

Bertha Morral walked briskly up and down the hollow, covering miles in a short time. She carried the mail in a back sack and delivered mail twice daily to the Roaring community.

"Howdy!" Bertha said as she allowed the sack to slip from her shoulders. Opening it, she searched for the bundle and handed it to Lora. "Guess you get to sort the mail and find out if there's any fer you."

"That's Aunt Nellie's job," Lora responded, "she's the one who takes care of the post office for Anna."

"Any mail going out?" Bertha asked.

"Good morning." Aunt Nellie appeared and handed her a stack of envelopes.

Bertha placed them in the sack. "Anything much happening up Roaring?"

"Not much," Aunt

Bertha Morral, the mail carrier in Roaring community.

Nellie spoke. "Anything special going on in Onego?"[1]

"The usual bizness, people comin' fer mail and such. Well, I best be goin'. People want their mail. See ya this afternoon."

Bertha flung the sack over her shoulder. In a few moments she had vanished from sight. Lora followed Aunt Nellie to the porch and settled on a chair just as the rhythmic clopping of a horse's hooves sounded from up the valley. Lora leaned forward to see who was coming. The man on horseback trotted up to the gate and stopped. It was Sister Polly's husband, Noah.

"Howdy, folks," the mountaineer called to the ladies. He spit a stream of tobacco juice in an arch that landed on the

---

1   Pronounced "WON go"

lawn. "I'm goin' down t' the store. I'll stop on the way back fer my mail."

"Sure thing," Aunt Nellie called. "I'll have it ready."

The rider trotted off while Lora and Aunt Nellie watched him go. *O God, touch this man's heart. Bring him into the fold,* Lora prayed. Silently Lora followed Aunt Nellie inside the mission home where Aunt Nellie sorted the envelopes and packages for people to pick up.

Lora pulled the hoe through the dirt, tearing away the weeds that sprouted beneath the potatoes. Aunt Nellie and Rhoda also worked the long rows. When they had finished hoeing, Lora stepped over a few rows to the cabbage patch.

"Looks like kraut time is here." She pressed her finger against the firm cabbage. "Wonder if Anna is ready to start sauerkraut."

"The peas seem about ready for the last picking." Aunt Nellie bent down to look under the pea vines.

"I'll help," Rhoda volunteered. "May we pull up the vines, Mother?"

Anna tossed table scraps into a pan for the cats. "Yes, we can. I'm so delighted to have all this help."

"Looks like plenty to do," Lora said as they put away the hoes and headed back to the house.

In a few days, shredded cabbage and salt filled crocks on the kitchen counter, and the last fresh peas filled the serving dishes on the table.

Summer days brought additional responsibilities for the mission workers. One day Anna Benner approached her helpers.

"Rhine wants me to go with him on a visit. Would you mind keeping the children?"

"Not in the least," Lora responded.

"You go along," Aunt Nellie agreed. "We'll watch the children."

When Brother and Sister Benner had left in the buggy, little Elva began to cry. Lora took the child on her lap and tried to distract her with a story.

"I want Mama," Elva whimpered.

"Now listen," Aunt Nellie said in her no-nonsense manner, "your Papa and Mama went away, but they are coming back. You must be good for Lora and me."

The crying stopped, and Elva tearfully surveyed Aunt Nellie.

"Will you be good for us?" Lora asked, wiping away the tears.

The child nodded and a hint of a smile quivered on her lips.

Lora gave Elva a hug. "Now listen while I sing you a song."

One afternoon after the work had been completed, Lora sat down at the table with colored pencils and clean paper.

"What are you doing?" Rhoda leaned across the table.

"I'm making some pictures for Sunday school class."

"Oh-h!" Rhoda watched the careful drawings and the process of coloring. "That's nice."

"Thank you," said Lora. "I hope the children will like them too."

Aunt Nellie studied a catalog. "Look here, Lora." Her aunt shoved the catalog across the table.

"What?" Lora paused and looked at the page.

"Pictures for our classes—Bible story pictures. We wouldn't have to draw them."

"I don't mind drawing though," Lora stated as she surveyed the catalog.

"You are good at drawing," Aunt Nellie mused, "But here they are already done in color."

"These are attractive and colorful." Anna Benner smiled as she inspected the assortment of Bible illustrations.

"You have a wonderful idea," said Brother Benner with a nod of approval. "I wish we could have Sunday school quarterlies for our people here, but there just isn't money to reach around. Illustrations will add a nice touch to your lessons."

Aunt Nellie searched for the order form. "I will order some and see how that works for teaching."

Ma-aa-aa. What was that? Lora hurried to the door. Gracie, a Sunday school girl, and her older brother were at the gate.

"Hello," Lora said. "I thought I heard goats."

Sister Benner came outside. "Hi there, Ezekiel and Gracie. I'm so glad your mother had goats for us. We will have goat milk now! I'll run inside and get the money for you."

Lora chuckled at the frisky goats that the boy and girl held in check with ropes.

"Where do you live?" Lora asked.

Gracie pointed at the mountain. "Up there. Mother would like you to come see us sometime."

"I would love to," Lora responded.

The tall slender boy took the money Anna placed in his hands and shifted his hat lower so his eyes were invisible. "Wonder if there'd be any mail fer us?"

Anna smiled kindly. "Just a moment and I'll have Nellie check for you." Anna cupped her hands to her mouth and called toward the barn. "James, could you come get the goats?"

Aunt Nellie placed some envelopes and a catalog in the boy's hands and laid her hand on Gracie's shoulder. "I believe I saw you at church on Sunday."

Gracie nodded and smiled shyly.

"Oh, I almost forgot," Gracie said as James took the goats toward the pasture. "Mother said she needs another bonnet awful bad."

"All right," Lora answered. "I'll see that your Mother gets a new one."

Anna nodded with understanding. "It's pretty difficult to keep a bonnet nice when you have to walk so far in the rain sometimes."

"C'mon," the boy nudged his sister. "Gotta go."

"Good-bye," the women chorused.

Ezekiel had already started to go. He looked back and shifted the hat off his eyes. "The name's Zeke."

"Zeke," Aunt Nellie repeated. "Good-bye, Zeke and Gracie. Give your mother hello for us."

Gracie waved. "I will." Then she skipped away, keeping up with her brother's long stride.

Lora shoved the mop swiftly under the bed, into the corners, and across the floor. With a cloth she dusted the furniture and shelves and shined the lamp chimney on the mantle. Pulling clean sheets from the dresser drawer, she stretched them on the bed, smoothing each wrinkle until the bed stood complete with its patchwork quilt. For a moment, she paused to inspect the bedroom that visitors would soon occupy. Stepping over to the window, she shined the glass. In the yard below, she noticed Aunt Nellie and James Benner plucking a chicken. Tomorrow the chicken would rest upon a Sunday platter.

The bleat of goats in the pasture jogged her memory. Spinning on her heels, Lora gathered her cleaning supplies and swished downstairs to where goat's milk dripped from a cloth into a bucket.

Lora poured some milk into a pan. Then she added a chunk of wood to the stove, and measured flour and sugar into the pan. As the milk heated, she stirred the mixture and beat eggs. The pudding thickened slowly under her expert hand. Lora smiled as she scraped the dessert into a container. Tomorrow, their guests would enjoy a tasty milk dish for dinner.

By afternoon the house had been scoured clean. Beds awaited the arrival of visitors, and the table had been stretched to accommodate extra people. Anna carried a pretty bouquet from the garden to set on the white tablecloth.

Lora went to the door and listened. Were they coming? Letters had informed them of the expected arrival. The children pressed against her as she listened. Between the scuffles and chatter she heard the sound of a motor down the hollow.

"They are almost here!" Lora said as she smoothed the hair of one of the girls. Brother Benner slipped from his bedroom to meet the guests.

When the car rolled into view, Lora saw that two familiar friends had accompanied the minister and his wife.

"Josie! Maggie! You surely know how to surprise us!" Lora grinned as she pumped her friends' hands.

"Welcome, good friends!" Aunt Nellie greeted each one warmly. "Come right inside and make yourselves at home!"

"Have some mountain mint tea," Lora offered as she poured drinks for each of the guests while Aunt Nellie served cookies.

"Mmm, so refreshing." The guests consumed the treat with pleasure.

"What a trip!" Josie said. "It's unbelievable, all those mountains between here and home."

"I'll never forget it," Maggie sighed, "but I'm so glad to be here."

Lora beckoned. "Come upstairs to our room and we'll find a place for your things. Already she knew that she and Aunt Nellie would give up their bed for the visitors. Perhaps they could concoct a bed on the floor for themselves.

"You may place your things there." Aunt Nellie pointed as she poured water into the washbowl. "Here, freshen up a bit."

Lora pulled out washcloths from the dresser. "This is delightful to have you join us. Perhaps you could teach my class. Would you, Maggie?"

Maggie dropped the cloth into the water and wrung it tightly. She drew the cloth across her face, her eyes tightly shut. "I'll just sit in the class and listen."

"You must see what we want to do with Sunday school." Aunt Nellie pulled out a drawer and opened the catalog. "We ordered these pictures for the children to paste in their books as we teach the lessons."

Josie eyed the book. "That looks enjoyable."

"We've been drawing a lot of the pictures for the lessons," Lora said. "It takes a lot of time."

"But you have an artistic talent, if I remember." Maggie grinned.

Lora smiled and said, "Just a few scribbles. Seriously, you would find it a privilege to teach. Will you?" she asked.

"I could try."

"Come on, girls, let's hike up to the falls," Lora suggested. "We can talk more on the way."

"I'm ready," Maggie said.

"Anything to get the cramps out of my legs," Josie agreed. She descended the stairs behind Lora to where the Benner family was visiting with the guest minister and his wife.

Good-natured talk flowed freely as the visitors were made to feel at home. The weekend sped much too quickly, filled with fellowship, good food, sharing of burdens, prayer, services, laughter, singing, and more. Monday arrived much sooner than Lora wished. The visitors departed and the duties returned.

One day Rhine and Anna suggested that Lora and Aunt Nellie go visiting. Anna would stay home with the children.

"We have invitations," the women acknowledged. "And Gracie's mother needs her new bonnet."

Rhine encouraged them. "The people are friendly, and they enjoy fellowship. You will need some sturdy shoes," Rhine said. "The trails are steep and rugged, but the people will welcome you."

"We might as well get started," Aunt Nellie said.

"Get a good stick to lean on as you go up the mountain," Rhine advised as he sketched a map for them.

Lora put on her most comfortable shoes, placed a Bible in her oversized bag, and tied on her pink-gingham sunbonnet. Aunt Nellie did likewise.

Lora looked at Aunt Nellie. "Are you ready to go?"

"If you are." Aunt Nellie nodded.

"Mountain trails, here we come," Lora chuckled. Then she launched into a song with Aunt Nellie's strong alto blending the duet.

"Scattering precious seed by the wayside,
Scattering precious seed by the hillside . . ."[2]

---

2 "Scattering Precious Seed," *Church and Sunday School Hymnal,* No. 325

Chapter Five

Community

1926

Brambles arched the slopes with half-ripened berries. From a limb overhead, a squirrel swished his bushy tail and considered whether to scurry away or linger in the presence of humans. As the women pressed up the hollow, the harmony of their voices blended in song.

"Sowing in the sunshine, sowing in the shadows,
Fearing neither clouds nor winter's chilling breeze . . ."

Aunt Nellie stopped singing and looked at the sky. "I don't see a threatening cloud or any danger of snow."

Lora stopped a moment and pretended to investigate the sky through a thin part of the forest. "Not today, but maybe tomorrow." Lora grinned at her aunt, who could invent humor from almost any situation. "We haven't time to waste, comrade. Let's be on our way." She poked her stick into the ground and walked on, singing.

A sharp voice came from a cottage just ahead. Lora stopped singing and listened.

"You get out of here, you good-fer-nothin' . . ."

The door opened and a thin man fled up the hillside, away from the sharp tones that cut him to the heart.

Lora looked at Aunt Nellie. "Should we go on or should we stop and visit here?"

Aunt Nellie hesitated a moment and replied, "We are out to visit the community. Yes, let's make a visit."

The two crossed a foot log and walked toward the home. Dust whirled under the vigorous thrust of the woman's broom as she swept the porch and steps.

Millie welcomed them as if nothing had happened. Inside, Lora and Aunt Nellie found a tidy home and a girl lying on a cot.

"Hello." Both women shook hands with the girl whose eyes brimmed with tears.

Did the harsh words spoken between her parents bring the girl heartbreak? Some questions one did not ask.

Aunt Nellie loved to connect with school. She knelt beside the girl and asked, "What grade are you in at school?"

"Haven't been to school in a long time. Don't know."

Millie's friendly voice explained, "She has rheumatic fever and must stay home to rest, but maybe she will go to school in the fall."

"I hope you will be able to." Aunt Nellie squeezed the girl's hand warmly. "Do you like to read?"

"I can't read very well," the girl murmured.

"Practice will help you improve." Aunt Nellie smiled. "I'll bring you some books to read."

The girl's eyes glinted with hope as Aunt Nellie spent time with her. The women ventured on to other topics with Millie. They explored subjects of homemaking and godly living taught by the Bible. When Aunt Nellie ventured to spiritual things and mentioned forbearance and forgive-ness, Millie leaped from her chair, livid with anger.

"It might be how you live, but I've got a no-good hus-band, that's what! There's no way I'm gonna forgive him fer messin' up th' place. No sir!" Millie paced as she ranted.

On the couch a sad face turned away from the visitors and a stifled sob escaped. Lora and Aunt Nellie spoke softly to the upset woman.

Millie bristled. "You ain't married, so you can't know what I've got to put up with!"

The two nodded in silence. It was true. They were not married; neither did they have all the answers to life's per-plexities. But one thing they did know without a doubt, and Aunt Nellie proceeded with confidence, "Life isn't always easy, but God's Word is truth. Those who practice what the Bible says will find their life much better."

Lora nodded her support.

Millie stuffed another log into the stove. Then she swept up the wood particles on the floor.

"We'll be going," Lora said. "We'd like to visit some others too."

Aunt Nellie patted the girl's shoulder. "I'll be back with books for you."

The girl smiled faintly, and Millie nodded her apprecia-tion. The two left the house, happy that the Lord had given them a soft answer to Millie's angry outburst.

The women noted that clouds had moved in while they had been visiting, and the crack of thunder brought rain. They found a haven and a hearty welcome at the elderly Sister Sarah's house.

"Who would have thought the weather could change so

quickly?" Lora asked, chuckling.

"It's something, I tell you," Aunt Nellie replied. "When we left home, there wasn't a hint of rain in the sky."

Sister Sarah rocked contentedly. "You never can tell what's its gonna do. It's such a narrow piece of sky to look at 'round here."

For a while they chatted as Sister Sarah rocked in her chair and discussed the Scripture with them. Sarah often coughed hard into her handkerchief. Even though tuberculosis made her life quite miserable, still she remained a loyal follower of Christ and loved to discuss spiritual matters.

Soon it was time to move on and visit others. Such good times made it hard to depart.

Sister Sarah leaned back with a sigh. "I'm so glad you have come. So many need to hear the Bible that us older ones have heard preached for years. We know it is true and right, but the younger ones are too busy to interest themselves."

"We are glad to teach the Holy Book," Aunt Nellie said. "It is a privilege to share what God has given to all mankind."

With encouraged hearts, the two ventured up the winding trail that disappeared into the mountain. As the trail grew steeper, the women found their walking sticks a definite aid for the climb.

The twittering of birds sweetened the steepness of the trail. Eventually, trees thinned and gave way to a clearing where a worn house and barn sat surrounded by small buildings. Chickens squawked and geese honked as the newcomers approached. Several dogs barked in earnest, and as they drew near, a curtain fluttered and children's faces peeked at them, then suddenly disappeared from view. The door burst open and a woman yelled at the dogs.

"Hesh up, dogs! Howdy, folks. Come on in." The woman tugged her curious youngsters out of the way. "Glad you came. Let's sit and talk a spell. Joe's at the lumber camp workin', you know," she apologized.

The smell of fried grease drifted through the dimly lit room. As the women visited, the children peeped from behind their mother's skirt. Eventually a girl became braver.

"I'm going to school this year," she announced with pleasure.

"You are?" Lora asked. "Has your mother made you school dresses?"

"Not yet," the mother commented. "There's too many things t'do. Gertie needs dresses bad."

Lora offered, "I have sewn for my sisters at home, and I think I could make one to fit her."

The little girl jumped up and down. "I'd like that!"

"Oh, Lorie." The mother breathed a sigh of relief. "You can't imagine what a help that would be to me!"

Lorie? That was the first time she had been called by that name. Lora grinned. "I'd be happy to sew for you. If you have material, I'll get started on it."

"This is plain wonnerful. Now let me git you folks some dinner. You must be hungry from trampin' up this way."

A strong aroma filled the air after the woman opened a can of food. Lora visited in the kitchen and helped prepare the meal. Along with more tasty foods at dinner, she encountered a dish of ramps, a strong onion harvested from rich woodlands. Natives who had grown up with this spring delicacy loved the dish, but Lora's stomach fluttered during the meal. She laid down her fork and hesitated before taking another bite. Her stomach churned. Suddenly she shoved back her chair and dashed from the room. The screen door banged. Not until she had released her meal across the fence did her stomach settle.

By the time she was ready to leave, all of them had a hearty laugh over the ordeal. Lora carried a piece of fabric in her bag, a new friendship, and the determination to avoid any future servings of ramps.

Brother Benner had joined the visiting pair, and he led the way to another house.

"Is Myrtle here?" Brother Benner asked. "We'd like to visit her."

"She's not around right now." The woman at the door pressed her lips together. "She don't wanna talk to y'all no how."

"We've been missing Myrtle at church," Brother Benner ventured when the woman of the house refused to invite them in.

"She's not comin' to church no more." The woman glared at the preacher, spitting out the words.

"What changed?" Brother Benner asked. "Myrtle was so happy with her faith in Jesus."

"Just a minute," the woman said, not answering the question. She stepped back out of sight and then appeared again. "Here. You can have this ol' thing back." She shoved the wrinkled head covering into Lora's hands. "She won't be needin' it now."

Sadly, Lora placed it in her bag.

The rain had disappeared and the sun shone into the clearing when Lora and Aunt Nellie reached the steps of the next place.

"Come go in," Sis Polly welcomed with the customary community greeting.

"Thank you," Lora echoed Aunt Nellie as they followed Brother Benner into the tidy house.

"May I git you some dinner?" Sis Polly asked.

"We had dinner. Thank you."

"Surely you want some water?"

Up and down the trails, Lora and Aunt Nellie stopped in homes to visit and share the Gospel.

All three travelers nodded. The cheerful hostess carried a cup of water to each guest before she sat down to visit.

Friendship and spiritual encouragement entwined the hearts of the women as they visited around a tub of beans. The visitors helped string whole beans together with a needle and thread. They would hang by the stove to dry for winter use. The children warmed quickly to the visitors who had come to visit, but soon they were ready to go outside and play.

"I appreciate my church friends," Sis Polly expressed.

"You are an encouragement and example to all of us at Roaring," Brother Benner said.

The slender woman smiled slowly, and her eyes met each of the visitors with a wistful look. "I wish my husband would be a believer of Jesus and a part of the church."

"We will continue to pray for Noah," Brother Benner sympathized as he thumbed through his Bible. He read Scripture to encourage her to be a faithful Christian example that would convince her husband of the power of the Gospel.[1]

Sis Polly nodded her head. "I try, but sometimes I fail. I wanna be th' wife God wants me ta be."

Brother Benner offered encouragement. "We can ask the Lord to help you be the wife you should be, and to make your husband want to know the Lord."

"Yes. Please do that for me." Sis Polly clutched her hands together.

Quietly the little group lifted petitions to the Almighty. A heavy heart was lightened and peace filled the hearts of those in prayer. Sis Polly sighed and wiped a lingering tear. "We will keep praying and watching for God to work in your husband's life," Aunt Nellie said as she gave a kiss of charity.

Lora followed likewise. She whispered in Sis Polly's ear, "God can do a miracle."

---

1   Read 1 Peter 3:1, 2

Sis Polly gazed into Lora's eyes, a tear glimmering on her eyelash. "Y'all come back again. You always help me go on living."

Brother Benner put on his hat and smiled at their sister. "That's what Christian fellowship does to us. It's the Spirit at work in our lives."

Shadows crept into the forest that afternoon as the missionaries descended the trail and stopped for one last visit. Abe and Lizzie lived close to the mission home. Their family still grieved the loss of a ten-year-old son who had died in a freak accident some months earlier.

Over glasses of lemonade, Lizzie explained what had happened. "He was playin' hide'n'seek, but nobody could find him. My husband found him behind a buildin'. The boy had fallen from a roof onto weed stubbles that pierced his jugular vein. Abe brought him in and laid him on the couch." Lizzie paused before she continued solemnly. "Twasn't a thing a body could do."

Lora could almost visualize the little body, limp and bleeding as his young life ebbed away. Silence filled the room as each one sat thinking of the loss.

Lora gave Lizzie's arm a gentle squeeze. "How sad. I'll be praying for you and your family," she whispered.

"We need that," Lizzie said, and her husband nodded in agreement.

There was silence as they sipped the refreshing drink, and Aunt Nellie said, "This is real lemonade, isn't it? Where did you get lemons?"

"Down at the store," Lizzie replied.

"It's mighty good lemonade," Aunt Nellie complimented and the rest agreed.

When they finally reached home, Lora and Aunt Nellie removed their shoes to find blisters on their feet.

"These mountains will toughen up you tender folks," Brother Benner said with a chuckle.

"You think so?" Aunt Nellie replied. "It'll be weeks before I can put these blistered heels into shoes again."

They all shared a good laugh. Then Lora picked up her shoe and examined it. "Looks like these shoes need repair."

Anna Benner nodded toward her husband's patched shoes. "Shoe repair is a necessity in these parts. Keeps my husband occupied more than you would think, just fixing shoes."

Rhine Benner held up his ragged shoe with a twinkle in his eye. "These mountains are hard on shoes and tender folks."

Chapter Six

Vision

1926

"Lora! Guess what came in the mail?"

"What is it?"

Aunt Nellie tore open the package. "The pictures I ordered from Perry Picture Company."

"Really?"

Aunt Nellie spread the pictures on the table as the family crowded around to see.

"They are nice," Anna Benner said.

"Let me see," Elva grasped a picture.

"No, no," Anna corrected. She took the picture away. "We must not touch them."

"Pretty." Elva sighed.

"What will you do with these pictures?" Rhoda asked.

"Use them for Sunday school lessons," Lora explained.

Aunt Nellie gathered up the pictures and put them in the envelope. "We'll paste the pictures in a book for each student. Then we will have them write a few lines about the story underneath the picture."

In spite of her sore muscles and chafing feet, Lora set about making the dress for Gertie. She placed the fabric on the table and smoothed the wrinkles. Using scissors, she began to cut the fabric without a pattern.

"This looks about right," she said as she cut a hole for the neck, then cut across the fabric for a shoulder, then around an armhole. Carefully she eyed the piece as she cut the front bodice. Then she cut the back bodice, sleeves, and skirt. As she sat and began to sew, a song came to her lips.

"There's work for the hand and there's work for the heart,
Something to do, something to do;
And each should be busy performing his part,
There's something for all to do."[1]

The machine hummed as Lora sewed the pieces together. In a few hours a new dress hung in her room upstairs waiting to be worn by a growing young girl.

A cheerful voice called through the screen door. "Any mail fer me?"

Lora looked up. Tillie stood grinning, her chubby baby on her hip.

"Just a moment. I'll see." Aunt Nellie shoved some envelopes into the cubicles.

Lora walked over to the door and invited the girl inside. "Your little boy is growing so fast."

Tillie grinned. "I know."

---

1 "Something to Do," *Church and Sunday School Hymnal,* No. 520

Anna Benner carried her small-featured baby into the post office. "Hello, Tillie. Your baby is so robust. How do you girls do it?"

"Don't know, ma'am. He drinks lotsa milk. Eats good too."

Lora squeezed the toddler's chubby hand. The child giggled and hid his face in his mother's neck, then he peeked again.

Tillie gave a cocky flip of her hair. "Yep, he's as healthy as they come."

Lora laughed gently while Aunt Nellie handed the girl her mail.

Tillie turned to go. "See ya later."

Aunt Nellie placed an envelope in Anna's hand. Anna's face lit up as she read the familiar address. She hurried toward the kitchen to enjoy news from home folks.

"Heh, Lorie." Tillie was back at the screen door. "Could ya help me can tomatoes? I don't know why mine always spoil."

"Sure, I'll help you. Just let me know when you are ready."

"I'll let ya know."

Lora's heart tingled with joy as she watched the young mother head for home. Now there would be an opportunity to work closely with a friend. She loved this girl's youthful spirit and her sweet baby.

"We need notebooks for the children to put their lesson pictures in," Lora stated as she looked at the pictures spread on her bed.

"And glue to paste them on the page," Aunt Nellie added.

"I think I'll go to the store and get some things for our class." Lora picked up her purse.

"I think I'll go along," Aunt Nellie said. "I need supplies too."

"Would you need anything from the store, Anna?" Lora asked when she entered the kitchen.

"Let me think," Anna said. "Yes, there are a few things I need. I'll make a list."

James Benner had the horse and buggy hitched and ready when Lora and Aunt Nellie came out of the mission house carrying their purses. Lora climbed into the buggy while Aunt Nellie helped little Elva in. She settled into her seat and pulled the girl onto her lap. Lora flopped the reins across the horse's back. The buggy moved forward with the horse clopping slowly down the dirt road.

"Git up!" Lora slapped the reins, but the steady trot did not hasten. When they reached the ford, the horse slowed and hesitated at the water's edge.

"Git up," Lora called. The horse shook his mane and neighed rebelliously, but refused to move.

"He doesn't want to go," Elva said.

"That's right. He's a bit stubborn." Aunt Nellie chuckled.

Lora touched the buggy whip to the muscled flanks. "Git up!" Reluctantly, the horse lunged forward.

Elva bent forward and watched the horse's feet splashing in the water.

"See, he's getting his feet wet," Lora explained to the child. The youngster looked at Lora with wide eyes.

"Git up!" Lora said more firmly, with a tap of the whip that brought only a measure of speed.

"The mission horse is a little sluggish, isn't he?" Aunt Nellie commented.

"Perhaps this horse is a little like some church members," Lora said, hiding a smile.

"Like church members?" Aunt Nellie asked in disbelief.

"Yes, a little slow and inactive."

Aunt Nellie laughed. "I'm thankful not all of them are."

"That's right. Some Christians are active and useful in God's kingdom," Lora said. "I wish all were inspired to be involved in the work of the church."

At the store the ladies selected items for Anna Benner along with supplies for Sunday school. Lora fingered a bolt of fabric while the storekeeper waited on a customer at the counter.

"How many yards did ya say?" the storekeeper asked the woman.

"Three."

"Let's see." The proprieter grinned as he snipped the material and folded it. "Any men comin' to ask fer yer hand yet?"

Lora glanced at Aunt Nellie and raised her eyebrows at his boldness. In a moment, the woman shook with uncontrollable sobs.

"I'm so sorry," the storekeeper apologized. "Here, you just run along and don't ya bother to pay one cent."

The woman nodded, blew her nose, and scurried out the door, head bent.

Lora bristled inside. He'd better not ask them any nosey questions. She need not have worried; the man kept strictly to business when she paid for her articles.

"I wonder who she was?" Aunt Nellie mused on the way home.

"Poor woman. That man was insensitive, I think," Lora said.

When they reached home, Anna asked if they had met Lilly. "She seemed troubled when she passed by here."

Lora explained what had happened at the store.

"Oh." Anna clapped her hands over her mouth. "She lost her husband back last winter. He had TB."

"So she's a widow," Aunt Nellie stated.

Lora looked at her aunt. "Maybe we can visit her and give her some encouragement."

"Yes, I think we should," Aunt Nellie said in agreement.

The coolness of evening stole into the hollow as Lora relaxed on the porch with Aunt Nellie and Anna. Brother Benner played tag with his children. A few lightning bugs flickered in the dusk while the sound of softly rippling water came from the creek. Just beyond the lawn a figure approached.

"Hey, folks," Neighbor Abe greeted. "Why don'tcha c'mon over to our house. We're churnin' ice cream right now."

"Ice cream!" the children chanted.

"Sure. C'mon over and eat it with us," Abe insisted.

"That's too good to turn down, Abe." Brother Benner chuckled. "Mother, do we have any cookies to take?"

"Yes," Anna answered. "We'll bring some cookies when we come, Abe."

"All right. See you in a bit."

That evening Lora felt warmed by hospitality as Abe's wife Lizzie dished up bowls of ice cream for all. Abe chatted with Brother Benner, and Lizzie's gentle laugh and humor spiced the conversation. But as Lora walked home beside Aunt Nellie, some new thoughts swirled in her mind. Could Abe and Lizzie's bachelor son be taking a special interest in Aunt Nellie? Those two had found a lot to discuss together. The evening had been most delightful. Abe and Lizzie had seemed to enjoy the visit too.

Lora handed each child a new notebook.

"For me?" one child gasped as he thumbed through the pages.

"For you. We're going to paste a new picture in every Sunday."

Young eyes watched in wonder and excitement. Lora smiled at them and began the lesson.

"While we paste the picture in your books, I will tell you the story."

The children leaned in closely while Lora helped them paste the picture on the page. They listened to the story and studied the picture.

"You may write a few lines under the picture about the story."

Some quickly wrote the parts they remembered. Others wrote slowly and stopped to think. Lora helped the younger ones recall the story as she wrote for them.

"Now let's learn a verse with our lesson," Lora said. "I'll say the verse and you repeat it after me."

"Lorie, I like your class," a young boy said as the class ended.

"I'm coming next Sunday." The little girl nodded her head with emphasis and clasped the new notebook to her chest. "I like the stories."

Lora smiled. "There are still many more to tell you."

Another grasped Lora's hand. "I wanna hear all the stories."

"Good," Lora replied as she squeezed the child's hand. "Keep coming and you'll hear more stories about how great our God is."

She smiled at the students as they filed from the classroom. How she longed to show them God's wonderful plan for all His children! Would the lessons bring about a difference in their future? The words of Scripture slipped into her mind, "And they brought young children to him, that he should touch them."[2] Oh, that He would touch these little children too, and those in all the world.

---

2 Mark 10:13

Chapter Seven

Questions

1926

At the end of the service, Lora made her way outside the church. Tillie's husband, Bill, gathered up his toddler and gave him a kiss. Lora smiled. How special to have fathers come to church with wives and children!

The preaching that morning had been direct. Brother Benner had presented the Gospel and pled with them to trust in Jesus. Those who trusted Him would find their lives satisfied and fulfilled. Would the listeners accept the invitation? Would their souls receive Light and Truth?

Lora moved into the dappled sunshine where Tillie stood alone with a perplexed expression. Lora approached the young woman.

"Does something trouble you?"

Tillie nodded. "Just thinkin'. What does the preacher mean 'bout trustin' Jesus?" Tillie's blue eyes searched Lora's face.

Gracie had stopped to listen. The girl raised her eyebrows with curiosity.

Lora took a deep breath before she addressed the question. "It means you allow Him to take care of absolutely everything in your life."

"Ever'thing?"

"Yes. Christians ask the Lord Jesus to guide them and show them answers for their questions. They can trust Him to do what is best for them."

Tillie hesitated a moment. Then she asked, "But how will I know God's answers for me?"

Lora responded, "When a person has the Lord in their heart, the Spirit tells them God's answers. You know what He wants you to do."

Tillie seemed serious. "How do you get Jesus in your heart?"

Gracie looked from Lora to Tillie, her hands behind her back. She licked her lips and bent forward.

Lora spoke tenderly. "First you need to confess your sins to the Lord. Then you repent and turn away from sin, and ask Jesus to come into your heart."

Tillie pondered. "I'm not really bad," she countered.

Gracie giggled. "I'm not either."

Lora took her time as she continued to explain. " 'All we like sheep have gone astray; we have turned everyone to his own way.' [1] You see, every person is sinful and needs Jesus to save them from sin."

Gracie started to walk away, but skipped back again as Lora quoted the Bible. "That if thou shalt confess with thy mouth the Lord Jesus, and shalt believe in thine heart that God hath raised him from the dead, thou shalt be saved." [2]

---

1 Isaiah 53:6
2 Romans 10:9

Tillie nodded that she understood, but perplexity was etched on Gracie's brow.

Lora continued. "But there's more. Christ comes into the believer's heart to live. Jesus will bring complete satisfaction and peace in the inner soul." Lora shared several verses.

Gracie lingered and listened. Tillie blinked and squinted as the sun broke through the shade and beamed in her face.

"It sounds good," Tillie said.

"It is good. The Lord loves to guide His children in His ways." Lora turned to Gracie. "I hope you will answer the Lord when He calls you."

Gracie bounced with energy. "How will I know?"

"You will sense unrest in your heart. You will know something is not right."

Gracie cocked her head and grinned. "That's nice to know."

Lora laid her hand on Gracie's shoulder. "When the Lord asks you to follow Him, be open to His call."

Gracie nodded and skipped toward her family, who was leaving. Lora waited for a response, but Tillie didn't say more.

"Are you thinking about becoming a child of God?"

Tillie shoved the blonde hair away from her sweaty face. "Maybe."

Lora smiled. "The Lord is always waiting with open arms."

"I wanna think 'bout this," Tillie replied.

"You do that. Would you like to start reading the Bible? God speaks to people from His Word."

"Yes, I'll start readin'."

"The book of John is a good place to begin. I'll be praying for you. "

Lora counted the bills in her wallet. She had stretched her money carefully by only spending for the most necessary things. Would her stockings hold out until she returned to her job in the fall? She had patched them as well as her dresses. It had taken more shoes and stockings than she had expected. So far, Brother Benner had repaired her shoes, but she would have to buy another pair soon. The many miles of walking in the hill country took its toll on shoes and stockings. Would her money reach?

She breathed a prayer and put her wallet away. God had promised to supply every need, but how would He do it?

One day while Lora was baking bread, Rhoda fished a pickle out of the wooden tub and gave it to her little sister.

"Try it. It's good."

Little Elva took a bite and puckered her mouth.

"It's supposed to be sour," Rhoda explained.

Elva bit into the pickle again. She ate all of it and reached for another one.

"Heh," a man called from the screen door where he waited for Aunt Nellie to give him mail. "I'm needing a tub to make kraut. Mind if I borry it?"

"I suppose you can borrow it," Anna agreed. "I think we could put the pickles in some crocks."

Lora dished out the pickles, washed the tub, and gave it to the man.

"Did you say kraut?" Rhine Benner asked when Anna explained that the tub had been borrowed. "Kraut season has been over for weeks. Now I wonder what he would need a tub for? That seems a bit odd."

"Maybe they are just late with cabbage this year," Anna suggested.

"Which reminds me," Rhine commented, "the hoe and saw I loaned last spring never came back. I'll have to buy new tools when we have the money. I think I'll keep two sets of tools—one to loan and one to keep."

Later, Brother Benner came upon the kraut tub and a borrowed water hose, but it was not kraut in the tub. Making whiskey brought in cash for men to pay the bills, but also brought problems to the families. Women and children suffered, and so did the men as the drink trickled into the homes of the community. The mission workers prayed hard.

"Do you think you are being watched when you travel up and down the mountains?" Anna questioned.

Lora looked from Aunt Nellie to Brother Benner. Were they in danger if they stumbled upon a still?

Brother Benner pointed up. "My trust is in the Lord. We are His workers and He can keep us safe."

"I'm not afraid," Aunt Nellie spoke up. "However, it seems wise to be careful."

Lora agreed. "My job isn't to find the stills, but I can teach the children the dangers of drink."

The workers prayed for wisdom and fresh ways to teach the Bible. They prayed that the Almighty would come into the community and into people's hearts. How long, O Lord, until these souls would be rescued from sin?

Lora's heart felt as if a stone were lodged there as she walked to the stable, hitched up the horse and buggy, and started on her way.

A cloud of dust puffed from each clop of the horse's hooves. Lora snatched her handkerchief from her pocket and wiped the beads of sweat on her brow. With a click of her tongue she urged the pokey horse to keep his pace on the winding road. The streams over which she crossed rippled more gently now that summer was advancing. A few leaves fluttered down, but Lora wasn't focused on nature. The burden on her heart grew as she neared her destination.

Lora breathed a prayer while she tied the horse. *Lord, help me show Sadie Your way.* Sadie had attended the services often with her family and community friends. All summer Lora had prayed for this girl and sought the Lord for wisdom to share with her.

The simple-minded, unmarried girl welcomed Lora delightedly. "I'm s'glad you come ta see my new baby. Mom thinks the baby look jus' like me. What do you think, Lorie?"

"She does look like you," Lora agreed as she exchanged her gift for the infant placed in her arms.

"Oh!" Sadie exclaimed as she fondled the soft, crocheted cap. "A pink lil' baby cap. Didja make it, Lorie?"

"Yes," Lora said, cupping her hand over tiny fingers. "She looks the picture of health. Must be this fresh mountain air."

Sadie grinned broadly. For a while they chatted as Lora rocked the little one. Finally Lora asked the girl to join her outside. A gentle breeze swept through the trees as the two walked slowly in the meadow. In the distance, thunder rumbled. She would have to hurry while the opportunity was here.

"I've been wanting to talk to you." Lora stopped and looked fully into the girl's face. She paused. What should she say that could be understood and yet not offend? She breathed a prayer until she noticed the girl waiting to listen.

Awkwardly Lora began with a smile. "Babies are a very special blessing from the Lord."

Sadie grinned and cocked her head sideways. "I know. It's so special to have my own baby."

Lora continued. "Babies bring a big responsibility: to care for them and teach them right from wrong."

Sadie nodded with enthusiasm. Thunder rumbled louder.

Lora paused. Would Sadie understand the concepts of Scripture that God had laid on her heart to share? Carefully Lora proceeded to explain God's plan that babies be brought into homes where man and woman are husband and wife.

Sadie's gentle eyes grew stormy. The girl stiffened and spat words at Lora. "Well, git this, Lorie! My baby is jus' lik' Jesus. He had no father either!"

Lora caught her breath. She looked away and prayed intensely for wisdom while Sadie glared into the distance.

Lora breathed a sigh. She thought the Lord had impressed her with the need for this visit, one that she preferred not to make. Was it untimely?

She bent down and picked daisies and gently placed them in Sadie's hand. Without a word the two walked back toward the house. Thoughts raced through Lora's mind. How could she get through to a girl with limited understanding? Or did Sadie understand far more than she realized?

"I'll be going," Lora said softly. "I hope you will think about the things we talked about. This is God's way, not mine."

Sadie swallowed and looked at the daisies in her hands.

"Good-bye." Lora turned toward the buggy. "Hope to see you at church on Sunday."

"Bye." The girl watched Lora walk to the buggy. Then she walked to the house, her head bowed.

Lora untied the horse, climbed in the buggy, and began earnest prayer for the precious folks she had come to love. The burden for girls weighed on her soul. How could she help girls understand God's plan for children, homes, and godly marriage? Ministers taught what the Bible said about these issues, but some seemed unable to grasp these teachings which so differed from their culture. She and Aunt Nellie had begun visiting girls and women to help them understand and practice God's Word in everyday life. The seed of truth had been cast forth, falling on assorted ground. She knew some ground was hard and rocky, some was weedy, but she believed some had fallen on fertile ground and was germinating within receptive hearts.

The clop of the horse's hooves beat a rhythmic sound down past the creek. The words of a song came to Lora.

"Help me the slow of heart to move
By some clear, winning word of love . . ."[3]

A crack of thunder brought a torrent of rain. Lora pulled up the blanket to shield herself from the wetness. She

3   "O Master, Let Me Walk With Thee," *Church and Sunday School Hymnal,* No. 467

tapped the horse's flanks with the whip, and the horse reluctantly picked up a slow, steady gait.

A song floated on the air as the two missionary sisters walked home from the store.

An elderly man dressed in bib overalls and a straw hat heard the song as he worked on his front porch. He was a man of ingenuity, clever and creative. Like many mountain men, he could invent things to meet any need. He especially loved to make birdhouses, and he liked to sing and play his fiddle. But today he listened to the harmony of feminine voices while he worked.

"Howdy," the man greeted.

"Hello, Solomon," the women greeted.

"Jus' call me Sol. That's my name."

The women knew Brother Benner often used the names commonly used by the community if the people preferred it that way.

"What are you making, Sol?" Aunt Nellie asked as they paused on the road.

"Birdhouses." The wrinkled face turned toward them. His smile revealed the scant teeth he had left.

Lora scanned the display of assorted birdhouses on his fence. More of them perched on trees and the front of the house. "You have quite a talent I see."

"Keeps me busy and outta trouble," Sol said as he pushed a mug out of sight.

Aunt Nellie had seen the movement. "That's good. We had better move on."

"Wait a minute," Sol laid down his work. "I have some-thin' fer Benner."

In a moment the bent, slender figure came down the path. "Give this to Benner."

Aunt Nellie reached for the book and recognized the title. "Did you read it?"

"A little. But I don't have no in'er'st in religion. Nope, I don't."

Aunt Nellie made a few polite attempts to continue the subject, but Sol didn't want to hear.

"You can have it fer you. It's not fer me."

Lora knew Brother Benner had made many visits to this house with no results. Solomon was getting older. Would he enter eternity like so many others before him—unsaved, unprepared to meet his Maker, and unable to receive the joys of Heaven? God's Word was powerful and could accomplish what persuasion could not.

"Good-bye, Sol," Lora said. "Jesus said 'I am the way, the truth, and the life: no man cometh unto the Father, but by me.'[4] I hope you will find Him."

Sol shook his head in disagreement and bent over his work.

As the women walked home, they talked in subdued tones. What more could be done to reach the souls of the young, the old, the careless, the seekers, and even the non-seekers?

"It's God's work," Lora said.

"Yes," Aunt Nellie responded. "Like those in the Bible, we plant and water the Seed that goes forth."

---

4 John 14:6

Both chimed in with the familiar Scripture. "So then neither is he that planteth any thing, neither he that watereth; but God that giveth the increase. Now he that planteth and he that watereth are one: and every man shall receive his own reward according to his own labour. For we are labourers together with God."[5]

The mission house was just in sight. They would press on in the work of winning souls for Jesus.

---

5 1 Corinthians 3:7-9

Chapter Eight

An Idea

1926

Bang! The screen door at Sister Sarah's house slammed shut behind the grandchildren.

Lora jumped and chuckled. "Children have so much energy."

Sister Sarah rocked in her chair as the chatter of children's voices faded and the sound of bare feet pattered down the path. "I know. Wish I had just a little of it." The elderly woman coughed into her handkerchief.

Lora wished there was more she could do to help Sister Sarah with her health. The visit turned to spiritual things, and for a while the two encouraged one another with words of Scripture.

Lora beamed a bright smile at Sister Sarah. "It's a blessing that some of your family have found the Saviour."

"Oh, yes," Sister Sarah agreed. Still her brow furrowed. "I wish ever'one of 'em loved the Lord, but they don't. Some of 'em have turned to things Satan offers. Worries me somethin' awful."

Lora studied the concerned woman. "Yes, those who accept those tricky lures don't realize how miserable their lives will be."

Sister Sarah sat forward. "Why can't folks just accept God's rich gift—Jesus—and have the good life!" Her eyes were moist.

"We sow the Seed," Lora consoled. "Some souls receive it and grow. Others need more time to prepare the hard soil in their hearts."

Sister Sarah Vance loved the Word and desired that others would know its power in their lives.

"That's right," Sister Sarah gave a wan smile. "Some are coming to the Lord Jesus." The woman leaned forward and gazed into Lora's eyes. "My grandchildren love the lessons you and Nellie teach. If children had more teaching, maybe it would make a difference."

Lora blinked. "You may be right."

Sister Sarah persisted. "They love to learn."

Lora stood up to leave. "They are good students."

All the way home and upstairs to the room she and Aunt Nellie shared, Lora mulled over what Sister Sarah had said. Finding a comfortable spot to sit on the bed, she spoke up, "You know something?"

"What?" Aunt Nellie glanced up from her Bible study.

Lora contemplated how to voice her thoughts. Then she spoke, "There are so many spiritual needs here in the community. There is so much to teach, and the people are eager to learn."

Aunt Nellie leaned back in her chair, folded her arms and looked squarely at Lora. "What are you getting at?"

Lora told about her visit with Sister Sarah.

"I know what she means," said Aunt Nellie. "It seems we can't teach them fast enough. Some are good students and want to grow in spiritual things."

Lora nodded and hurried on, "Remember how much we learned in Bible classes at Eastern Mennonite School? Every day we had lessons that expanded our Christian faith."

Aunt Nellie took off her glasses and rubbed her nose. "You and I have had the advantage of years of Bible teaching from parents and faithful ministers, and we are thankful for it." She set the glasses back in place. "Our dear mountain people have much to appreciate too. Some are faithful even though some family members object to their commitment. They need encouragement."

"So, what are you thinking?" Lora asked.

"If we could have Bible lessons in the summer . . ." Aunt Nellie paused for a moment.

Lora felt a spark ignite in her soul. "That's it! We could do it now, couldn't we? The children are out of school and summer isn't over yet."

She went over to the drawer, pulled out pictures and lesson notes, and spread them on the table.

Aunt Nellie's eyes twinkled. "We could use these for Sunday school and make other pictures for the summer classes."

The minds of both raced with the flicker of growing inspiration. If only their neighbors could enjoy long periods of Bible study like she and Aunt Nellie had enjoyed. Perhaps more could grasp the teachings of Scripture. The idea had more than ignited. The potential before them burned like a candle in their minds.

"Let's see what Brother Benner and Anna have to say," Aunt Nellie suggested.

The workers sat in the living room and discussed the idea together. Rhine and Anna's eyes glowed. Additional teaching could lead more souls into the kingdom. Exposure to the Bible could provide opportunity to teach practical Christian living, and could add greater fulfillment to the Christian life.

Rhine Benner looked from Lora to Aunt Nellie. "There is much potential here, but it will take work."

Both women nodded with enthusiasm. "We know."

"There's something else," Brother Benner said. "We should have our bishop's consent. Bishop S. H. Rhodes has oversight of this work. Write to him and explain what we want to do."

"Aunt Nellie is a good letter writer," Lora said.

Aunt Nellie wasted no time in finding a piece of paper. Lora followed her to the table. The flame in the lamp burned brightly. Aunt Nellie dipped her pen in ink and wrote, "Dear Brother Rhodes." Lora watched the pen move across the paper.

Please, Lord, show us Your will about Bible school. Please send the answer soon, before summer is ended.

Direct the work . . . Her prayer would go on, a constant plea in the days to come.

Aunt Nellie read over the words again and signed her name. Then she folded the letter and sealed it in an envelope. Lora smiled as Aunt Nellie placed a stamp on the envelope and put it on the pile of mail Bertha Morral would carry out of the hollow. Tomorrow morning this letter would be on its way to Bishop S. H. Rhodes.

Chapter Nine

Waiting

1926

Lora felt the smooth fullness of an ear of corn attached to the stalk. She parted the husk carefully with her fingers and peeped inside. Plump round kernels appeared. Lora smiled and called across the garden rows to where Anna and Aunt Nellie stooped over the cucumber vines. "Here's some corn that's ready."

"Really?" Anna answered, standing up to face Lora. "Is there enough for dinner?"

Lora checked further. "There's enough for everyone." She twisted several ears from the stalks.

"We're having corn?" Rhoda shrieked with joy while her siblings jumped up and down.

Lora carried an armful of husked corn to the back porch while Aunt Nellie and Anna followed with a bucket of cucumbers. Little eyes peered over the table while Lora removed the silk.

"Do we have plenty of butter?" Lora asked Rhoda.

Rhoda shifted the baby in her arms and responded, "You mean 'cow butter'?"

Lora raised her eyebrows. "What's 'cow butter'? I thought all butter came from a cow."

Anna laughed. "Not all butter comes from a cow, Lora. There's apple butter, and pear butter. The mountain people call butter, 'cow butter'."

"I see," Lora said. "I've learned something new. Well, Rhoda, do we have cow butter for dinner?"

"I'll check the springhouse." Rhoda giggled. She handed the baby to her mother, clasped her sister Elva's hand and skipped off toward the springhouse.

While corn simmered on the stove for dinner, Lora helped Aunt Nellie slice cucumbers into salt brine in a huge wooden tub. At dinner the mission workers and the Benner family sank teeth into the first crop of corn, served with "cow butter" and sprinkled with salt.

Summer was advancing, and no letter had come from the bishop.

Lora rolled over and shut off the alarm. Aunt Nellie sat up and reached for her glasses.

"Wonder if we'll get our letter today," Lora said.

"I wonder too," said Aunt Nellie as she lit the lamp by the bed.

Lora combed her brown hair into a thick bun and pinned on her covering. The two ladies slipped quietly down the stairs where only silence met them.

"Brother Benner came in late last night, didn't he?" Lora whispered.

"Yes. I'm amazed how that man gives a helping hand day or night."

"The people love their minister," Lora said.

"They most certainly do," agreed Aunt Nellie. "The baby fussed last night. I'm sure Anna needs extra rest."

"I'll get some eggs and milk at the springhouse and start breakfast." Lora turned the knob and stepped through the back door.

The springhouse was a handy place to keep milk and other foods from spoiling.

The morning air felt cool as she walked through the early dawn toward the springhouse. A rooster crowed. Through the darkness, the cow watched her from across the fence, and the soft bleat of goats floated on the air. A hint of light hovered above the mountain.

When Lora returned to the kitchen with ingredients for a tasty breakfast, Aunt Nellie had a fire crackling in the stove. Lora broke eggs into a bowl and stirred in some milk and salt while Aunt Nellie mixed up the biscuits and placed them in the oven.

Overhead, a thump and scuffles sounded in the bedrooms. Then bare feet pattered down the stairs. One by one the children entered the kitchen, wiping sleep from their eyes as they plopped into chairs at the table. Brother Benner appeared and began singing while the family and missionary sisters joined in. *"Bright and roaring where you are . . ."*

Warm, foamy milk dripped through a cloth while Lora finished cleaning up the kitchen. She took the milk to the springhouse, washed the milk bucket, and set it near the door for the next milking. She stepped into the post office where Aunt Nellie sorted the mail.

"Did our letter come today?" Lora asked, her eyes bright with hope.

"I'm looking." Aunt Nellie shuffled rapidly through the stack.

Lora held her breath. Just maybe the letter had come. Aunt Nellie started through the pile again. When the last envelope had been checked, she turned slowly and faced Lora.

"I can't understand why the bishop doesn't answer."

This place, these people, this spot, had found a special place in Lora's heart.

"I can't either," Lora responded. As she turned to go, her shoulder drooped with disappointment. "Maybe it will come in the afternoon mail."

"Several women need new coverings, Lora," Anna Benner said one morning while Lora stirred soda cheese on the stove. "Do you think you could make some new ones?"

"Yes, I can."

"Coverings are not easy for the sisters to keep neat," Anna explained as she dressed the baby. "Rain often ruins them."

"Lora is quite the seamstress," Aunt Nellie responded with a nod in Lora's direction.

Anna Benner smiled. "Good! Some women need new dresses and bonnets too."

"I'll do what I can," Lora answered while scraping cheese from the edge of the skillet. "I think I'll write and ask Mother to send materials for coverings and bonnets. Maybe she could send thread and buttons too."

"I don't know how I could handle all the needs if you and Aunt Nellie weren't here." Anna set the baby on the floor among some toys.

"I want to sew for your family too," Lora said as she turned the soda cheese into a bowl.

Rhoda leaned against the table watching Lora dish out the cheese. "May I have the brown cheese left on the edge of the skillet?" she asked.

"Sure." Lora handed her the spoon. "Help yourself."

Rhoda scraped the brown cheese from the skillet and took a bite. "You make the best soda cheese, Lora."

"Thank you, but I don't know that mine is better than anyone else's."[1]

Throughout the year, various ministers from Virginia arrived at the mission home for scheduled preaching. With the preparation for the visitors came anticipation.

Lora set an extra plate on the table. At any moment the guest minister would arrive. Anna did last minute straightening and combed the children's hair. Aunt Nellie checked the oven.

Anna paused a moment to survey the waxed, well-worn linoleum. "Lora, these floors look so much better. I'm delighted at the improvement."

Lora brushed away the compliment as she checked to see if the guest had come. "All the scrubbing and preparation is worth it," she said. "I always enjoy visits from home folks. Wonder what he will bring this time?"

Moments later, a vehicle halted outside and a man in a black Sunday suit walked to the house. The minister took off his hat and shook hands with each one. He turned to Lora with a warm greeting and placed a box in her arms.

"From your mother," he explained.

"Thank you," Lora said, setting down the box to open it immediately.

"What is it?" The Benner children crowded close to see.

She found covering and bonnet material, long black ribbons, thread, and other sewing supplies inside.

Lora closed the box with gratitude. "Now the women will get new coverings and new bonnets too," she said.

---

1   Lora's soda cheese recipe is found in Appendix A.

"Did you have a letter for us from Bishop Rhodes?" Aunt Nellie asked the minister.

The minister shook his head. "No, I do not." He turned from the disappointed women to join Brother Benner in the living room.

"When will our letter come?" Aunt Nellie's brow wrinkled with concern.

"I don't know," Lora said worriedly. "The summer will be over if we don't hear soon."

The community creeks attracted both visitors and workers, especially on Sunday between the morning and evening services.

"You've got some lessons ready, and so do I," Aunt Nellie said.

"There's plenty to do until we get an answer," Lora said.

"And we can keep praying," Aunt Nellie added.

Sweet harmony floated throughout the mission home as the workers completed morning chores. Summer days sped by with no letter of permission for Bible school.

"It's time to visit again," Aunt Nellie said.

"Let's do," Lora agreed as she finished sweeping the floor. "We've been so busy with garden and company lately."

Anna wiped off the counter and hung up her dishcloth. "I wish I could go along, but it's hard for the children to walk that far."

"We will tell the women how much you would like to visit them," Aunt Nellie offered.

"Please do," Anna said, her eyes brightening.

"Of course, we haven't forgotten your prayers for us as we visit," Lora added.

"It seems I can do so little for the mountain people these days," Anna said.

"Perhaps you underestimate your part in the mission work here, Sister Benner," Lora encouraged. "You are an example to others of how godly mothers and wives should live."

"I know," Anna responded.

"It's a very important role." Aunt Nellie laughed good-naturedly. "It's one that Lora and I cannot fill since we have no husbands!"

"Aunt Nellie!" Lora stopped sweeping and stared at her aunt.

"It's true," Aunt Nellie said with a mischievous grin. "However, Lora could change that if she would give a certain young man a chance."

"Aunt Nellie!" Lora raised her broom in a playful manner as if to swat her aunt.

That afternoon Lora and Aunt Nellie climbed the steep ridges and knocked at several doors.

"What is the matter?" Aunt Nellie asked Lora. "Has everyone gone into hiding?"

"Someone is usually home," Lora said.

"Howdy," an elderly voice called across the fence.

"Hello, Minnie. We came visiting. Where is everybody?"

"Pickin' huckleberries."

"Huckleberries?" the ladies chorused.

"Yep. It's miles up ta th' plains. Folks'll be back late, 'bout dark, with plenty of burries to can up."

"Well, that explains things," Aunt Nellie said.

As dusk settled in the hollow, a knock sounded at the mission door.

"Anybody wanna go huckleburryin'?" The young woman asked. "More folks are goin' tomorr'."

"I'll go," Lora offered.

"Bring some buckets, yer dinner, and purty good shoes. It's a lo-o-ong way up to them blueburry plains."

Early the next morning, Lora trudged out of the hollow with a lantern in her hand. Barking dogs faded in the distance as the pickers started up the steep trail. It was an intense hike, and as Lora struggled to keep up with the mountain people, she had no doubt who would win in a race.

Her aching muscles, the threat of snakes, and the hot, blazing sun on the open plain made Lora think twice about ever coming back. Hunger gnawed her stomach while her muscles protested every movement. By late afternoon, Lora longed to be back at the mission home instead of facing the three-mile return walk.

In the gathering darkness, lights flickered in the windows along the way. Home was almost in sight. By the time she stepped onto the porch, she had made up her mind about one thing.

"Never again," Lora said with a sigh as she set the buckets in the kitchen and dropped into a chair.

"What?" Aunt Nellie asked, standing over Lora.

"I'll never go up to the huckleberry plains again," Lora stated.

"Are you sure?"

"Absolutely sure." Lora grimaced as she took off her shoes.

"You've got blisters," Aunt Nellie positioned a pillow for Lora to rest her legs. "Some reward for all that hard work."

Anna went for ointment. "Thank you for your hard work, Lora. This is a lot of berries."

Lora sighed wearily. "I just need a good night of sleep after my supper. I'm starving. What do you have to eat?"

Aunt Nellie set a plate of food on the table. "Eat up, mountain comrade."

While Lora ate supper, the children investigated the full bucket.

"Yummy!" Little Elva's bright eyes and grin gleamed through purple smears on her face.

"We'll have lots of huckleberry pies, Lora," Rhoda encouraged, tasting the berries for herself.

Lora moaned. "Who cares about huckleberry pie? I don't want to see huckleberries for a long time."

The following day, jars of deep purple cooled in the kitchen. On Sunday, two huckleberry pies smothered in whipped cream sat on the table. Anna cut the pie and handed it to Lora.

"I think you deserve the first slice," Anna said.

"Me?"

"Of course. You did the hardest work."

"Thank you." Lora lifted the first thick purple slice onto her plate.

Aunt Nellie took the pie from Lora and helped herself. She glanced at Lora with a hint of mischief in her eyes. "Are you going back to the huckleberry plains anytime soon?"

Lora took a bite while she deliberately delayed a response. Wild, sun-ripened huckleberry pie was so good! But she must answer Aunt Nellie's question.

A smile turned the corners of Lora's mouth. "I don't believe so."

"Do you mean it?"

"I mean that I shall never hike to the huckleberry plains again," Lora said with certainty.

The memory of gathering wild, mountain-grown berries high on the plains was satisfactory enough that Lora never did return to the huckleberry plains.[2]

---

2 The recipe for Wild Huckleberry Pie is in Appendix A if you would like to try making it.

Chapter Ten

More Than an Answer

1926-1927

"Why didn't Bishop Rhodes answer our letter?" Lora asked as she and Aunt Nellie packed their luggage to return home in the fall.

"I can't understand it," Aunt Nellie responded, "but it's too late anyhow."

Lora sighed. "There are so many needs here. 'The harvest is past, the summer is ended, and we are not saved,'" she quoted.[1]

"I know." Aunt Nellie placed her clothes in the suitcase.

"I'm going to keep praying," Lora said as she packed up her ragged shoes. "I hope we will be able to teach Bible school next year."

"I hope so too." Aunt Nellie checked each drawer and closed her bags. "Brother and Sister Benner concern me," her aunt whispered. "Brother Benner is run ragged, and the family is not very healthy."

---

1 Jeremiah 8:20

Lora turned to her aunt and whispered in return, "Should we pray for willing hearts and hands to help them?"

Aunt Nellie nodded.

Back home, Lora adjusted to her job in the silk mill where she worked second shift. Each afternoon she drove to work with several single women who shared the ride. Through the afternoon and evening hours, wheels and belts churned with a rhythmic hum. Lora handled her machine carefully, watchful that the threads spun correctly.

As she worked, memories of the mountain people mingled with her job. She wondered about Tillie and her family, and Sadie and her baby. Was Anna Benner getting along well? A new Benner baby would soon join the family. She thought of Della, the widow up the mountain with several children. Did they have enough provisions for the winter? Would there be enough money to see the mountain folks through the winter while the lumber camp closed until spring? How were the new Christians faring in their walk with God? She breathed a prayer for each one and asked the Almighty for help to meet the many needs.

One day a Home Mission Board member approached Lora, "Would you be willing to return to Roaring Creek next summer?"

"Sure," Lora responded without hesitation. "I would be happy to go."

In a short time, she learned that Aunt Nellie had also been asked to return to Roaring Mission. But what about the privilege to teach Bible lessons outside of Sunday school? *Lord, please send us an answer soon!*

During the winter of 1927, Lora attended Bible school at Eastern Mennonite School in Harrisonburg, Virginia. There she interacted, sang, and studied with students from many states. Godly teachers directed by the Holy Spirit taught lessons with clarity and enthusiasm. As the Bible lessons lodged deep in souls, students grew in faith and conviction. Some, like Lora, prepared to serve in missions.

In class, Lora absorbed the Scriptures. Like a building under construction, each brick of knowledge added to her edifice of faith. The class motto, "Building for God," reminded her of the process.

One day Aunt Nellie stopped her in the hall. "Have you heard the good news?"

"What news?"

Aunt Nellie clasped her hands together in glee. "Oh, Lora! We have permission from conference to have Bible school next summer! Think of it!"

Other students had crowded around to hear what was happening. "I'll be praying for you," some whispered.

Another gave Lora a pat on the back. "Keep up that cheerful smile and faithful work. God will bless you."

Aunt Nellie leaned over and whispered to Lora. "You know we have to get working on lesson ideas. Summer will be here soon."

Lora's eyes sparkled. "I'll work on some lessons in my spare time. I can't wait until summer!"

She picked up her books and walked to class with her perpetual smile. She would praise the Lord, for He did answer prayers. He would meet their needs somehow. In the evening, Lora jotted notes and sketched drawings for the vacation Bible school.

A friendly voice interrupted Lora as she studied one day.

"Yes?" Lora looked up into the pleasant face of Esther Moseman, a student from Pennsylvania.

Esther's eyes beamed. "I've been asked to help you and Nellie this summer with the vacation Bible school."

"Oh, Esther!" Lora exclaimed. "That is good news and a definite answer to prayer. The harvest field is white and ready to harvest."

"I'm thrilled to help you, but I'm nervous too," Esther said. "I never did this before."

"We haven't either," Lora replied, "but don't you worry, those people love Bible lessons. We just need the Lord's help to prepare and teach what He directs."

Enthused fellow students promised to pray for God's direction and blessing on the new work. Lora marveled at the Lord's answers to their prayers, but Aunt Nellie's news capped them all.

"What, Aunt Nellie? You've been asked to teach school at Roaring?"

"Yes." Aunt Nellie grinned so wide it seemed her face would crack. "Why Lora, we've been begging the Lord to send help to West Virginia, and now He is sending you and me there with more work than ever to do."

Lora began to laugh. "Do you think we got more than we bargained for?"

"More than we had in mind!" Aunt Nellie chuckled.

"But God's sending us helpers," Lora said.

"That's right," Aunt Nellie replied. "The Lord has answered our prayers far better than we imagined."

Lora placed the printed graduation leaflets in her dresser drawer. The past three days had been filled with graduation ceremonies, speeches, and fellowship. She smiled as she pushed the drawer shut. Now with weeks of Bible study, assignments, and graduation behind her, she must turn her focus to the upcoming months.

She examined her repaired shoes. Would they hold together for another season of mountain climbing? She opened her brand-new suitcase and filled it with new dresses, stockings, personal belongings, lessons she had prepared over the winter, and more.

Her things were ready to go. Downstairs a new table and two folding chairs she had purchased waited to be hauled along somehow. She and Aunt Nellie would use them for Bible school preparation.

She sighed. Tomorrow she would be at Roaring Mission Home for the busy summer months. Her heart gave a leap. She turned back the sheets and prepared for bed, checking her alarm clock. She would need to rise earlier than usual for the big trip.

With the table strapped to the vehicle, suitcases, bundles, and bags in the trunk, and passengers within, the burdened car groaned across winding, steep roads. Couldn't the miles go by faster? Lora peeked out the window to see if her new table and suitcase were still intact. The rough road curved and intersected a river. The vehicle eased into the ford and bounced through the rocky river bottom.

Thump! Clatter! Splash!

Lora gasped as she watched her suitcase tumble into the river. "Stop! I lost my suitcase!"

The driver stopped. Lora kicked off her shoes and waded into the water. She hauled the precious cargo to the bank and inspected the contents.

Lora breathed a sigh of relief. "It's not too bad. Clothes will dry and so will my papers."

Then she tied the suitcase tightly into place. Once again the overtaxed vehicle moved into the hill country. After miles of rough riding and with a throbbing headache, Lora scrambled out of the backseat and took a deep breath. The sounds of rushing water and squeals of delight from the Benner children warmed her heart as she rushed to meet them. Anna placed the baby in Lora's arms.

"He's hardly a newborn," Lora remarked as she held four-month-old Millard.

All of the Benner children had grown. James stretched inches beyond his previous height while Rhoda, on the

The Rhine Benner family.

verge of thirteen, seemed like a young lady. Little Elva was three and young Timothy toddled about and hid in his mother's skirt when the newcomers spoke to him.

"Somebody has been making changes around here." Lora looked at each of the Benner family. "Somebody built a new fence around the garden and yard."[2]

Anna answered with a pleased smile. "My husband has been busy."

One of the children took Lora's hand and pulled her toward the stairs. "See, Lora? New stairs."

Lora looked at the staircase. "Your papa is a good hand at such things."[3]

Lora handed the baby to Anna. "Aunt Nellie and I will try out those stairs. We'll unpack and get right to work."

Anna Benner smiled and nodded gratefully.

In the room upstairs, Lora hung up her damp clothes, set up the table, and spread out the lessons to dry. Which lesson should she use first? Did she have enough lessons prepared? Would the children understand and learn to know the Almighty One?

On Sunday morning at Roaring Church, a familiar woman engulfed Lora in an embrace.

"How good to have you back," Sister Sarah spoke sincerely. "We've missed you."

"It's so good to be back," Lora and Aunt Nellie agreed.

---

2 Middle District Minutes, Home Mission Board, December 28, 1926. "Decided to let Bro. Benner get fence for lot around house and truckpatch."

3 Middle District Minutes, Home Mission Board, December 1, 1926. "Decided to let Bro. Benner take out the one staircase and build new one . . . Decided to pay for work on house and church."

The chatter of children mingled with the sounds of the creek. There was a splash and the squeals of wet children. *Clop! Clop! Clop!* A man on horseback rode up to the hitching post, slid off, and tied the horse. Because he was lame, Jason often rode to church. He was there for almost every service, helping with church responsibilities.

Familiar faces brightened as they came to renew friendships with the Virginia women and issue a volley of invitations.

"When can you come visit us again?"

"Will you stay for dinner?"

"Will you bake me a cake?"

Aunt Nellie held up her hand. "Wait a minute. We just came. Give us a little time to settle in, and we'll be around to see you."

Lora chuckled too. "'Course we will. You couldn't tie us two codgers at home."

Several children clung to Lora and Aunt Nellie like flies on sticky pies.

"Will you tell us more stories?"

"We sure will. Lots of stories."

"I'm glad you've come back. I hope you will stay."

Lora placed her finger to her lips. "Sh-sh-sh. Now it's time to go into God's house. We must be reverent when we go inside."

Some of the children scooted onto the bench beside her.

"Shh," Lora whispered again, but her attempts to still little voices, hands, and feet seemed futile. The children wiggled anyway. Some craned to see which baby cried. Bare feet pattered up the church aisle. The benches creaked as the children scooted into place.

"Ow-w!" a child whimpered. His mother bent over and pulled a splinter from his hand.

Then the songs came forth in full volume. Oh, what joy! It was so good to be here with the friends she knew and loved. The summer lay before them—full of activity and potential.

Chapter Eleven

Vacation Bible School

1927

Lora placed the last Sunday dish into the cupboard. The Pennsylvania guests had come and gone. The John Moseman family had brought their daughter Esther, approximately age twenty, to assist with three weeks of vacation Bible school. Esther's special friend, John Mumaw, had come with the Mosemans and had brought the Sunday morning message.

That afternoon the three teachers lounged in the upstairs bedroom. A whiff of mountain air swept through the window screen and fluttered the freshly-turned July calendar page. Esther seemed quiet since her folks had gone.

Lora sat down at the table where Esther penned a letter and Aunt Nellie paged through her Bible. "Our guests showed a lot of interest in the mission work here," she said.

Esther nodded. "Yes, John is supportive of this work and the beginning of Bible school."

Lora agreed. "John's message was well-received this morning. The people could understand his presentation."

Aunt Nellie cleaned her glasses. "It is a blessing to have the support of other Christians. Your family and John are an encouragement to us."

Esther attempted a smile. Then she wiped her eyes with a white handkerchief.

"Let's plan the order of the Bible school," Aunt Nellie suggested. "You help me. We never did this before, so let's have some ideas."

"The children love singing," Lora said. "We should have lots of singing."

Aunt Nellie nodded. "Good idea. Each day we will take turns being in charge of singing."

The three women discussed their plans, and Aunt Nellie jotted down each decision they made.

Singing, devotions, prayer—20 minutes
First class period—30 minutes
Intermission: classes meet together for music and
      memory work—25 minutes
Second class period—30 minutes
Dismissal [1]

"Now who will teach the primary children? Lora, would you do that?" Aunt Nellie asked.

"Sure," Lora agreed.

"Esther, could you teach the intermediates?"

"I think I could."

Aunt Nellie mulled some thoughts, then looked at Esther. "If you and I swapped classes, we could teach two groups the same lessons."[2]

---

1 Esther Moseman, July 8, 1927, letter.
2 Esther Moseman, July 14, 1927, letter explains who taught what groups.

"What do you mean?" Esther asked.

"You teach the intermediates the first period, and then you teach the youth the next period. I would take the younger ones the second period." Aunt Nellie waited for an answer.

"I think I could." Esther squeezed her lips together as she mused on the idea.

Aunt Nellie leaned back in her chair. "This sounds like a good plan. Let's seek God's direction on what we are to teach."

With a gleam in her eyes, Lora shuffled through her collection of drawings. Which one should she use for the first night? She selected one and began to find Scriptures to accompany the lesson.

"Please tell me what to do." Esther's voice quivered. "I'm mighty green at this."

"All of us are green," Aunt Nellie chuckled as she looked over the rim of her glasses. "But these folks are harmless. I'm sure you will be comfortable with them."

"I don't know," said Esther uncertainly.

"You just wait and see," said Lora.

Esther lamented, "If only I had the artistic talents of those two Eastern Mennonite School students, Ernest Gehman and Russell Mumaw. My art would never measure up to the abilities of those two."[3]

"I wish for a dose of that talent too." Aunt Nellie nodded at Esther. "But these folks are more interested in the Bible than a talent show."

"Just do your best," encouraged Lora.

---

3 Ibid.

On Monday morning, Lora smoothed her clean dress and gathered her supplies.

"This day has finally come, Lora!" Aunt Nellie scooped up her books, ready to descend the stairs.

"Don't we look like EMS faculty members?" Esther crowed as she shuffled her books and examined Lora and Aunt Nellie.[4]

"Only a little more feminine, I'd say," Aunt Nellie quipped.

The three burst into laughter.

"Come on," said Aunt Nellie starting for the stairs, "Let's see what Brother and Sister Benner think of the vacation Bible school faculty."

Aunt Nellie tried to appear serious when she approached Brother Benner. "What do you think of the VBS faculty that has come to serve at Roaring?"

"Well now," Brother Benner caught the humor, "I think there is potential here. I don't believe we could have found a more qualified faculty."

"I quite agree," Anna Benner offered with amusement.

"The VBS faculty had best be off to work," Lora said as she headed for the door with her usual punctuality. "As I recall, Bible school is scheduled to begin at 10:00 a.m." [5]

Lora's determined stride brought her to the church quickly and slightly ahead of the others.

"Where do they all come from?" Esther asked as she watched children throw stones in the creek.

---

4   Esther Moseman, July 4, 1927, letter.
5   Esther Moseman, July 8, 1927, letter.

The three teachers ready for Bible school. From left to right:
Lora, Aunt Nellie, and Esther Moseman.

"From many places." Lora grinned. "In time, you will see for yourself where some of them live. I'm going to check my classroom."

When Aunt Nellie rang the bell, nimble feet sprinted for the church door.

"Sh-sh." Lora tried to hush the noisy, incoming students. "Wait here until we divide you into classes. What grade are you in, Johnny?"

She caught sight of several mothers standing in the churchyard. They came closer after the children had gone inside.

"I know you said classes are fer the children, but I came to see that mine b'have," one mother explained.

"I'm gonna check on my young'un too," another offered as several more mothers lingered at the door.

"Come in and join us," Lora said as Aunt Nellie waved them inside.

"Welcome to all of you!" Aunt Nellie said above the chatter and laughter as the children pressed through the door. "You may sit here, and here." She divided the students into the groups.

Then Aunt Nellie stepped to the front. "I'm glad you have come today. We are going to have Bible stories and lessons from God's Holy Word as we meet together each morning. We will have a wonderful time learning lessons to help us grow and love Jesus. Listen as I read you some words from God's Book.

'But Jesus said, suffer little children, and forbid them not, to come unto me: for of such is the kingdom of heaven.'[6]

"You see, Jesus was interested in children. Come along to Bible school each morning and learn what Jesus wants us to know about happy living. Another verse tells us what God says about those who love Him. It says this:

'I love them that love me; and those that seek me early shall find me.'[7]

"The Lord loves children and older ones who come willing to seek Him. He likes us to come as youngsters to learn of Him. Now Lora will lead us in some singing."

"What would you like to sing?" Lora surveyed the enthusiastic faces. A boy in a blue shirt waved in earnest.

"You in the blue."

The words burst out like a popped balloon. "Death Shall Not Destroy My Comfort!"

"All right. Let's sing." Lora led in singing about the joys of life hereafter. She focused on the bright faces of the children while the song rose to a crescendo. Let Esther see how

---

6   Matthew 19:14
7   Proverbs 8:17

well these children sang, even of topics such as death.

After the preliminaries, the children scuffled into their classes: primary, intermediate, and youth. Lora led the primary children to her classroom in the front of the church. She smiled into their eager faces. Finally the great moment had arrived! Now she could drop the seeds of truth into the hearts of the listeners. It was a privilege that thrilled her.

"What we gonna do?" the curious children squirmed with delight.

"We will have a Bible lesson each time you come to class," Lora explained. "You will learn how God wants people to live and how to behave in church. Living God's way brings happiness and joy in life."

The time sped by much too quickly. Reluctantly, the children and mothers departed, excited voices recounting the morning's activities as they left for home under the noonday sun.

"Why did they choose such songs?" Esther questioned, her voice almost a wail.[8]

Aunt Nellie smiled at the young teacher. "They are familiar."

"Perhaps we can teach them some new songs in Bible school," Lora offered.

"That sounds like a good idea," Aunt Nellie said. "You have to agree though, Esther, these people love to sing."

"Yes," Esther nodded, "they surely can sing. I thought the roof might lift off the rafters."

"How did the VBS faculty manage?" Anna asked as she set food on the table.

---

8 Esther Moseman, July 8, 1927, letter. "Their two favorite hymns here are 'Death Shall Not Destroy My Comfort' and 'Our Friends on Earth We Meet With Gladness.'"

*Children of all ages, and mothers, too,
turned out for the new Bible school in 1927.*

Lora said, "My students were eager to learn. They seemed to enjoy class."

"My students were enthusiastic," Aunt Nellie added, "but I wasn't expecting adults."

Esther sighed. "What do you think of a youngster like me teaching the older students? The adults looked at me strangely when I taught that class in the second period. Some of them are older than I am!"

Lora patted Esther on the shoulder. "We really were not expecting adults. But you managed?"

"Yes. I was frightened, but they listened well and took part in class," Esther said. "I learned something too. These people are not ignorant like I thought."

Lora added, "And the children know quite a lot about the Bible. Others have been teaching them years before we came."

Brother Benner added, "Some parents read the Bible and teach it to their children."

"How many attended?" Anna Benner asked while everyone sat up to the table.

"Around thirty-five, plus babies," Aunt Nellie answered.[9]

"A good number," Brother Benner commented. "I think you teachers have a wonderful opportunity to teach the Bible. And it seems that there's plenty of enthusiasm."

The teachers nodded in agreement. Then Brother Benner led the group in prayer.

"Lord, bless the Bible school and bring many souls into Thy kingdom. Bless the teachers as they seek to know what Thou wouldst have them teach. And bless the hearts of all who come to hear Thy Word. In Jesus' name, Amen."[10]

---

9 Esther Moseman, July 4, 1927, letter.

10 The contents of Esther Moseman's letter differ from Harry Brunk's reporting in *History of Mennonites in Virginia 1900-1960,* p. 209, concerning the first Mennonite vacation Bible school. The letters, as well as photos, indicate that Roaring was the location. During this time, the teachers visited people in the Roaring community. Also, the attendance given by Brunk does not match the information in Moseman's letter. The Brushy Run Bible school did not begin until 1929 or 1930, according to information in *Leaders and Institutions of the Southeastern Mennonite Conference.*

Chapter Twelve

Lora's Lessons

1927

The days skimmed by, filled with regular summer duties, class preparation, and Bible school. Lora smiled at the eager students who clamored into her classroom. What precious children they were, and what energy and potential lay in their hearts! Lora knew that the King of kings and Lord of lords wanted to grasp each young hand and walk with them through life. She must lead them to know Him and show them how to live as His children. "Here's a seat, and there's one," Lora directed as she prepared to begin the lesson.

"Guess what, Teacher?" Billy's teeth showed a gap as he hammered on Lora's arm for her undivided attention.

"What?" Lora asked as she helped the boy find a seat on the bench at the table.

"A fox got a couple a chickens, and my Daddy's gonna shoot him up good fer that!" Billy nodded for emphasis.

Lora patted his shoulder and grinned. "We have to get rid of foxes that eat chickens. All right, class, let's begin with a story today about bees."

"Hey, Teacher," a little girl in pink interrupted, "we just got some new honey. My daddy found a bee tree."

"A bee tree?" Lora questioned.

"Yep. Daddy followed the bee to the tree and found a heapin' stash of honey. He burned the tree to get the honey and almost burned up the mountain!"

"I see," Lora commented. "I'll have to learn how that's done. Well, let's learn about bees." She held up her picture.

"They look real!" someone gasped.

Lora laughed. "Let's see what these bees do. The bees we will talk about are different from honey bees. These are bees for church."

Lora pointed to the first bee. "*Be always there.* Be there for church on the Lord's Day. Be there when the church doors are open. God has such good things He wants you to learn, so be there when church time comes."

Several little heads bobbed in agreement.

"I like to come to church." A little girl grinned up at her teacher.

"Me too," several children chorused.

"Good," said Lora. "Now here's another bee. *Be on time.* Get ready ahead of time and start for church in plenty of time so you are not late. Be there on time."

Heads nodded, their eyes riveted on the picture Lora held.

"This bee is *be prayerful.* When we speak to God, He hears and wants to answer. He knows what is best for us, so we can pray and ask Him to help us.

"*Be reverent.* When we come to God's house, we must remember that He is here. He wants to speak to us while

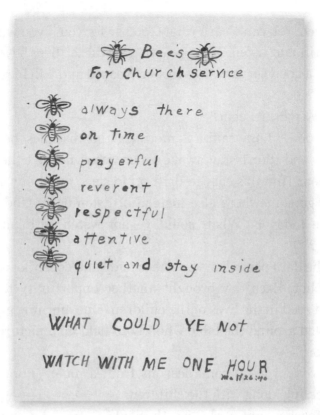

Lora's "bee" lesson.

we worship in God's house. We must listen to His voice and be reverent."

Lora pointed to the next bee. "This one is *be respectful*. We should respect our parents, our teachers, our minister, and God. God teaches us in the Bible to respect those in authority."

She tapped the shoulder of one boy who gazed out the window. Some squirmed in their seats and others listened.

Lora stooped to the children's level and made eye contact. "Here's another one. *Be attentive* and learn what God wants you to know. And *be quiet* and stay inside during the service. You can't learn what God has for you if you will not sit still and listen. If we practice all these "bees," we will have a good service. God will be pleased and will bless our lives."

"We will, Teacher."

"Good," Lora said. "Sometimes the disciples became tired and didn't stay awake when Jesus needed them to be near Him. It's easy to drift off to sleep or let our attention go somewhere else instead of listening to God. Our verse today is 'What, could ye not watch with me one hour?' "[1]

The days passed one by one, cloudy and cooler, or sunny and hot. Each day brought another opportunity to sow good seed in the lives of the children. One morning giggles rippled around the table when Lora held up a picture of a mule.

"We can learn some lessons from a mule," Lora said, chuckling along with the children.

"Teacher, my uncle has the bad-dest bad mule ever!" The boy opened his eyes wide with expression. "My uncle said he's a good fer nothing . . ."

Quick as a flash, Lora hushed the conversation and moved on with the lesson. "A mule is quick, stubborn, tricky, and strong-headed. You don't always know what to expect from a mule. Sometimes he cooperates with the farmer; sometimes he is stubborn and will not behave. He can kick his feet high in the air."

Laughter filled the classroom, but Lora pressed on with the lesson. "Humans can be like a mule too. Jesus wants to live in our hearts, to master our lives and make us useful for Him.

"Some people will not allow Jesus to live in their hearts. Instead they choose to be selfish, just like the mule. Their lives become difficult when they do whatever they want. The Bible says, 'The way of transgressors is hard.'[2]

"So children, if we live like a mule, our lives will be difficult and unhappy. But if we follow Jesus and allow Him to control our lives, we will be happy."

Around the table, young heads nodded and faces lit with smiles as they chanted the memory verse. Would they remember the truths they had been taught as they grew older? When the Lord called them to follow, would they respond with gladness or insist on living life their own way?

Happy voices sang to the Almighty. How He must have smiled at the songs of praise presented to Him!

"Can you say the verse?" Lora leaned over and asked little Elva Benner.

Her small mouth twitched but no words came. Lora paused a moment, still no answer. So she called on the next child, and the next, to say the verse until the circle had been completed.

Lora tried to encourage. "Now it's your turn."

Still the lips pressed tightly together while innocent eyes peered back and blinked. Attempting to speak, the saliva drooled from the corners of Elva's mouth. She snapped her

2 Proverbs 13:15

lips shut, but not before Lora caught sight of a tiny clove on her tongue.

"Come," Lora said, grinning at the perplexed child. "I know what we can do."

Taking the child by the hand, Lora slipped through the back door and paced a few steps from the building. "Now you can spit it out."

Cloves grew on bushes and could be used as mints to freshen breath. Elva spit into the weeds and wiped a fist across her mouth, then turned to smile at Lora.

Lora grinned in return and patted her shoulder. "Did someone give you a clove?"

Elva nodded. Lora took the small hand and led her back into the classroom, wondering who had given it.

"Can you say the verse now?" Lora asked as Elva slid onto the bench.

Little Elva nodded enthusiastically, quoting the verse without any mistakes.

Lora pulled the picture from her stack of materials and held it up for her students to see. "Today's lesson is about the wheelbarrow."

Cheerfully, Lora dug into the lesson. Some giggled, some wiggled, and others propped their chins in their hands to listen, their eyes bright with anticipation.

"That looks like our wheelbarrow!" one child said.

"Like ours too," another said.

"I'm sure all of you have one at your house. Now listen

as we learn some lessons from the wheelbarrow. The wheelbarrow must be pushed to make it go. Let us not be a person who needs to be pushed to do his part. We should do our duties willingly, cheerfully, and well. Another lesson about the wheelbarrow is that it is easily upset and can't get back up. Let's not be wheelbarrow people who are easily upset. We need Jesus to help us not to become angry and disagreeable."

Lora looked around the room at the innocent, loving children. Surely they couldn't be such people, could they? But time and history had proven that all people have a fallen nature. Every innocent child possessed a human heart, its devious and carnal ways known to all mankind. Only the transforming of human nature by divine power could bring about radical change.

The young faces gazed back at hers, waiting for more teaching. She hurried on.

"Let us not be idle, unable to be up and about, like a wheelbarrow on its side. Let us wake up and help our minister. Don't ask your minister to carry your load; help to lighten his. Do your part to encourage him and others. Your life can encourage the ones around you. Now everyone, let's sing a song."

As Lora walked home from church, questions filled her mind. Would these children grow up to be helpers in the church? Would these lessons make a difference in the lives they might live for Jesus' glory? Would some of them become believers and stand for truth even when others refused? She prayed that they would.[3]

---

3 The lessons and illustrations in this chapter are copies of the original lessons handmade by Lora during these years at Roaring. See Appendix B for more of Lora's lessons.

Chapter Thirteen

Rain!

1927

"Oh, no!" Lora moaned as she sat up in bed one morning.

"What's wrong?" asked Esther in the darkness.

Lora replied, "Can't you hear? It's raining!"

"I hear it," Esther said as a rhythm drummed on the roof.

"Rain," Aunt Nellie murmured as she sat up and lit the lamp.

"What's the problem?" Esther asked. "It rains in Virginia and Pennsylvania too."

"Too much precipitation in these mountains can be dangerous." Aunt Nellie sounded like a teacher standing before her classroom. "These local folks speak about floods in the past that swept away homes and property, even people."

Lora crawled out of bed and dressed. "It seems there are more rainy days here than at home, but maybe the rain will stop soon," she said hopefully.

"I hope so," Esther said. "We have all our lessons prepared for the children."

The rhythmic drumming of the raindrops increased as the ladies dressed, combed, and made beds. They slipped down the stairs, and soon the smells of breakfast drifted throughout the kitchen and up the stairway. Sounds of bare feet shuffled down the steps. Rhoda Benner set the table while bleary-eyed children plopped into chairs.

Brother Benner's raspy morning refrain broke into the kitchen clatter. *"Bright and roaring where you are . . ."*

Half giggling, half singing, the children and workers joined in while Esther listened.

"What a cute song," Esther commented.

"Might as well be cheery and bright even if it's a rainy day," Rhine Benner said. "The creek will be roaring before long anyhow."

Rain pounded on the roof as everyone ate breakfast.

"Will the children come to Bible School in all this rain?" Esther wondered.

"I don't know," Brother Benner responded. "Sometimes we cancel services because of heavy snow. We'll just have to wait and see."

After the breakfast dishes had been washed, Lora went to the window. Gray skies still dumped rain.

"Is the creek rising yet?" Brother Benner asked.

"Yes," Lora answered. "I doubt the children will come in such a downpour. I may as well get busy sewing."

The scissors snipped quickly through fabric as she cut out the pieces of a dress. The back and front bodice appeared, then sleeves and a wide piece of material for a gathered skirt. She placed the pieces by the sewing machine, threaded the machine, and began to sew. The machine hummed while the sound of rain on the roof droned on. Rhoda leaned across the table, watching the seams speed through Lora's skilled hands.

"Watch out, or I'll catch your nose in the needle," Lora teased.

"Ouch!" Rhoda giggled. "You wouldn't do that, would you?"

"It might happen if you get too close."

Rhoda ran off to help her mother.

"Do you sew for lots of people?" Esther asked as she watched Lora work.

"A good many. Seems there are always needs," Lora answered.

"Don't the women know how to sew?"

"Some do; others are too poor to buy fabric even if they can sew. We just help wherever we can."

"Let me sew on the buttons when you finish so you can start on another one," Esther offered.

"Thanks, Esther."

The minutes ticked on as the household buzzed with morning activity. The house had been tidied, and the children combed and dressed.

Aunt Nellie ventured to the window and said, "It looks like the storm is breaking up."

Lora looked at the clock. "It's almost starting time for Bible school and some of the children walk an hour to church. Surely they wouldn't come even if it stopped raining now."

Lora lifted the presser foot from the dress, snipped the threads, and held up the little girl's dress for inspection.

"Lora, you are fast," Esther said.

"Am I?" Lora grinned as she laid the garment down to mark the buttonholes.

"Ladies, guess what," Aunt Nellie gasped. "There are children over at the church."

"What?" Lora hurried to the window. "Well, there they are! At least a few of them came. Now isn't that something."

Aunt Nellie turned to the minister. "Brother Benner, the children are here. Should we have Bible school?"

Brother Benner peered through the window at the children. "The rain has stopped and the children are here. Why not have Bible school for those that have come?"

Lora folded her work and stashed it away in her room. She gathered her bag of prepared lesson materials, her Bible, and a sweater. Then she joined the other teachers and the Benner children as they slipped out the door and headed for the church.

In spite of gray clouds that smothered the mountain peaks, childish laughter drifted through the damp foliage.

"Are more coming?" Lora's eyebrows lifted.

"Sounds like it," Aunt Nellie responded with a grin.

Children gradually emerged from the forest only slightly wet. Some crossed the bridges with caution and watched the wild currents churn below. Several waded in a puddle, and a young girl cleaned a spot of mud splattered on her skirt.

"We didn't think you would come in the rain," Lora said, smiling at the youngsters.

"'Course we came." The little eyes twinkled with enthusiasm. "Y'said we'd get a Bible if we came every time."

Lora whirled around to face Aunt Nellie.

"That's right," Aunt Nellie responded.

"Did you get soaked coming down the mountain?" Lora asked the children.

"Not much." The boy smoothed his unruly blond hair. "Mama made us wear jackets and gave us flannel to wear."

"A good mother she is," Aunt Nellie commented. "And you don't seem too wet either."

"Nope, not when you have lots of trees to walk under." The youngster held onto his little sister's hand and grinned. "We wanted to come."

Lora felt her heart swell in gratitude for lovable children who wouldn't let weather deter their enthusiasm for Bible teaching. She could imagine them stepping carefully down the mountain trails. Just like birds and furry critters find shelter from storms, so these children found the Creator's natural protection from rain.

More children continued to arrive. "Come in, everybody," Aunt Nellie called from the door. "It's 10:30, so we should get started."

The children scampered from puddles and lined up to enter the church. Lora counted the children.

"Do you know what I think?" Lora asked the other teachers.

"What?"

"I think all the children are here."

Lora followed Aunt Nellie into the church with the children skipping behind. There was a scuffle as little bodies filled the benches. No rain pattered on the roof. But the creek rushed wildly on in its downward course while the children sang.

They chanted memory verses, listened to Bible stories, and sang more songs. Lora had the perfect story for the situation. She cleared her throat and began.

"Our lesson today is about feet. There are different kinds of feet—noisy feet, lazy feet, and busy feet. Feet can be quiet or noisy. When we are in God's house we must keep our feet still and not run in and out during the service. We can be reverent when we worship God. Today you children allowed God to direct your feet to the church to learn more of His ways. That pleases the Lord Jesus."[1]

The faces brightened with smiles. Some recounted the happenings of tramping down muddy trails that morning. Lora saw the opportunity and took it.

"Sometimes in life the way becomes slippery and difficult, maybe even dangerous. We need the Lord to guide us in our daily walk. He will be our help and guide no matter what comes in our path."

Would these innocent lambs always follow the teaching they were hearing today?

Lora opened her Bible. "Now let us learn our verse: 'Walk humbly with thy God.' "

When the children had gone home and the teachers sat at the dinner table in the mission house, the patter of falling rain began again.

"More rain," Brother Benner commented as he looked out the window.

"I hope the children make it home," Esther said.

"They will," Lora stated. "I've learned not to underestimate what these mountain people can do."[2]

---

1 Taken from Lora's homemade lesson.
2 Esther Moseman, July 8, 1927, letter, p. 11.

Chapter Fourteen

Problems

1927

With two weeks of rigorous Bible school schedules behind them and another to go, the teachers felt fatigued. One afternoon the teachers and Rhoda ventured to the creek for some relaxation. The ripple of water awakened childish inner urges, and in short order each one had removed stockings and shoes for the sheer joy of wading.

Playfully, Esther picked up a big rock and aimed it deliberately and precisely in front of Lora, who stood knee-deep in the creek. "Gotcha!"

Lora shrieked as cold water sprayed onto her dress and face. "Who did that?" Lora sputtered to regain her composure as she surveyed Rhoda, Aunt Nellie, and Esther doubled over in laughter.

Esther laughed so hard she could barely get out the words. "I'm . . . not . . . telling."

"I'm not telling," Aunt Nellie mimicked, her eyebrows upraised with mischief.

"And I'm not either," laughed Rhoda.

With a playful scheme in mind, Lora wiped her glasses and put them back on her nose. As she reached for a rock, another wave whaled her face.

"Somebody has something coming!" Lora teased as she aimed and carefully directed a rock to the intended spot with a delightful splash. "Got all of you!"

The three squealed with laughter. Suddenly Esther lost her balance and plopped backward into the creek.

"Looks like we're all in the same boat now," Lora chuckled as she gave Esther a helping hand.

"It's better than being wet hens," Aunt Nellie countered with a chuckle.

"This water is so cold!" Esther lamented as they wrung water from their skirts.

The lighthearted moment brought a welcome change from the serious responsibilities of Bible teaching. Even so, mirth cannot last forever.

"Come on, let's go see Stone Camp Run," Aunt Nellie suggested as she sloshed out of the water.

"That is a beautiful place," Lora agreed. She wiped her feet dry on the grass and sat on a log to put on her shoes and stockings.

"And I'll take some pictures," said Esther. "I'll go get my camera."

The group walked up the hollow just beyond the church where Stone Run gushed into Roaring Creek.

Esther gazed at the water spilling down the mountain. "What a lovely place this would be if the trash could be cleared."

"Let's clean it up," said Lora, pulling away some of the brush.

"Let's do," agreed Aunt Nellie.

Esther tugged at a big branch. She pulled and pushed until the limb broke loose. Together they worked until the natural beauty had been reclaimed. Then Esther took pictures of the improved scenery.

When the girls returned to the mission house, they found Brother Benner studying his Bible and Anna dressed in Sunday clothes.

"Could you girls keep the children while we go to a funeral?" Anna asked. "Rhine has been asked to preach."

"Sure," Lora answered.

Aunt Nellie had other ideas. "May I go along? I'll hurry and get ready."

"Sure," Anna responded as she cleaned Rhine's best shoes.

Aunt Nellie and the parents had hardly been gone when one of the children began to cry. Rhoda took them out to play while Lora's needle stitched a hem.

"Why do the children cry so much?" Esther asked.

"I don't know," Lora answered. "Some have had health problems."

"I think I'd spank them."

"That's what Aunt Nellie says," Lora responded. "Probably parents don't always know the answers either."

Lora's needle flicked in and out of the dress, her thimble thrusting it through the folds with precision. She had almost finished when she noticed Esther reaching for the wall to steady herself.

"Are you all right?"

Esther sat on a chair and held her head. "I don't know what's wrong. I feel dizzy and achy. Maybe I pulled some muscles when we cleaned up that brush."

"You'd better go upstairs and lie down."

"Are you certain you can handle the children?" Esther asked weakly.

"I'll do my best," Lora answered.

When Rhoda brought the children inside, Lora read stories and sang them to sleep. Later the Benners and Aunt Nellie returned, bringing letters from the Onego post office.

"Another letter for Esther?" Aunt Nellie pretended to be surprised as she sorted the letters.

"She's upstairs and isn't feeling well," Lora explained.

Aunt Nellie called up the stairs, "More mail from John." She wandered back to the table to place several envelopes on a stack for Esther.

Esther came downstairs looking rather pale and reached for her stack of mail.

"Didn't you get a letter from John just this morning?" Aunt Nellie's voice mellowed with good humor.

Esther smiled weakly and answered, "Yes." She clasped her letters possessively to her heart.

"I think you should tell John he's writing entirely too often," Aunt Nellie teased.

Esther grinned sheepishly and changed the subject. "How did the funeral go?"

"Not as we expected," Aunt Nellie offered, looking from Rhine to Anna Benner with a grin playing at the corners of her mouth.

"Rhine didn't even get to preach," Anna said.

Lora looked puzzled. "But I thought that's what he went to do."

"He was supposed to speak," Anna explained, "but another minister came and *he* gave the message."

"So Anna finally got her wish to hear another preacher," Aunt Nellie declared with jovial laughter.

Lora joined in with amusement. "Don't you like to hear your husband preach, Anna?"

Anna chuckled. "Of course I do, but a change is nice once in a while."

"What did the preacher speak about?" Esther looked at Aunt Nellie for an answer.

"I'm ashamed; I can't remember anything that was preached. I kept watching something crawl in the head of hair in front of me. I kept fidgeting because I thought the critters had me too."

Everyone laughed except Aunt Nellie, who went into a coughing spell.

"Maybe some critter did get you," Rhine Benner quipped.

Aunt Nellie responded, "Come to think of it, my throat is a little scratchy."

The humor died as Esther scanned her letters. "Oh, no! John writes that his cousin Russell Mumaw is sick in the hospital."

The mention of Russell brought back memories of days at Eastern Mennonite School. The three ladies chatted about the good times with their friends and hoped Russell would soon recover. Then Esther excused herself and went back upstairs to bed.

When the household awakened the next morning, all humor had vanished.

"Can't talk," Aunt Nellie whispered with a raspy voice when Lora spoke to her.

"I'll make some coffee and see if that helps soothe your throat," Lora said.

"Are you feeling any better?" Lora asked when Esther stirred.

"I won't be needing any breakfast," Esther said, rolling over in bed. "I feel hot and faint."

Lora descended the stairs and started a fire in the kitchen stove. Just as she put the kettle on the hottest spot, slight nausea stirred in her stomach.

Anna joined Lora in the kitchen. "Are you all right, Lora?"

"I'm beginning to feel sick."

"We must have a germ," Anna said, her face looking tired from broken sleep. "The children were sick last night."

When Lora had finished making breakfast, she set the platter of eggs on the table and sat down to keep from losing her balance. She held her head and spoke to Aunt Nellie who was already sipping hot coffee at her place at the table. "How can we have Bible school when we are sick?"

Aunt Nellie shrugged her shoulders instead of answering.

"Aunt Nellie is very hoarse this morning." Lora explained to Rhine and Anna Benner the reason for her aunt's inability to talk.

Brother Benner led in prayer, asking God for direction in Bible school and for recovery from sickness. When class time arrived, the teachers had decided to shorten the lessons and practice the program. By God's grace they got through the day, with enough improvement to write letters home and study for another lesson.

However, better days did not return immediately. Sad news arrived when a phone call brought startling news about their classmate.

"I can't believe it!" Esther stared at Aunt Nellie and Lora.

"I can't either," Lora and Aunt Nellie echoed.

Dazed by the sad news, the conversation fumbled.

"Russell Mumaw passed away?"

"He had such a talent for art."

"I just can't understand why God would take him home, but God's ways are not our ways."

In desperation, Esther tried to connive a way to get home for the funeral. But the distance and time to travel to Pennsylvania proved too great, and she was left with the stark reality that she could not go.

Upstairs in their bedroom, the teachers wiped their eyes and noses. They prayed and tried to plan for the next classes. Lora fingered her drawings, wondering which one to select. Still, the shock and grief fogged their creative energies.

"Do you know what?" Aunt Nellie clicked her fingers as a thought came to her. "We could tell our students about Russell's life and how his mother prayed faithfully for him."

Lora brightened as she blew her nose. "Yes, Aunt Nellie, that's a wonderful idea."

Aunt Nellie continued. "The fact that his mother's prayers were answered could encourage those who are praying for wayward ones. Now he is in Heaven with his mother who prayed for him."

Esther smiled through her tears. "Do you think we could sing 'Tell Mother I'll Be There' for the students?"

Lora questioned, "Do you think we could do it without getting choked up?"

"We could try," Esther offered as she dried her eyes.

The teachers sang softly with husky voices.

"Tell Mother I'll be there in answer to her prayer:
This message, blessed Saviour, to her bear!
Tell Mother I'll be there, Heaven's joys with her to share;
Yes, tell my darling mother I'll be there."

Aunt Nellie mused aloud. "Maybe we could also sing 'Where Is My Wandering Boy Tonight?'" She began the song with the others blending in harmony.

"Where is my wandering boy tonight,
   the boy of my tender years,
The boy that was once so dear to me,
   and none was so sweet as he?

Oh, where is my boy tonight?
Oh, where is my boy tonight?
My heart o'erflows, for I love him, he knows.
Oh, where is my boy tonight?"

Lora suddenly jumped up and searched in her drawer for her memory book from EMS Bible school days.

"Russell wrote something in my memory book." She thumbed through the pages until she found the words he had penned to her. Solemnly she read,

"Measure not life by the hopes and enjoyments of this world but by the preparation it makes for another; looking

forward to what you shall be rather than what you have been."[1]

Tears glistened in the eyes of each as they pondered the words. It seemed that Russell's life spoke even more clearly in death than in life.

Aunt Nellie looked tenderly from Lora to Esther as she whispered, "You know, perhaps we should be glad he could go."

"What if death had called one of us?" Lora asked.

Aunt Nellie nodded in agreement. "Or someone else in our classes, or here in the mountains, who was not ready to enter eternity?"

"Oh, time is short," Esther lamented, "but we still have a little while yet."

"And we can make the best use of the remaining days," Lora said with determination.

Aunt Nellie picked up her Bible and paged to a Scripture for her lesson. "I can hardly wait for the next class."[2]

---

1 From Lora Heatwole's Eastern Mennonite School Memory Book, a book of friends' autographs and inspirational words.
2 The information in this chapter was taken from Esther Moseman's July 14 and 18, 1927 letters. It is thought Russell died after an appendix or gallbladder surgery. His mother had died previously.

Chapter Fifteen

Growth

1927

Three weeks of vacation Bible school had come to an end. The children had just completed a program of songs and verses for the mothers. Boys and girls squirmed in their seats and whispered with excitement. All eyes fastened on the Bibles stacked on a table at the front of the church.

Aunt Nellie smiled as she addressed the audience. "Thank you, students, for your program and thank you, mothers, who have come to listen. Now we will present prizes to those who had perfect attendance. Please come forward when your name is called."

One by one the children slipped from the pews to claim the rewards. Eyes twinkled and smiles shone as the new Bibles came to rest in the hand of each child. Some gasped with joy.

A young boy grinned, hugged his Bible, and whispered, "This is so special!"

An older student whispered, "Thanks. I'll try to read it."

"It's your very own," Lora whispered to an excited student who returned to sit beside her, new Bible in hand. "Now you may read the stories for yourself."

After a closing song, the students scampered the short distance to the mission home for a picnic. Mothers contributed food they had prepared in advance. Lora placed a plate of Lebanon bologna on the table. After prayer, everyone filled plates and found a spot to eat.

"Bible school was so much fun," the students said repeatedly.

"We learned so many things," Gracie said. "I liked the classes."

Tillie added, "You taught the Bible in a way that we could understand."

Aunt Nellie adjusted her glasses and said, "Thank you for coming and making our first Bible school a very good year. I hope we can have classes again next year."

Lora and her class of Primaries.

Esther and the Intermediate class.

Aunt Nellie and her students.

When the last child had reluctantly gone home, the teachers cleared the table and shook the crumbs from the tablecloth. Lora picked up a blanket that had been spread for the children to sit on.

"Here's a piece of Lebanon bologna someone didn't eat." Lora picked up the meat with a precise bite in the edge.

"Must not have liked it," Aunt Nellie surmised.

"But why not?" Esther Moseman questioned. "Lebanon bologna is good."

Anna Benner said, "I thought everyone would like this Pennsylvanian specialty."

"Maybe the mountain people never had this kind of meat before," Lora suggested.

"And I thought I had served something special," Anna lamented.[1]

With Bible school over, the mission clicked into frenzied preparation for guests. On Sunday, Anna's pretty zinnias graced the center of the table. John Mumaw had come to take Esther home. In addition, evangelist J. E. Suter and song leader W. M. Heatwole joined the mission workers around the table. Suter and Heatwole planned to follow the Bible school work with a week of evangelistic meetings, beginning that evening.

After dinner, Lora and Aunt Nellie and the Benner family said farewell to Esther and John.

"We will pray for you," John said.

"Now I know much more about the work than I did before," Esther added. "I'll miss you."

---

1 Lebanon bologna, a special meat processed in Pennsylvania, was likely introduced to the States when Mennonites migrated from Germany. After the meat is smoked and preserved, it can be served as a cold cut. The student who took a bite of the bologna related to the author that she could not finish eating it nor did she ever want to try it again. Likely the Mosemans brought it when they came to visit.

"May the Lord bless you as you serve Him here," John said as they turned to go.

Lora and Aunt Nellie retired to their room to rest and pray for the meetings.

Lora asked, "Aunt Nellie, do you remember that verse in Matthew about two who pray together?"

"Yes. There's a promise in that verse." Aunt Nellie paged to Matthew 18:19. " 'If two of you shall agree on earth as touching anything that they shall ask, it shall be done for them of my Father which is in heaven.' "

Lora studied Aunt Nellie. "That's a wonderful promise. I know Brother and Sister Benner are praying, and we can too."

Aunt Nellie agreed. "Let's do. After three weeks of teaching, I feel in need of soul refreshment."

"Our grief has not been easy," Lora added, "but the Lord will meet our needs."

Both prayed for revival for themselves and salvation for the lost.

That evening, W. M. Heatwole led singing and shared a children's meeting. Little children filed to the front of the church to hear the story. Then the evangelist presented light from God's Word.

Each evening the little church filled with people. The speaker opened the Gospel message to all who listened.

For all have sinned, and come short of the glory of God (Romans 3:23).

For the wages of sin is death; but the gift of God is eternal life through Jesus Christ our Lord (Romans 6:23).

That if thou shalt confess with thy mouth the Lord Jesus, and shalt believe in thine heart that God hast raised him from the dead, thou shalt be saved. For with the heart man believeth unto righteousness; and with the mouth confession is made unto salvation (Romans 10:9-10)

Now when they heard this, they were pricked in their heart, and said unto Peter and to the rest of the apostles, Men and brethren, what shall we do? Then Peter said unto them, Repent, and be baptized every one of you in the name of Jesus Christ for the remission of sins, and ye shall receive the gift of the Holy Ghost. Then they that gladly received his word were baptized (Acts 2:37, 38, 41).

The Spirit moved among the audience and brought conviction to hearts. Many youth and adults responded to the call. Some older ones also knelt to receive forgiveness of sins. James and Rhoda Benner responded, along with a teen-aged mother who carried her chubby toddler. Tillie had joined the family of God.

At home in the mission house, the workers praised God and committed themselves afresh to the work of guiding new believers.

"Truly, God is working here," Brother Benner rejoiced at the table with his family and mission workers.

"He certainly is," Brother Suter agreed. "Several people have helped you sow the seed and nurture faithfully. Now God is reaping a harvest."

Brother Benner chuckled as he quoted a portion of Scripture so familiar to him. "So then neither is he that planteth any thing, neither he that watereth; but God that giveth the increase. Now he that planteth and he that watereth are one: and every man shall receive his own reward according to his own labour. For we are labourers together with God."[2]

---

2   1 Corinthians 3:7-9

With the satisfaction of a farmer who gathers crops into his barns, the workers delighted in the gleaning of God's great harvest. Lora felt as if she could burst with the joy that flooded the mission home.

With the birth of new Christians, the sewing needs soared. Each afternoon the sewing machine hummed while new dresses and coverings formed under Lora's skillful hands. Several new dresses hung on hooks, ready for young ladies to try on.

Rhoda Benner watched Lora sew. The machine hummed while the white netting passed under the needle. As Lora worked she always had a song on her lips.

Lora lifted her foot from the treadle. She cut the threads and pressed the completed covering. After setting the hot iron on the stove, she added the new veiling to the stack of finished ones.

"You are a fast seamstress," Rhoda commented.

"It is a joy to need so many coverings!" Lora rejoiced

A walk into the highlands brought views and refreshment for the sowers of the Seed.

as she placed cut pieces together and set them under the machine needle.

"New Christians are such a blessing," Aunt Nellie said while she cut out a dress. "It's wonderful to see people find joy and peace."

"The Lord's work brings much reward," Lora commented with a smile as she kept sewing.

"I could not handle all the sewing needs without your help," Anna said as she jostled her baby and watched the women work. "You both are such a blessing here."

"It's good we can all work together," Lora responded while the machine still hummed.

"Is that one mine?" Rhoda asked.

"Yes," Lora answered as she kept the treadle moving rapidly. "You are becoming a young woman so quickly. I'm so glad you became a Christian."

"So am I."

"And you are becoming such a help to your mother."

"I try to be."

The seams passed with swiftness as Lora sang song after song. She stopped the machine, snipped the threads, and stood up. "Let's see how this fits."

Rhoda glanced at her new reflection and blushed. "I look so different."

Lora turned the girl around, sizing up the fit. "The Lord has something special for you to do in His vineyard."

"But I'm only thirteen."

Lora looked deep into the girl's eyes and smiled with affection. "He has a plan for you," she insisted.

"Thank you, Lora." With that Rhoda went to find her mother.

Young women and older ones stopped by the mission for new coverings. With a pleasant smile, Lora handed them crisp, new coverings and wished them the Lord's blessing in their new walk with Christ.

God worked powerfully in their midst each night. The faithful felt encouraged, and the weary were strengthened to keep laboring. Though some had refused the Lord's call, by the end of the revivals forty-one had responded in faith for His salvation.

The meetings ended, and Brothers Suter and Heatwole returned to Harrisonburg, Virginia. In a few weeks the bishop would arrive to receive the new Christians into fellowship and to conduct Communion services.

A joyful heart carried Brother Benner up steep trails to visit those who had responded. Most visits brought encouragement. However, the faithful minister sometimes returned with shoulders slumped with disappointment. Some questioned their choice to follow the footsteps of Jesus. As Jesus foreknew, some seed had fallen on stony ground, to quickly sprout but soon wither in the face of opposition and temptation.[3]

The bishop knocked at the door of the mission house.

Brother Benner threw open the door. "Come in, Brother Rhodes."

---

3 Read Matthew 13:3-8

"Thank you." S. H. Rhodes smiled as he stepped inside and removed his black hat. "How are you folks?"

"Rejoicing in the Lord," Brother Benner responded.

"Yes. I hear good things are happening here in Roaring."

"The Lord has been working, but so has the devil," Brother Benner said with sadness.

"When the Lord is working, Satan gets busy," S. H. Rhodes said. "It happens wherever God's work is prospering. But don't be discouraged, brother. We will continue to pray for those who are uncertain."

Brother Benner lamented, "But souls are at stake."

"Yes," the bishop agreed, "but we must continue to invite people to Jesus. Some will refuse but we must labor on."

Brother Benner smiled at the bishop. "Well, brother, there are many to visit. Shall we get started?"

Upstairs Lora and Aunt Nellie sang as the ministers set out on their visits.

> *"Have you sought for the sheep that have wandered,*
> *Far away on the dark mountains cold?*
> *Have you gone, like the tender Shepherd,*
> *To bring them again to the fold?"* [4]

On Saturday, August 13, 1927, Bishop S. H. Rhodes received thirty people into church fellowship: twenty-six by baptism and four by acknowledgement.

Lora and Aunt Nellie watched Rhoda and James Benner kneel for baptism with the other new believers. S. H. Rhodes baptized them by pouring water onto their heads. Later, the congregation gathered by Roaring Creek for those who chose to be baptized there.

---

4 "Have You Sought," *Church and Sunday School Hymnal,* No. 526

The congregation lifted their voices in song and smiled through tears of joy. The next morning, fifty-one souls participated in the Communion service in Roaring Church. Perhaps one day, the eleven who had hesitated would want to take that final step too.[5]

5 The information concerning the 1927 revivals and this baptismal service was taken from *Gospel Herald*, September 15, 1927, p. 532; *Records of Proceeding of Ministers' Meetings Book II,* June 1, 1918-Sept 8, 1928, and from the memories of Rhoda Benner Hertzler. Rhoda recalled that some were baptized in the church and some in the creek, according to their preference.

Chapter Sixteen

Chances

eet pounded across the mission house porch, and the door vibrated with loud knocks.

"Whatever is the matter?" Sister Benner rushed to the door while the children and workers froze. "Is something wrong?"

"Yes." The man's eyes darted nervously as he spoke. "Noah's hurt bad up at the lumber camp. A tree fell on 'im and crushed his leg. Tell Brother Benner to pray."

"He's up in the hay field, but I'll let him know right away," Sister Benner assured the caller.

The man seemed hesitant to leave. His fingers trembled as he bent over to whisper. "Really we don't know if he'll live. They're bringin' him down the mountain and takin' him to the hospital. He's bleedin' pow'rful bad."

"But the hospital is miles from here," Anna's eyes were wide and fearful. "Noah might not make it that far."

"I know." The eyes shifted. He turned to go.

"I'll tell Rhine right away," Anna called after him. "And we'll be praying." She turned to Lora. "Please go tell Rhine."

Lora rushed to the fields to tell Rhine and James what had happened. Breathless, the men followed her to the house just as the clopping of horses and the rattle of wagon wheels sounded up the way. Lora's heart thumped as the wagon rumbled into view, carrying solemn men bent over a limp man. The driver slapped the reins over the horses' back. The momentary staccato of horse hooves broke into a rhythmic pace.

Lora bit her lip and stared at the wagon until it disappeared around the bend. Few mountain people considered going to the hospital until life was threatened and, even then, medical advice was not often sought. Countless accidents in the lumber camps had taken men's lives or maimed them for life. Would this be yet another one?

Rhine burst into the mission and grasped Anna's arm. "Anna?"

"Yes?"

His voice quivered with emotion, "Noah is not ready to meet God. I've got to go and speak to him if there's any chance at all. James, please saddle the horse immediately."

Anna's worried eyes met her husband's. "Yes, dear. You go right on. We'll be praying for you."

Rhine clasped his Bible tightly and hurriedly kissed his wife. In a flash, the dedicated minister was off and riding at a gallop after the wagon.

Noah had been exposed to the Gospel for years, yet he had not surrendered to God's call. Would it be too late to rescue his soul? How was Sister Polly holding up with the shock of the accident?

Brother Benner did not return that night. In vain the mission workers tried to get back to normal. Still, their minds and prayers revolved around poor Noah and his family. The hours passed slowly, and still Brother Benner did not return.

"These people need a doctor and nurses," Lora stated.

"They've needed medical help for years," Anna replied. "I've seen too many deaths that could have been avoided if help had been here."

"More than just Noah need help," Aunt Nellie added. "So many have tuberculosis and other ailments. Surely God can meet this need."

Rhine did not return for quite some time, but when he did, he was exhausted.

Anna asked, "Will Noah make it?"

"He's very weak, but I think he'll make it. At least he's in the hospital, but we must keep praying for him."

"They're sure?" Lora asked.

"Yes, but his leg had to be amputated. Recovery will take a long time."

"Oh!" Lora groaned.

"Did Noah commit his life to Christ?" Aunt Nellie leaned forward, eager to hear his response.

"I'm afraid not. I spent some time showing him Scriptures about man's need of salvation, and I pled with him to repent. He said he'd think about it. So let's keep praying that God will speak to his heart." Brother Benner's brow carried the marks of worry.

Aunt Nellie lamented, "Why do people have such little regard for their eternal destiny?"

"Because the devil blinds them to their sins." Brother Benner shook his head sadly. "But Noah said he would think about becoming a Christian, so don't give up praying."

"Oh, wouldn't Sis Polly be happy if he did?" Lora sighed hopefully.

The summer days spun by quickly. When Lora opened her purse, she gasped. Only coins remained, and summer was not yet ended. She rarely dipped into her wallet even for necessities.

"Oh, Lord," she prayed, "please meet my needs. Thank You, Lord, for the help You will supply."

Lora closed her purse and tried to recall the ways God had answered her financial requests in the past. He had provided a job with good wages, but life in the mountains took its toll on dresses, stockings, and shoes. She discovered that her shoes needed repair more times than she had imagined possible. The poor, tattered shoes would soon need replacing—and shoes cost dollars!

Another rip in her dress needed repair. She applied a patch to the dress, and once again allowed Brother Benner to repair her torn shoes. Must she leave the mission early to make more money to pay her bills?

Lora often pondered her limited finances. Then an idea flashed into her mind. Should she do it? She spread a piece of fabric on the table and smoothed the wrinkles.

"Sewing today?" Anna asked as she changed the baby's diaper.

"Yes," Lora answered as she picked up her shears and began to cut. "What do you think about charging a small amount of money for sewing for the mountain people?"

"Money is rather limited for most here in the mountains," Anna commented.

"I know, but some have enough money for cigarettes or snuff."

"You could ask and see what happens," Anna offered.

The opportunity came not long afterward when a mother handed Lora a piece of fabric.

"Could you make Maggie a dress, Lorie? She needs dresses s'bad."

"I think I could."

Lora paused to consider how to ask for money. She had never asked the women for money when she sewed for them. She would not ask an unreasonable amount. She smiled at the woman as she ran a hand over the material.

"Thanks, Lorie. You don't know what this means."

"Would it be asking too much if I charge a quarter for a dress?" There, she had bravely asked as courteously as she knew how.

"A quarter? I don't know, Lorie. We just can't afford that."

"All right," Lora agreed.

Nearly everyone's response was the same. "We just don't have money to pay."

So Lora sewed and prayed that God would make her shoes, stockings, and dresses last a little longer. Whenever the women handed her a few coins, she was thankful for whatever was given.

There were still some trails she wanted to climb and people to visit before she went home in the fall. One of those visits would be to Noah and Sister Polly.

The weeks of canning and weekend visitors kept Lora and Aunt Nellie tied to the mission home. When Noah arrived home from the hospital, the family temporarily moved in with relatives in the hollow. Rhine Benner announced his intention of going for a visit.

"I'd love to go along," Anna sighed, "but I must stay here. Maybe Lora and Nellie could go."

"There's canning to do," Lora objected.

"Those tomatoes will keep another day," Anna replied. "You girls go. Give Sis Polly and Noah my best wishes. Tell them I'm praying for them."

Sis Polly had just flung a pail of slop across the pig fence when the mission workers arrived.

"Well, looky here! You folks came jest to see us? And it's cannin' time," Sister Polly exclaimed as Lora placed a plate of cookies into her hands. "It's s'good ta see ya."

"How's Noah?" Brother Benner asked.

"Come and see."

Noah sat on the front porch, his bleary eyes avoiding the preacher.

"We've come to see you, Noah." Brother Benner stretched out his hand warmly.

Noah smiled stiffly as he wiped his whiskers and allowed the compassionate preacher to shake his hand. "I'm healin' right smart."

For some time they shared Scripture and encouragement.

"Could we sing you a song?" Lora asked.

"Why sure." Noah nodded and wiped his nose with his hanky as the group began to sing.

"Tell me the old, old story
Of unseen things above,
Of Jesus and his glory,
Of Jesus and his love.

Tell me the story simply,
As to a little child,
For I am weak and weary,
And helpless and defiled."[1]

Noah had heard it countless times. Would today's encouragement make a dent in his hardened soul?

"Have you considered letting Jesus into your heart, Noah?" Brother Benner asked.

"I'm thinkin' on it," the man responded.

"The Lord spared your life and has given you another chance. He would love for you to join His family."

Old favorite songs floated across the porch, the mixed voices blending in harmony.

"Open wide thy heart today
At Jesus' call;
Bid him enter and abide,
Thy life, thy all."[2]

Noah listened and rubbed his stub leg, which was covered with a pinned-up pant leg. After a short while, the workers said good-bye and returned down the mountain. The invitation had been extended one more time.

---

1 "Tell Me the Old, Old Story," *Church and Sunday School Hymnal,* No. 521
2 "Open Wide Thy Heart," *Church and Sunday School Hymnal,* No. 505

Chapter Seventeen

Cucumbers, Chickens, and Cake

Lora leaned on her stick to push herself higher on the beaten trail that wound up the mountain. Young Rhoda Benner followed her and Aunt Nellie brought up the rear. One more afternoon had been snatched from the days of hard work. Lora sighed with joy at this rare opportunity.

An hour of climbing brought the hikers to a clearing where chickens pecked at the ground between the house and buildings. Lora shooed them out of her path. With squawks and a flutter of feathers they made way for the visitors. Sheep grazed in the meadow, and beyond the fence, hogs slept in the shade. Lush cucumber vines sprawled across the end of a large garden, and a few flowers bloomed brightly. As Lora approached, gruff barks announced the unwanted invasion of a dog's territory.

Two girls scampered out of the house, hushed the dog, and grasped Rhoda's hand.

One said, "Hi, Rhoda. You've come just like ya said ya would."

"Let's go play!" the other girl pled. "We got some wild grapevines to swing on. Come on."

"Sure." Rhoda quickly skipped off with the girls while Lora and Aunt Nellie joined Della in the house for a time of good fellowship.

Lora commented. "You have quite a walk to church, Della. And a steep climb back home."

"Yes, but the children love ta come to church."

"We love to have you come," Aunt Nellie offered. "Your young boys take an interest in the classes we teach. They are becoming fine young men."

"They love yer classes. I'm s'glad you've come to teach 'em the Bible. I wish my husband and son could of heard yer teachin'."

"How long has your husband been gone?" Aunt Nellie asked.

"He died in 1921," Della explained. "Died on the operatin' table at th' hospital with 'pendicitis. How I've missed him!"

"I'm sure you have." Lora's voice was warm with sympathy.

"And now Denver's gone," Della mentioned her oldest son who had died in the army.

"What happened to him?" Aunt Nellie asked, trying to recall the particulars.

Della's brow wrinkled as she spoke. "They say Denver and sum of th' boys ate ice cream and got TB of th' intestines. We buried him 'bout a year ago with a flag draped over his coffin."

The ladies encouraged one another with comforting Scriptures. Then Della had an idea.

"Nellie, won't you make a cake and s'prise the children? I've heard you can make good cakes."

"Sure, I'll be glad to make you a cake. Do you have eggs?" Della nodded enthusiastically. "Plenty of eggs."

"Some flour and sugar?"

"No sugar."

"Honey then?"

"Yep."

"Some lard?"

Aunt Nellie took the varied ingredients and with them concocted a cake. While Aunt Nellie mixed up the cake, Lora helped Della wash cucumbers.[1]

"Looks like you will have plenty of pickle come wintertime," Lora commented as she dropped cucumbers into a wooden barrel of brine.

"This year I'll have cucumbers 'til spring," Della said. "If ya just knew half th' trouble I had gettin' 'em ta grow."

"What was the problem?" Aunt Nellie asked as she stirred the ingredients in her bowl.

"The problem? 'Twas a hen, I tell you." Della placed her hands on her hips and pressed her lips together in feigned disgust.

"A hen?" Lora exclaimed.

"Yep, a hen. I planted half a pack of cucumber seeds I'd ordered through th' mail. But ya know, one day I spied a hen out ther' in th' garden a-peckin' up all my cucumber seeds."

Lora started to chuckle.

"Must have been a tasty meal," Aunt Nellie said with amusement.

---

1 Naomi Swartz told the author about the cakes Nellie could bake.

"That ain't all," Della exclaimed with a laugh. "I planted th' other half of the cucumber seeds. Lo and behold, the hen found those and et them too!"

"Smart chicken!" Lora said with a quirk of her mouth.

"Too smart fer my likin'," Della retorted. "An' ya know what? I went out ther' and chopped that hen's head off, I tell you. I dug them seeds right outta her craw and planted 'em right back in the garden."

"What? These cucumbers grew after they had been a chicken's dinner?" Aunt Nellie stopped stirring and stared at Della.

"Yes-siree! And we've had dandy cucumbers a growin' all summer. Best cucumbers I ever growed!"

The ladies cackled like hens.

Lora asked, "What about the chicken?"

"That chicken made a splendid dinner!" Della retorted as hearty laughter filled the house.[2]

Della insisted the ladies stay for supper and for the night. "I'll fix ya some chicken and fried taters."

"You wouldn't happen to know what your chicken had for dinner now, would you?" Aunt Nellie asked with an eyebrow raised in pretended seriousness.

"I hardly think she had cucumber seeds," Della grinned. "An' I'll fix up a cucumber salad and some red 'maters."

The hard climb and afternoon work made Lora hungry. Sure, they would stay. While Aunt Nellie poured the cake into a pan to bake, Lora helped their hostess kill and clean a chicken. She plucked feathers quickly as the chatter of little girls neared.

---

2 Gae Arbogast told about this chicken and how her mother butchered the chicken and retrieved the seeds.

Lora glanced at Rhoda. "Did you have a good time?"

"I watched the girls swing way out over the ravine on those grapevines, but I didn't do it." Rhoda clasped her hands together and shivered.

"Cuz she was scared. We told her she could do it," Della's two girls explained as they pranced with delight.

Lora stared at the girls. "You swing out over the ravine?"

"Sure we do. Do it all th' time."

"But what if you fell?" Lora shuddered to think what would happen if one lost hold of the vine or if the vine should break.

"I didn't do it, Lora," Rhoda assured. "I really was too scared."

Lora didn't say more. She carried the chicken into the kitchen for Della to fry. Then she grabbed a knife and began to peel potatoes.

By suppertime a tall thin teen entered through the screen door, followed by his brother. Della's boys loitered in the kitchen, playfully matching Aunt Nellie's good humor. While Aunt Nellie frosted the cake, the boys grinned and licked their lips in anticipation of such good fortune.

At supper, Lora bit into the fried chicken that Della served. "Mmm. This is so tender."

"And flavored just right," Aunt Nellie added.

With fried potatoes, tomato slices, and crunchy cucumbers to complement her tasty chicken, Lora's hunger was satisfied.

"Well, Della, seems to me you do mighty fine at raising cucumbers and chicken," Lora said while Aunt Nellie sliced the warm cake heaped with fluffy icing.

"That cake is plain downright scrumptious," the tall thin boy complimented the baker.

"Um-huh!" the rest nodded in agreement, each mouth stuffed with the tasty dessert.

"Thank you," Aunt Nellie said, a twinkle forming in her eye. "But I think Della's fine art of growing cucumbers that have been a chicken's dinner—well, that just plain takes the cake!"

Chapter Eighteen

Heartstrings

L ora sat on the bed in her nightgown and picked up her Bible. The night air drifted through the window. She read the Scriptures to nourish her soul after a hard day of work. "Because the love of God is shed abroad in our hearts by the Holy Ghost which is given unto us. For when we were yet without strength, in due time Christ died for the ungodly."[1]

Lora sighed. It had been a wonderful experience to become a child of God. God had so abundantly blessed her. He had shed His love abroad in her heart and had brought manifold richness to her life. But others still did not have that for themselves. She read on. "But God commendeth his love toward us, in that, while we were yet sinners, Christ died for us. Much more then, being now justified by his blood, we shall be saved from wrath through him."[2]

Lora knelt in prayer. Her heart ached for those she loved. Some had accepted Christ as Saviour and had received

1 Romans 5:5, 6
2 Romans 5:8, 9

God's rich love and salvation. But some still waited on the sidelines, contemplating the cost. She prayed for Sadie, the unmarried mother with the sweet baby. She prayed for some who had courageously accepted Christ but had become discouraged by the taunts and scorn of others. She prayed for youth who had been hustled into the realities of parenting responsibilities at a young age.

Her spirit agonized over Noah's need for salvation and Sister Polly's longing to raise a godly family. She pled for Abe and Lizzie, who mourned the loss of a son. She sought the Master Teacher for Solomon, who saw no need for spiritual light. Then came a long list of little children, youth, and adults who eagerly listened to the words of God. *Lord, grant each of these wisdom and direction. May they find the Light of Life and the path out of darkness. May they experience true joy and peace in their hearts.*

For a long while Lora stayed on her knees. She prayed for the faithful to remain true, for the mission workers to endure the hardships. Then she prayed again for supply to her scanty pocketbook. In the quietness, she found refreshment.

"They are coming! I can hear them singing," Rhoda Benner said as she burst into the mission house.

Aunt Nellie pushed open the door and listened. "They are."

Lora cupped a hand over her ear. Sure enough, the harmony of men's voices and the faint hum of a car drifted up the hollow.

"Let's go meet them and make sure they find this place," Aunt Nellie said, pulling Lora after her.

The maidens hurried down the road to meet their old friends from Eastern Mennonite School who were coming to give a singing program. While the men sang at full volume, the auto chugged toward them, then groaned and ground to a stop.

"Hello, friends!" Some of the men lifted their hats in politeness.

"Welcome to Roaring Creek," Aunt Nellie greeted.

The door flew open and two young men stepped out and gestured with mimicked politeness. "Won't you come aboard?"

"Sure," Aunt Nellie accepted as Lora quietly slipped into the backseat beside her with a broad grin.

The two men stepped on the running board and hung on. As the car moved forward, rich tones floated into the air, a blend of men's voices with Lora and Aunt Nellie joining in the harmony. They rounded the last bend to see Brother Benner and his family waving a welcome.[3]

"Well, folks. I can tell we have a store of blessings coming our way," Brother Benner crowed as he greeted each of the brethren.

"What a lovely spot this place is," one of the brothers stated.

"You just wait until you meet the people," Brother Benner said.

That evening, people drifted down the trails and filled the church benches. The quartet stood at the front of the

---

3 Rhoda Benner Hertzler recalled the details of the quartet's arrival at the mission.

church and sang song after song, mellow tones and sacred words blending to lift the downhearted and encourage the believers. Some songs touched seekers' hearts. The hour slipped away and the singers mingled with the mountain people afterward.

"Come sing for us again," someone requested.

"The songs encouraged me," another said.

"Wish my children could learn to sing like that."

The hearty laughter, singing, and visiting ended much too quickly. Once again the mission was back to routine until another round of visitors came.

When Brother Benner returned from a visit on the mountain, he joined the women in the garden.

Anna asked, "How is Noah?"

"He's quite discouraged. He wants to work," Brother Benner answered. "You know, any man feels a responsibility for his family."

"And how is Polly?"

"It's discouraging for her, too, when Noah can't provide."

"Is there anything we can do?" Lora asked.

"I'll write a letter and see if some brethren could give money for an artificial leg. There is no way Noah could afford one."

"That would be such an encouragement to Noah and Sis Polly," Lora remarked.

"It certainly would," Aunt Nellie added.

Rhine Benner hung up his hat and grinned at Anna. "Mother, we've been invited to Jake's house for eel."

Anna exclaimed, "Eel? Why, I've never eaten that before."

Startled by Rhine's announcement, Lora quickly peeped into the oven, closed the door, and paused to listen.

"I haven't either," Rhine said. "Jake caught the eel himself and said we should come over for supper."

The children clustered close to hear what their father had to say. Rhoda shuddered.

"Do we have to go? I thought Jake is a mean man, and he doesn't like us." Rhoda looked almost ready to cry.

Rhine placed his arm around his daughter's shoulders. "Jake seems to have changed his attitude toward me. I don't know what it is, but he seems kinder than he used to be. I think it would be just fine to go visit them."

"That's sure nice of him," Lora commented.

"Lucy will have a table full with all of us," Anna commented.

Aunt Nellie quizzed, "Do you think the eel will be long enough to feed us all?"

Lora gave her aunt a playful swat. "I imagine so, if everyone takes the portion I think I'll take."

Around the table with Jake, Lucy, and children, the Benner family and mission workers discovered genial hospitality and a warm relationship.

"That's mighty good eating," Rhine said to the cook after the meal.

"Yep. Nothin' wrong with eatin' eel," Jake said, rising from the table and pressing his hands into his overall pockets.

"It tasted just like fish," Lora said. "Lucy, thank you for fixing supper for all of us. You must have cooked all day."

Lucy smiled in appreciation. "You folks are welcome any time."

"We'll have you to our house sometime," Anna said as she helped clear the table.

Aunt Nellie placed some dishes into a tub of soapy water. "This has been a special evening for me, and quite enjoyable. I'm glad we got to eat eel."

Grateful for a positive turn in this relationship, the Benner family and workers returned to the mission house with warm hearts, encouraged to keep reaching out to souls. Some were cold and indifferent toward spiritual issues, but occasionally a surprise awaited them. For this they thanked their heavenly Father.

Aunt Nellie slid the iron back and forth to press the wrinkles from a shirt. Supper simmered on the stove while they waited for Brother Benner to return from a visit. Out of the blue, Aunt Nellie said, "Brother Benner needs a car."

"A car?" Anna exclaimed as she stirred the contents of the kettle.

Lora met Anna's gaze with confidence. "Why, sure he does," she said, remembering how her parents valued time management. "Think how much quicker he could get to places he visits."

Anna smiled at the thought. "And we could drive home to Pennsylvania and we wouldn't have to take the train."

"And you could attend conference in Virginia," Aunt Nellie suggested.

Anna looked out the window as if in a dream. "But that is unthinkable for missionary folks like us."

"Well, could we ask God to consider your need?" Aunt Nellie asked with a grin as she continued ironing.

"I suppose so," Anna agreed.

"Hello, Miss Coffman," a bright voice greeted Lora and Aunt Nellie at the store in Onego.

Lora spun around and met Gracie holding a stack of books.

Aunt Nellie spoke first. "Hello, Gracie. Looks like you have plenty of books to read."

"Yep. I love readin'."

"What do you have in your stack?" Aunt Nellie asked.

The girl handed a book to her teacher. Aunt Nellie scanned the pages as furrows knit her brow.

"Where did you get these books?" Aunt Nellie asked as she read the titles on the spines.

"Sam gives 'em to me after he reads 'em."

"Sam?"

"Uh-huh. Sam says I can have 'em and I'll read all of 'em too."

Aunt Nellie was concerned. "You are a very good reader, but these do not look like reading material that builds good character."

"But I love 'em, Miss Coffman. They're so excitin'."

"I'll try to find you some better books to read," Aunt

Nellie promised. "I don't think you should read any of these."

Gracie politely said good-bye, tossed her head to throw the hair out of her eyes, and trudged home with her stack of books.

On the way home Aunt Nellie discussed her concern with Lora. "That kind of reading undermines all we are teaching these people."

"Satan is so busy," Lora said. "What can we do about it?"

"I'm going to hunt for some character-building books. Our reading material is pretty scarce. Some of the students are good readers."

Lora determined to pray about the matter and see what God would provide.

One day a delegation from the mission board stopped for a visit.

"Brother Benner, your account at the store is paid in full."

"Brethren, how can I thank you enough?" Brother Benner surveyed his supporters. Then he dropped his gaze to the floor, fighting tears.

The brother continued, "We know you and your family have sacrificed much for the sake of the mission."

"Thank you," Anna whispered and nodded gratefully, tears in her eyes.

"Another matter we want to take care of is the support for the sisters who live with you. We will pay you room and board for them, and we also plan to provide them with a small allowance."

Lora drew a deep, deep breath. "Thank you," she said as the brother placed some bills in her hand.

"Thank you," Aunt Nellie repeated. "This is much appreciated."

"And here is money for Noah's prosthesis." The board member handed over a roll of bills.

"Brethren, this is so encouraging." Brother Benner wiped his eyes. "Noah will be speechless."

Lora climbed the stairs and put the money in her purse. Then she thanked the Almighty for answering her prayer. Now she could buy that pair of shoes she really needed.

Later, Brother Benner carried the cash up the mountain with a light heart. Some weeks later, Noah was adjusting to walking. He even traveled on horseback sometimes to church, much to Sister Polly's delight. And Noah's children smiled because Pap had finally come to church.

One morning Lora cracked eggs into a bowl while Aunt Nellie stirred up biscuits.

"Anna has been so tired lately," Lora said to Aunt Nellie. "She said to let them sleep a little late."

"I had hoped to go visiting today," Aunt Nellie said with disappointment.

Lora nodded with agreement. "And the women keep asking us to come. Wonder if they want you to bake them a cake?" She began to titter and Aunt Nellie looked away to stifle her own laughter.

"We have baked a few." Aunt Nellie turned the dough on the counter and kneaded with expertise.

"Aunt Nellie, you are something," Lora whispered. "I never saw the likes of someone who could make a cake out of almost nothing."

Aunt Nellie laughed softly while she rolled the dough to perfect thickness. "Well, I just try, and somehow the cake turns out."

Word had traveled up and down the mountain trails that Aunt Nellie could make good cakes. So wherever the missionary sisters went visiting, Aunt Nellie was called on to exercise her talent. Many times her intelligent mind was stretched as she decided what ingredients to use in place of the missing ones. Sometimes there just was no substitute.

"But a cake made from three things?" Lora hid her face in her sleeve to muffle the giggles.

"And the chocolate cake..." Aunt Nellie sputtered, unable to control herself any longer.

Lora restrained her mirth, wishing she could let it roll. "Who else could make a chocolate cake with little more than chocolate and water? Aunt Nellie, you are a wonder!"

Both women laughed. Aunt Nellie shoved the corner of her apron under her glasses to wipe the tears. Lora blew her nose and washed her hands.

"Shh. We must not waken the family."

Aunt Nellie remarked, "Why, Lora, I think the Lord must have helped some of those cakes to turn out. I don't know how else they could have worked."

Lora and Aunt Nellie found opportunities to speak to many girls about godly living. Some of the girls appreciated the one-on-one talks.

"Know what?" Aunt Nellie asked with an upraised brow.

"Tell me," Lora responded.

"We could start a girls' circle and teach more girls at the same time."

"Oh, Aunt Nellie, that's a wonderful idea! You know I love these girls. We could teach them how to develop Christian character."

Aunt Nellie smiled. "I know. We could show them how to strive for higher ideals. But time is running out. It will be time to start school soon."

"But we could do at least one and see how it goes."

"It's worth a try," Aunt Nellie said, paging through her Bible.

On Wednesday afternoon they came—Gracie, Bessie, Sadie, and Tillie. Tillie now held another baby in her arms, but she wanted to discover the secret these women had in their hearts. Gracie curled her short hair with a finger and squatted on the blanket to listen.

"Okay, girls, we're ready to start." Aunt Nellie smiled at her students. "Can you tell me where to find happiness and fulfillment in life?"

A chill crept through the hollow as summer advanced. Red and yellow tipped the edges of hardwood trees as if a giant paintbrush had splattered paint on a massive canvas. Farmers harvested crops and women gathered the last tomatoes and corn before frost could demolish them. Down the narrow roads and lanes, trucks from places beyond the mountains rattled into the communities, bringing buyers to purchase beef cattle and fruit from the orchards. When the trucks drove away, the farmers patted their pockets. Now they could pay up some accounts and maybe even buy something special.

Aunt Nellie visited the schoolhouse and prepared for the upcoming school year. Up and down the trails and footpaths, children in sweaters skipped to school for lessons. Aunt Nellie rang the bell and the classes came to order. The wise teacher adjusted her glasses and smiled at her students. She was but one in the string of many good teachers who delivered education to the mountain children. She loved teaching.

Aunt Nellie folded her hands together. "Let us begin our school year with a prayer."

At home in the mission house, Lora peeled and processed applesauce and peaches. She wiped the sticky jars clean and placed them on the shelves in the basement. Then she packed her bags. She could hardly tear herself from this place when so many needed guidance. But her job called her home, and she must go.

In late autumn, visitors arrived at the Roaring Mission. Rhoda sat by the window and looked at the two cars sitting out front.

"We brought you a car," said one of the relatives.

"You did?" Rhoda looked from the car to her parents, who beamed with joy.

"Which one do you think is for you?" Rhoda's uncle asked her.

"I don't know," Rhoda said, looking from the older car to the shiny blue one.

"Would you like the blue one?"

Rhoda nodded while the other children crowded around the window to see.

"Is it the blue one?"

The uncle nodded. "It's a gift from friends and family in Pennsylvania. Now we want you to come home and visit sometime."

"Oh, brethren," Brother Benner exclaimed, his lips trembling with emotion, "you don't know what this means."

Anna Benner's eyes glistened. She swallowed and hurried off to set the table for the guests. [4]

The Benner family could hardly believe they now owned a car. Truly the Lord had shed His love abroad in the lives of those who served in this mission field. But more needs awaited answers. With the possession of a trustworthy vehicle came new responsibilities that no one had expected.

---

4 Rhoda Benner Hertzler remembered this special gift and day at the mission.

Chapter Nineteen

Dark Shadows

1929

Something formidable hovered in the shadows even though a new president had taken the reins in the White House that March of 1929. "Ours is a land rich in resources; stimulating in its glorious beauty; filled with millions of happy homes; blessed with comfort and opportunity. In no nation are the fruits of accomplishment more secure," President Hoover had assured the nation in his inaugural speech.[1] In spite of his optimism, something seemed about to happen, but what?

Deep in the Appalachian Mountains, all was not well at Roaring Mission Home. Lora gathered a hint of what the trouble was when Aunt Nellie came home to Virginia in early spring for a visit.

After the service at her home church, Lora hurried over to Aunt Nellie.

"You and I need to talk," Aunt Nellie suggested. "Walk with me to the car."

---

1 *Inaugural Addresses of the Presidents of the United States: Volume 2*, p. 21.

"Sure," Lora agreed, eager to hear what her aunt had to say.

Aunt Nellie waited until they could not be overheard. "Sister Benner is not doing well. Besides, there is much work to do. If we go again this summer, I think we should have a separate place to live."

"Why?" Lora asked.

"We teachers and assistants add more work to Anna's load."

"I see."

"And besides, there is little time to do what we were sent to do." Concern deepened the lines in Aunt Nellie's face.

"I hope we can spend more time teaching the young girls," Lora said.

"We can't in the present circumstances. Sister Benner is swamped with work. The family has been sick. She needs lots of help and Brother Benner has his hands full with visits and teaching. The community needs are desperate. Lora, many have turned away from the faith! We have to get back to personal witnessing."

"I'm sorry to hear that." Lora gazed at Aunt Nellie's troubled face. "I must pray more earnestly for the souls and hurry back to help you."

"More than that, I want to speak to the board," Aunt Nellie resolved.

Lora blinked at the shocking words.

A meeting with the mission board could have been intimidating for some. However, both women had fathers who had served on the Home Mission Board over the years.

Still, Lora's heart beat faster as she followed Aunt Nellie into the room where men waited to hear their concern.

Aunt Nellie presented the matter. "We are often unable to visit the mountain families because of mission house duties. Sickness in the family keeps Sister Benner busy and she cannot board Lora and me any longer."

Lora quietly waited while Aunt Nellie went on. "So Lora and I would like to request a separate apartment. We could take care of ourselves and do more visitation, and the Benner family would have more privacy."

The board asked some questions and promised to get back to them with a response. A short time later, the board agreed to have a twelve-by-eighteen-foot building constructed below the Benner's garden near the springhouse.[2]

When Lora arrived at Roaring Mission that summer, no new building had been constructed, but a bedroom and separate kitchen had been arranged. She and Aunt Nellie settled into the new quarters and set right to work.

At church, change was evident. Some who used to attend faithfully did not attend the services. But Sister Sarah was there, Sister Polly, and others.

"Where is the Vance family?" Lora asked.

"They moved across the mountain," Anna explained.

Sometimes Lora met old friends in the community. Immediately she noticed the changed expressions and appearances.

---

2 Various Home Mission Board minutes in 1930 report the plans for an apartment to be built on mission property.

"Hello," Lora greeted a friend. "How are you?"

"Fine. You know I got married? Have a baby too." The eyes no longer met her own but searched the ground.

"I see," Lora ventured in a pleasant voice. "What about your faith and commitment to the Lord?"

The bride fidgeted and smoothed her short hair, cropped at the ears. "Well, Clyde wants me fer his wife and he don't see no need to be a Christian."

"Oh," Lora sighed. "You made a commitment to follow the Lord Jesus. A Christian wife is a great blessing to a home. Remember what Jesus told one woman in the Bible? Jesus promised, 'The water that I shall give him shall be in him a well of water springing up into everlasting life.'[3] Won't you need Him in your life to be a good wife and mother?"

The young woman furrowed her brows in thought. Lora paused a moment. It wasn't like her to be outspoken, yet she cared about this person's life. Just last year this young woman radiated with a glowing testimony.

Lora continued with earnest pleading in her voice. "It's a serious thing to depart from the faith. The Bible warns us to 'Take heed . . . lest there be in any of you an evil heart of unbelief, in departing from the living God.' To enjoy Christian blessings we must 'hold the beginning of our confidence stedfast unto the end.' "[4]

The woman pondered what Lora had said, then asked, "But what about Clyde?"

"Perhaps he can come to know the Lord Jesus too. It doesn't matter where we are or what we do, we cannot escape the eyes of the Lord God," Lora shared. "The Bible

3 John 4:14
4 Hebrews 3:12, 14

tells us, 'The ways of man are before the eyes of the LORD, and he pondereth all his goings.' "[5]

Tears glimmered in the woman's eyes as she replied, "I'll think about it."

But Lora saw the catalogs and magazines that were trickling into mountain homes. In addition, radios, news reports, entertainment in other communities, and better transportation enabled society's influence to infiltrate the remote communities. The battle for souls waged on.

"Aunt Nellie," Lora whispered one evening weeks later as they prepared for bed. "Anna is so weary with all the sickness and extra work. What more can we do to make life easier for her?"

Aunt Nellie looked up from her Bible. "I thought it would make a difference if we lived apart, but the family is still swamped with duties. There seems to be no letup at all even with us helping out."

Lora felt troubled. "And Brother Benner is gone so much, making visits or out tending the farm. We must pray harder for the family."

At breakfast, Brother Benner appeared weary even after a night of sleep. Still he went off to the barn with James. Some days he took people on a trip to the doctor or hospital, now that he had a car. The women pulled weeds, washed laundry, cleaned, cooked, canned, and humored the children.

One day Bertha Morral delivered a box. Lora stepped

into the post office just long enough to watch Anna open the package.

"Oh! Here are books for our Sunday school library." Anna brightened.

"Good!" Aunt Nellie exclaimed.

"So people have heard Brother Benner's plea for good reading," Lora commented.

Anna nodded. "Yes, they have. We occasionally receive shipments of books from people interested in donating them."

"Now we can actually offer good reading." Aunt Nellie pushed her glasses up on her nose and sorted the rest of the mail.

Lora hurried back to the kitchen with renewed joy in her heart. She picked up the mop and scrubbed the floor with added zest.

With her Bible and a worn blanket in hand, Lora swished down the stairs before this precious opportunity could be snatched from her. Aunt Nellie followed more slowly. Long strides took Lora to the shade tree where she had asked the girls to meet at two o'clock that afternoon. So often she and Aunt Nellie could not pursue girls' circle because of countless responsibilities.

The time had come—precious time that the two had longed to invest in youth girls. If these dear girls made godly choices in their youth, good consequences would likely follow. If they made ungodly choices, unhappiness would result. Whatever the choices, reaping would surely follow in the years ahead. The Bible said it best: "Be not deceived; God is not mocked: for whatsoever a man soweth, that shall he also reap."[6]

The women spread the blanket on the ground.

"I hope they will not forget," Lora said.

Lora watched young Rhoda sit down beside them. She had stretched up quickly and stood on the threshold of womanhood. She thought of Gracie and Bessie, who could quickly be ensnared by worldly things. But it wasn't too late to influence them. Even Tillie could be guided to make choices for her life and family based on the teachings of Scripture.

"Here comes Tillie," said Rhoda.

"No children today?" Lora questioned as Tillie grinned and sauntered to the shade.

"Nope. Mom's watching while they sleep."

Two slender teens sprinted across the lawn, giggling.

"Welcome!" Lora smiled as she made room for the girls. "I hope we will have a good time learning about God's purpose for us as girls and women."

Gracie pushed her short blonde hair behind her ears and dropped onto the blanket. Bessie sprawled beside her. Lora smiled at each one as she opened her Bible.

"Each of you would like to be the best girl you can possibly be. Someday you will be grown and perhaps have a husband and children. The Bible tells us about the wise woman and how she conducts her life. The Bible asks: 'Who can find a virtuous woman? For her price is far above rubies.'"[7]

"What's a ruby?" Gracie asked.

6 Galatians 6:7
7 Proverbs 31:10

"It's a beautiful red gem that is worth a lot of money," Lora explained. "Girls who live godly and upright lives are worth more than fine jewels. God sees them as valuable and precious, and He says a meek and quiet spirit is of great price.' "[8]

Lora looked deeply into each girl's face. Bessie's gentle brown eyes stayed fixed on hers and Rhoda listened intently. Tillie leaned against the tree. Gracie seemed more interested in a kitten and in waving at those who passed by.

"You know that girls like to be favored by others. They fix up their hair or try to look really pretty. God's Word says 'Favour is deceitful, and beauty is vain.' People are easily tricked by favor and beauty. But God says, 'A woman that feareth the Lord, she shall be praised.' "[9]

Tillie's eyes closed. *Perhaps the baby kept her up last night,* Lora thought. A crack of thunder startled them.

"It's going to rain," said Aunt Nellie with disappointment.

"And we are just getting started," Lora lamented. "Perhaps we can sit around the kitchen table."

Tillie jumped up suddenly. "I have wash on the line. I hafta run."

"I gotta go home too." Gracie sprang up and left.

Around the kitchen table, Aunt Nellie and Lora taught about the godly woman of Proverbs 31. The hour passed quickly and so did the rain. Bessie and Rhoda beamed with pleasure as the lesson ended.

"That woman sounds like my mama," Bessie said. "Mama works day and night fer us."

---

8 See 1 Peter 3:4
9 Proverbs 31:30

Lora grinned at the girl. "God is pleased with a hard-working woman filled with His Spirit. I hope you will be that kind of woman too."

Aunt Nellie stopped Bessie before she went. "Next time we will talk about some of the women in the Bible. You come and bring some other girls."

"I will." Bessie grinned. She slipped through the door and started off for home.

Aunt Nellie looked at Lora. "There are many lessons yet to teach."

"Do you have some ideas in mind?" Lora questioned.

Aunt Nellie nodded. "There are characters like Ruth, Hannah, Esther, Mary, Dorcas, and Lydia that contrast sharply with Jezebel, Miriam, Tamar, and Delilah."

Lora smiled at her aunt. "I hope we can find the time."

Brother Benner's new car offered dependable transportation, and he often took mountain people to distant places for medical assistance. In addition, he traveled to Virginia for ministers' meetings or to discuss mission concerns with the Home Mission Board. He was always busy.

Lora and Aunt Nelllie noticed that Brother Benner didn't seem his jovial self when he came in from putting hay in the barn. He spent more time in his bedroom. Was he praying for the needs of souls? He seemed burdened; but then the resident minister did carry an enormous burden for his flock. He felt the responsibility to reach those who resisted the call of Christ. He was the under-shepherd, leading the sheep to the Great Shepherd. However, he could not make the choice for them. He could sow the seed and point the way for eternal life, but they must choose or reject the opportunity. He must convince them that whatever choice they made affected their eternal destiny.

So much responsibility weighed upon Brother Benner. Lora and Aunt Nellie prayed long and earnestly for the Benner family. One Sunday Sister Benner told Lora and Aunt Nellie that her husband would not be able to preach.

"What will we do?" Lora and Aunt Nellie asked in unison as they gazed at one another.

Anna sought advice from her husband. "Rhine suggests you sing songs and have Sunday school. Jason Vance can read the Scripture."

Being a schoolteacher, Jason could handle the service appropriately, as well as teach Sunday school. But more Sundays followed with Brother Benner unable to attend. James, now a tall and lanky teen, attended to the farm chores. Anna seemed too weary to carry out summer duties. One day, Anna exposed her heart to the young women.

"I don't know what's going to happen."

Lora stopped chopping tomatoes into the kettle and stared at Anna.

"We are thinking about moving away from here."

Lora's mouth dropped open. Aunt Nellie stood speechless, waiting for Anna to go on. But Brother Benner walked in and finished the explanation.

"I think we need a change." His head bent down as he took a deep breath. "The responsibilities have taken a toll on our family. I must think of our future, possible work for James, and further schooling for the children. I need a dependable job too."

Lora swallowed and Aunt Nellie nodded.

Finally Aunt Nellie spoke. "I'll pray that you may know the Lord's direction."

"I can't imagine this place without you," Lora whispered. "I'll pray for your family."

"Thank you," Anna said softly.

Brother Benner went on. "I've been checking on some things over the mountain."

Lora swallowed again. Summer would soon be gone. How could the mission operate without dear Brother Benner? Who could possibly fill his role?

In September Lora packed her bags and said good-bye. Aunt Nellie would stay on to teach school. This time the Benner family packed too. They were moving to Harrisonburg, Virginia.[10] All the way home, Lora's heart wrestled with a burdened prayer. What would happen to the Roaring Mission and the people up and down the mountain trails? Who would continue to plant the seeds of God's Word and nourish the growth that had sprouted in those souls?[11]

---

10 Middle District Minutes, Home Mission Board, September 19, 1929.

11 In addition to Middle District Minutes other resources for this chapter include Rhoda Benner Hertzler and Minutes of Quarterly Ministers' Meetings of Middle District, Nov. 24, 1928-May 24, 1935.

Chapter Twenty

Changes

1929-1930

In the mountains leaves fluttered down, creating a carpet beneath the barren trees. Like colorful rugs, they matted along the edges of streams. At last the forest grew dull and the shrill wind whistled around the doors and windows of homes. Now and then flurries whipped through the hollow.

Though some hooted at the notion of economic disaster, more than simply change of season lay on the threshold of time. President Hoover didn't know the future when he said, "The fundamental business of this country, that is production and distribution of commodities, is on a sound and prosperous basis."[1]

Black, terrible, and undetected, an unknown monster crouched and waited for this moment. Suddenly, the great beast pounced upon the massive American economic machine, which had hummed with industry for the past decade. Mysteriously, gigantic wheels, disks, bearings, and

---

1 Robert S. McElvaine, *The Great Depression*, 1961, 1984, p. 47.

belts began to slow. On that catastrophic day, October 29, 1929, the stock market tumbled and kept falling. That historic day became known as Black Tuesday. It was the crash that initiated The Great Depression. Thousands of banks and businesses folded. Nationwide, people panicked as the reality of what had happened hit full force. People found themselves in poverty, their savings vanished and their investments devalued.

Even as the economy screeched to a halt and unemployment rose, President Hoover offered hope. Repeatedly he used optimism to keep faith in the American economy. In spite of his continued optimism, the President struggled to create a program to revive the country. He was not callous or indifferent to the needs of people, but he objected to government handouts to remedy the situation. Believing the economic recovery depended on the action of business and industrial leaders, he felt that to offer men and women a government handout would destroy their dignity.

Americans hoped that Hoover was right—that over time the situation would become brighter. They scanned the news reports for Hoover's solutions, but the situation did not improve. Months passed and the economic conditions grew worse.

Down in the hollow, the store proprietor added another log to the potbellied stove. Smoke chuffed from the store chimney and drifted into the woods. Seated around the stove, whiskered men in overalls propped their feet up to the fire. They puffed their pipes, chewed tobacco, and sipped at steaming mugs while they talked about national affairs. In the smoky haze, the rustle of newspaper pages mingled with harsh banter—words that would cause women to cringe if they heard.

"I tell you now, things is bad!" The speaker's shaggy eyebrows shadowed piercing blue eyes.

"Yes sir-ree," another agreed. "Did ya know 'bout all them people out there that have nothin' t' eat? I mean nothin'. No work! No money! That man up there in that there White House—he best git sumthin' done to change things!"

Grunts of agreement followed until another spoke. "We got right smart fam'lies to tend to! We gotta have money! We can't pay fer farms with nothin'." The man scratched his beard and shook his head with such emphasis his hat almost toppled from his bushy head.

Another squinted and spit a stream of black juice. "You think that plan the President's got goin' will do any good?"

An older man leaned forward, his hands pressing on his knees. "Them smart people up in Washin'ton don't know what they're a-doin'."

"I know, 'cause none of 'em can agree 'bout what's happened."

A younger man stuffed his hands in his overall pockets. "I hope the President is right. Prices go up and down. Mebbe it'll pass."

The talk went on, as it would for quite some time.

Meanwhile, folks in the mountains managed to exist on what they had, even though farmers had little chance for profits. They gathered eggs, milked cows, ate wild game, and butchered hogs to feed their families. Long years before, they had learned to survive on the resources around them. But times had turned tough.

The gears of the economy continued to decelerate. The buzz of saws in the lumber camps slackened as the need for lumber declined and businesses folded. Mountain people, like others nationwide, scrimped to make ends meet. Sometimes men ventured into the nearby towns in a vehicle co-owned by several people. It was there they could see entertaining shows, learn about the affairs of the country, and search for job opportunities. Sometimes someone did find a job, and the family moved to some town beyond the isolated, familiar place they had known.

The President continued to offer an optimistic view. "The nation is turning the corner," he said. The public continued to hope that Hoover's promise of brighter days returning would prove true.[2]

In some regions, small wheels of industry managed to keep turning. At home in Virginia, Lora worked in the factory and wrote letters to Aunt Nellie, who taught school in Roaring. Living among the people, Aunt Nellie saw firsthand the effects of their desperation. She sent a letter to Lora. When the letter came, Lora quickly hung up her coat and tore open the envelope.

Lora, you must pray for the people here. More of my students are moving away as their parents seek better

---

2 President Hoover made this statement in January 1930.

living conditions and jobs. The spiritual condition is on the decline. How we need a minister here to guide the people and lead them in this devastating time...

Aunt Nellie's letter came to the attention of the board, and church leaders and board members met to consider the needs that Aunt Nellie wrote about.[3] Home Mission Board worked urgently to find a replacement pastor for the Roaring Mission.

The need was urgent! Bishop S. H. Rhodes addressed the matter and laid the concern before the members of Home Mission Board on February 13, 1930. "We must call for a volunteer from among us. Brethren, are any of you willing to volunteer?"

The room was silent. The clock ticked and no one responded. The bishop cleared his throat. "Well then, let's take some nominations."

A short while later the newly chosen man swallowed as the men unanimously rose to their feet to vote for Brother Paul Good.[4]

"How soon am I to go?" Paul asked.

"How soon can you be ready?" Bishop Rhodes asked.

"I'll see what my wife says," Paul replied.

---

3 Middle District Minutes, Home Mission Board, February 13, 1930. S. H. Rhodes addressed the meeting by explaining why they had met.

4 Ibid. Mission board members were to "call for a volunteer from among them." "The call was then made for someone to volunteer. As no one volunteered, steps were taken to appoint someone. The Brethren Paul Good and J. E. Suter were nominated. They were then asked to withdraw from the meeting until decision was made. It was then decided to choose between the two by ballot. After a season of silent prayer, Brother Good received a decided majority of votes. We then made it a unanimous vote by all rising to our feet."

Across the barren mountain-scape, life stirred within each branch and twig. Treetops and bushes thrust forth buds of burgundy, brown, and bronze. In a few weeks those buds would burst into a green canopy. There was no time to think of such things. With the urgency upon them, Paul and Eula set to work immediately. Arrangements must be made for others to run the farm. Somehow in the flurry of plans and decisions, the young couple managed to pack clothes, store belongings, and finalize things for the move into the quiet hollow by Roaring Creek. In March 1930 a truck loaded with furniture and belongings groaned up the winding roads into the hill country.

At last Paul and Eula Good and little son Emory from Harrisonburg, Virginia, arrived at the mission home where Aunt Nellie lived alone. They unpacked and settled in, and Lora soon joined them. Together the workers dug in their heels to continue the work.

In addition to new workers, the board provided a phone for the mission and made conditions favorable for Paul to farm to support his family.[5] Instead of goats, a milk cow now grazed in the pasture.

White blossoms loaded the trees in the orchards scattered among the hills. In the weeks that followed, Paul pruned branches and hoped for lush fruit that fall. He hung the lopper-shears in the shop and stopped by

---

5   Middle District Minutes, Home Mission Board, February 19, 1930.

the clothesline where Lora and Eula unpinned the dry clothes.

"Guess what?" Paul lifted his hat and scratched his head.

"What?" Eula asked, clutching an armful of clothing.

"There's interest in preaching services over on Brushy Run," Paul replied.

"How will that be possible?" Eula asked as she gazed into Paul's eyes. "You already preach twice on Sunday."

"We could have afternoon services at Brushy Run every other Sunday," Paul suggested.

"That makes a full Sunday." Lora grinned as she pulled sheets from the line. "Aunt Nellie and I used to go there with Brother Benner on Sunday afternoon. Lots of children come."

Little Emory rode his tricycle up close to hear the conversation. "I want to go too."

"Of course you may go," Eula said. "We will all go."

Lora started to the house with a mound of wash heaped above her head. But that didn't keep her from singing.

"Walking in sunlight, all of my journey;
Over the mountains, through the deep vale;
Jesus has said 'I'll never forsake thee,'
Promise divine that never can fail."[6]

The busy spring days of 1930 evolved into a routine. One day Lora wrote the report for the *Gospel Herald.*

---

6 "Heavenly Sunlight," *Church and Sunday School Hymnal,* No. 471.

Roaring, W. Va.

Dear Readers of Gospel Herald: Our hearts are made glad when we see the folks of this community come out to Sunday school and services. For many of them have no easy way to get to the church. They have rough, steep paths to walk over. But their faces shine for joy as they tell us they are enjoying life. We have been very busy this spring with our patches, garden, and various other duties, with our visitation work. Almost every home has been visited and the people heartily invite us into their homes. Easter Sunday services were started at Brushy Run, which is about five miles from the mission home. At this place services are held only every other week on Sunday afternoons. The interest so far seems to be very encouraging. At these places of labor, as elsewhere there is much to be done. And only by God's guiding hand and the prayers of His children can there be anything accomplished. So don't forget your prayer life and definitely pray for the work. Sister Coffman who has been at home for several weeks on a short vacation expects to return with us when we come back from a few days' visit at home during commencement week at the E.M.S ... We heartily invite you to come and visit this small corner of God's great harvest field.

In His Service,
May 26, 1930 Lora Heatwole[7]

Lora dipped her paintbrush into the orange paint. Carefully she stroked the bristles just right until the petals of a daisy peered back from the paper. She dipped into the black paint and added a center on each flower.

---

7 *Gospel Herald Mission Supplement*, June 5, 1930.

"Very nice," Eula said as she stopped to watch Lora's handiwork. "The children will like colorful covers on their handmade lesson booklets."

"Thanks. I must have Aunt Nellie mimeograph some more lessons for the upcoming Bible school here at Roaring. I thought I made plenty of copies for all the Bible schools, but it seems I never have enough copies even though I make extras."

"I'm delighted so many children come," Eula said as Lora added green stems and leaves.

"Yes, so am I. Even if a few families have moved away, it seems more people come out for the Bible lessons."

She rinsed her brush, picked up a narrow-bristled one, touched it in the purple paint and carefully traced the words "Watch and Pray."[8] Then she set the copy aside and lined up a row of empty papers that she would paint just like the original.

Lora's artwork

"I'm glad for a little break between each Bible school," Lora said as she dabbed into the paint. "We can catch up on other work and prepare for the next Bible school."

"It's working out nicely," said Eula as she wiped the jars of freshly canned beans cooling on the counter.

---

8 Lora's original handmade lesson booklet is in the author's possession. It measures 4½" x 6" and contains twenty assorted lessons and Psalm 100. The lessons vary from Bible characters to spiders, bees, ants, and warnings about the use of cigarettes. See Appendix B for some of Lora's lessons.

Lora held up the picture to inspect her work. Just then Paul stepped inside the kitchen. His pants held a dab or two of white paint.

"Painting, are we?" He glanced over Lora's work.

"Yes. Looks like you are too."

"Yes sir-ree. It's looking better too." Paul sighed and took off his hat.

"Everyone is busy around here. Hardworking!" Eula poured tea and gave it to Paul.

Paul gulped down the tea. "Not everyone in these parts can find income. I'm just glad to have a job painting."

Lora worked on without stopping. "Yes, but I like to be busy." She looked at Paul. "Some mail just came for you."

"For me?" Paul asked.

"Uh-huh."

Paul tore open the envelope. "Well, what do you know— the board sent money to help pay for road improvements. That will make the community happy."

"It'll be a good improvement too," Lora replied. "It will be nice not to have to ford the creek, especially when the water is high."

"You can't call these people lazy even if there's not much work for pay." Paul set the glass on the table, put on his cap, and went back to painting.[9]

John R. Mumaw, his wife Esther, and baby Helen came for revival meetings. Esther had been secretly engaged

---

9 Middle District Minutes, Home Mission Board, June 4, 1930. The board "decided to pay Bro. Good customary wages for painting the house." They also sent money to help with changing the road on Roaring so that the creek need not be forded.

to John when she had helped Lora and Aunt Nellie in the beginning of the Bible school work. Brother Mumaw preached stirring messages that caused each listener to take heed. Each evening he expounded the purpose of Christ's coming and His plan to remedy man's condition.

Take heed, brethren, lest there be in any of you an evil heart of unbelief, in departing from the living God . . . lest any of you be hardened through the deceitfulness of sin (Hebrews 3:12, 13).

He died for all, that they which live should not henceforth live unto themselves, but unto him which died for them, and rose again. Therefore if any man be in Christ, he is a new creature: old things are passed away; behold, all things are become new. And all things are of God, who hath reconciled us to himself by Jesus Christ, and hath given to us the ministry of reconciliation (2 Corinthians 5:15, 17, 18).

But ye are a chosen generation, a royal priesthood, an holy nation, a peculiar people: that ye should shew forth the praises of him who hath called you out of darkness into his marvellous light (1 Peter 2:9).

Gracie sometimes came around to ask Lora and Aunt Nellie questions. She seemed almost on the verge of accepting the gift of salvation but something held her back. Tillie, too, came to the services, her hands busy with the little children who hung onto her skirts. Worry etched lines on the face that used to look so girlish, but each evening she came to hear the messages of hope.

After one service a mountain woman spat out the spice clove she had chewed on during the service. "I tell you now. That man can preach pow'rful-like. I can understand what he's sayin'. I always have liked that man's preachin'."[10]

At summer's end, some had renewed their confidence and faith in the Gospel and "fifteen souls were added to the church."[11] But Gracie still had not come to the light of salvation.

Aunt Nellie was beginning to think of schoolbooks and classes as the year slipped into August. Having a school-teacher in the mission house had some advantages for the children who resided there.

Aunt Nellie watched young Emory play with his toys. She stooped beside him and asked, "How many cows do you have in your barn?"

Little Emory pulled the cows out and lined them up.

"One, two, three," Aunt Nellie said pointing to each one. "How many sheep?"

Emory lined up the sheep and Aunt Nellie placed her finger on his and counted.

Lora scraped the soda cheese from the skillet into a bowl and gave the spoon to Emory to lick. "If you keep learning Aunt Nellie's lessons, school will be easy for you."

Emory grinned at her and licked the spoon clean.

"I have some primer books too," Aunt Nellie said with a smile. "I could start you in the reading and number books."

"But he's not even school age yet," Lora said.

"He can learn quickly," Aunt Nellie said.

"I don't mind," Eula said. "It seems like he enjoys it."

---

10 Esther Moseman's letter of July 1927 states that one of the women found Mumaw's preaching easy to understand.

11 *Gospel Herald Mission Supplement,* September 4, 1930, Roaring, WV report, August 22, 1930, Nellie Coffman.

Emory just grinned from ear to ear. It wasn't long until the boy was engrossed in primer books. School would come easy for Emory.[12]

---

12 Emory Good told the author that Nellie Coffman's coaching in his young years at the mission made him ready for school at an early age and that school was easy for him.

Chapter Twenty-One

Teardrops and Temptations

1930-1931

Boys and girls trudged to the schoolhouse, their overalls and dresses patched by work-worn hands. Aunt Nellie welcomed each student into her class and set them each on an academic pursuit. These children had good minds and much potential if she could channel their talents in the ways of the Lord. Some students were exceptionally bright, some found learning difficult, and some were limited physically because of health problems. She must challenge them to make the best use of time. She picked up the chalk and wrote a poem on the board for the children to memorize.

Gather ye rosebuds while ye may,
Old time is still flying;
For this same flower that blooms today
Tomorrow may be dying.

Aunt Nellie dotted the period and put down the chalk. A knock sounded at the door. Someone opened it, and an anguished messenger announced sad news.

"Guy Arbogast has passed away."[1]

"What?" The students' mouths dropped open.

"But he's only nine years old."

"He's our friend," another gasped in shock.

Grief writhed within Aunt Nellie's own soul. Guy had been her student, and Lora had taught him in Sunday school and Bible school.

Sorrow mingled with compassion as the mission workers helped the family lay another loved one in the ground. Aunt Nellie wiped her nose and stared at the fresh grave. There lay a young boy who could have lived a full and productive life, spared though he was from hardships of life and the lures of Satan.[2]

Solemnly, the teacher returned to the classroom and took up her work.

At home in Virginia, Lora drove a carload of single women to the factory each afternoon at three o'clock for the second shift of work. The clatter of wheels and the spinning of spools kept her hands busy. But while she turned the knobs and charted the progress at work, her thoughts turned to her summer friends.

---

1   This incident was remembered by a student who was present at the Roaring Creek schoolhouse when it happened. The person recalls that Nellie had written the poem on the board before the news came of Guy's passing.

2   Guy Arbogast was born June 24, 1921, died Sept. 22, 1930, and was buried in the Arbogast Cemetery #9 at Roaring Creek. *Grave Register, Pendleton County, West Virginia, 1977,* p.63.

Surely smoke spiraled from Janie's chimney these days, warming the log building Paul Good had improved for the elderly woman.[3] Snug and warm by the stove, she could peek from curtained windows and see travelers on sleighs or watch the stream course between its icy banks. Lora smiled. Janie's life had been improved by her move to this house near the mission. Now she need not shiver in the old drafty house up the mountain. She had new dresses, jars of food, a bed, warm covers, and mission folks to check in on her. She could hobble over to the church for services.[4]

Janie outside her home near the mission home.

Lora stopped the machine and loaded more spools. Then the machine was off to a rhythmic hum while more

3 The Middle District Minutes, Home Mission Board of November 1930 say that Paul was given permission to fix up a place for Janie to live.

4 It isn't known exactly when Janie came to live near the mission home. The Home Mission Board directed Paul Good to repair her mountain home, but the house was in such disrepair that the plan may have been abandoned.

thoughts and prayers ascended for the people she loved—
Abe and Lizzie, Sadie, Sister Polly, Noah, Sister Sarah,
children, the mission workers, and many more.

How did the families fare in this bleak economic situation
when farmers could not get a decent price for their commodities? Would they be able to make ends meet? The last
time she had visited, many had grown thin and haggard.
Some had lost farms and were looking for better places to
live. What would happen to them? Those who stayed would
subsist on what they had, since most had already learned
to do without. Lora's prayers included a long list of people
she held fondly in her heart. And there was more within
her soul than she dared utter to anyone.

She had heard and seen the woes of families who endured
the consequences of drink. The wreckage of homes and
hearts seemed more than the mission workers could mend,
even with the Lord's help. All this and more burdened Lora.

There was no question that carnal influences had filtered into the mountain communities. Hollywood ads
screamed from signs, magazines, and newspapers, luring
all ages to the latest shows in towns. Curiosity would surely
be aroused, even in those living in isolated communities.
There would be a desperate scrounge for money and a way
to the shows. Even at work and at shops in town, Lora
could not help but overhear talk about the dashing heroes
that danced and twirled across the silver screen. Whether
it starred a leggy blonde, a striking, square-jawed man,
or the dollish Shirley Temple, the moving picture stole
people's hearts. Cheap radios slipped into homes with fascinating stories and comedians to titter away the troubled
times.

It seemed that as times became tighter, people sought escape by flirting with the craze of the day. At first, the adventurous would only nibble at the bait of entertainment, then find it impossible to resist. In only a short while, these lost interest in spiritual things.

Lora had prayed long and hard for these souls, but some had plowed ahead, too ignorant to realize the dangers and consequences that would surely follow. What more could she do? How could she convince the young to avoid the pitfalls of evil? Even as her fingers moved with skill and speed, her mind was churning ideas. She would work up some new lessons for the coming summer classes. She must convince students that God's way was truly the best. She must warn them to avoid Satan's alluring packages.

When Lora returned to the mountains in the spring, the snowdrifts had melted. While women made garden rows and planted seeds, men checked their flocks for new lambs and planned what to plant in their fields.

One day Wayne, a new boy living at Abe and Lizzy's, stopped at the post office.

"Got any mail fer the folks?" Wayne stood at the door in bibbed overalls, the bottoms wet and rolled up.

"I'll check," Eula said, running her finger down the names on the slots on the wall.

"What's Lizzy doing?" Lora asked, since next-door neighbors often checked up on each other.

"Well, she's hoeing garden and Abe's a-takin' me up the mountain to graze sheep all by myself. There's a cabin up thar that I'm gonna stay at."

"I see," Lora said. "Have you ever done that?"

"Nope. But I'm big enough. Abe will show me the cabin and tell me what ta do. I might even shoot some squirrels."

"I hope you will be all right by yourself. You are still rather young," Eula said.

"There's nothin' to worry 'bout a'tall."

Eula handed Wayne the mail and the boy waved goodbye.

Several days later, Lizzy seemed worried when she stopped for the mail. "We don't know why Wayne hasn't come back. He was to come home yesterday and he didn't show up. Abe's a-goin' to check on him."

"Maybe the sheep gave him trouble or something," Eula suggested.

"I hope it's nothing." Lizzy took the mail and headed home.

An hour later, footsteps pounded across the porch and someone banged on the mission house door. The neighbor's eyes stared, glassy and dazed. He swallowed hard.

"They found Wayne up the mountain. He's dead."

Lora's mouth flew open. Aunt Nellie gasped and Eula fought tears.

"We must go see Abe and Lizzy. They must be heartbroken. They lost their own son and now another life is gone."

Numbly they tried to process the news. "Life seems so unjust."

The story came in bits and pieces, mingled with chokedback grief. When Abe reached the cabin, he found the boy shot by his own gun. Perhaps he had been squirrel hunting. It appeared to be accidental. A youth with potential had been transported from this life into eternity.

Amid the sorrow, men dug another grave. Women prepared the torn body for burial while friends comforted the best they knew how. At burial time men carried the coffin up the mountain while wails of sorrow echoed down the mountainsides.

One by one, souls faced eternity. Would the next one be ready to meet his Maker? Lora and the mission workers determined to pray more earnestly.

As one soul left the community, another joined the mission household. A tiny baby named Harley arrived on April 5, 1931. Neighbors and friends came to see the youngest member of the Good family and wish them well.

The house stood alone among the underbrush, under cover of thick forest. Some men were welcome there, but ministers who approached the house were accustomed to being sent off with gruff threats. Mountain men knew that in the hills beyond the house they could find what they wanted for small amounts of cash. There wasn't much danger of getting caught; the sheriff rarely patrolled this remote area. Even with times so tough and money so scarce, moonshine provided a little cash in the backwoods.

Jerry was a young teen, and he knew little except life in these parts. Every late summer he helped Dad gather the corn. They would take it up the hollow to a place hidden by brush and trees. This was the way Dad made extra money. It helped; most other times the family got by with almost nothing. Dad's business wasn't something to talk about, for some people were outright against such doings. He must never say a word to anyone—not at school and surely not at church. Of course, his family rarely darkened the door of a church—maybe once in a blue moon for a funeral or something. His folks had little use for religion.

One summer day, the boy plopped down on the creek bank near the church. He rolled up his patched over-alls and sank his toes into the water as children's songs floated through the windows. What went on in that church anyhow? He had heard religious people mocked plenty in his home. But these folks seemed real as he watched them come and go, spreading cheer wherever they went. What made them happy anyhow?

He had sat outside the windows and listened a time or two. What he could catch of the lessons sounded interesting. God's Word was like a treasure chest? Who wouldn't like to receive special things from a treasure chest? He must find out about it. The Bible was a sword? Sometime he might sneak into the church and listen, he told himself. He could leave if he had to. There was a sudden rustle of leaves, and a boy poked his head from behind a tree.

"Hey, Jerry. Wanna come to church?"

"Naw. Just messin' aroun'."

"Come on with me. The stories are good. Them teachers make it awful in'erestin'. Come on."

Jerry objected. "I'm barefoot."

"Don't matter. Heaps of 'em come that way."

"I might run off if it ain't fer me."

Reluctantly Jerry followed the shorter boy into church. When classes started, he found himself looking into the face of a cheerful woman. The teacher had pictures and a pleasant voice that made him almost forget that he was in a strange place.

Teacher seemed so sure of what she said, like it was true. He found the lesson quite captivating. That strange picture of a whiskey bottle had eyes, a nose, mouth, arms, and legs. Whatever was Miss Lora going to tell about that?

"See how friendly the bottle seems? But instead, the contents of this bottle will wreck you. Strong drink has ruined many people's lives and made unhappy families. It steals money from your pocketbook. It will rob you of a clear conscience and keep the Lord Jesus out of your heart. Strong drink robs homes of clothing, furniture, food, and things the family needs. It takes away a person's happy home, friends, and good reputation."

Miss Lora spoke in earnest. What she said was true.

The teacher went on. "And more than that, strong drink ruins the body. It destroys the stomach lining and creates liver problems. Boys and girls, don't take the first sip, and you won't find yourself addicted to it. Live for the Lord, and you will see that His way is much better than the one the devil offers."

Jerry peered at another picture that the teacher showed each student. What were those boys up to anyway?

"Have a look at these boys—Tom, Dick, and Harry. Do they look like they are in for fun?" The teacher's eyes met his and each of the student's gazes. "These boys are going into the world to do whatever they wish to do. They will drink and party until they cannot reason. Then they will be in the devil's clutches. They will find it very difficult to leave that place."

Jerry looked longer. The boys in the picture seemed to skip through the door. They wanted fun. He liked fun too.

"Remember, boys and girls, the popular way is not the happy way. It is better to be alone than to be in bad company. Following Christ will bring much more happiness even though it is not popular."

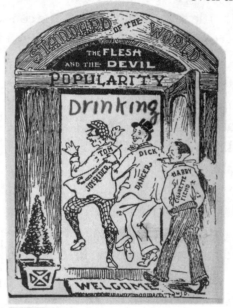

The seeds of truth lodged in his soul as Jerry trudged back home. He would have to think about all that he had heard.

Anyone who follows Tom, Dick, and Harry will find more than fun. Trouble, sorrow, regret, and much more awaits them.

Chapter Twenty-Two

Wild Currents

1931

"The garden is doing so poorly," Eula commented to Paul one evening.

"We'll have to keep praying for rain," Paul nodded as he answered. "The hay field is not amounting to much either."

Farmers surveyed their fields and worried about the crops. Even if the crops produced, there was no decent market anywhere in the United States. Mountain women coaxed their gardens to produce, but they refused to yield in abundance.

Across the nation the massive wheels of economy stood still, restrained by the foreboding fingers of the Great Depression. How much longer could it be until the gears turned again? Hoover's administration brought little hope that things would change. The public grew weary and angry. Hoover continued to send optimistic signals to the public. He said, "What this country needs is a good laugh." And comedians like Will Rogers did tickle the public with humor. "The United States is the only country in history to go to the poorhouse in an automobile," he said.[1]

Down home on the farms and in the mountains, people had subsisted on the land for centuries. They knew how to survive with hard work and the produce of the land. In by-gone years, hard work and diligent effort produced cash to pay the bills. But now, no matter how hard one tried, little progress could be made. Leaner bodies appeared at church, but gaunt faces grinned in spite of the hardships. Folks stretched their meager fare even farther.

Even in the mission house, where occupants had always lived frugally, the only option was to pull in the belt another notch and do without.

"Use it up, wear it out, make it do, or do without," Lora said with a chuckle as she sewed another patch on her dress. "Now let me have that old dress there, Emory. I think I can get a shirt or two out of it for you."

Dire times made people scrounge for new ways to meet the family's needs. Sometimes fathers ventured out of the hollow in search of a better future. If they found work, they returned to take their loved ones with them.

Lora hung diapers on the line and checked the garden with Eula. A row of scrawny cabbage appeared ready to harvest.

"Shall I take some to Janie?" Lora asked.

"Certainly," Eula answered. "And dig a few potatoes for her too."

---

1   H. Paul Jeffers, *The Complete Idiot's Guide to the Great Depression*, p. 48.

Lora filled her apron and walked across the road to Janie's log house. Janie invited Lora inside where a stove warmed the house despite the summer day.

"Thank ye, thank ye." Janie smiled, her eyes fastened on the cabbage that Lora placed on her table. "Y'know how I love boilt cabbage. That will be good with the squirrel meat soakin' over thar in the sink."

Lora lingered and chatted a few minutes. "I'm glad you live close," Lora said. "Now we can check in on you and chat regularly. Would you like me to clean your house this afternoon?"

"Wouldja, Lorie? These old bones don't work s'good anymore."

"Sure," Lora replied. She noticed that the elderly woman could use new shoes and stockings.

Later when the cabbage had been sliced into kraut, she returned to Janie's with a little money she could spare. It wasn't much, but she pressed the coins into the wrinkled hand and set to work scrubbing the log house.

One afternoon while Lora cleaned Janie's house, sudden wind rattled the window and chimney smoke drifted down across the view.

"That's strange," Lora said.

"A storm must be a-brewing," Janie forecasted. "Hain't seen a good rain in a long time."

Just then a crack of thunder crashed.

"I've got to run get the clothes in. Janie, take care of yourself now."

Lightning flashed, followed by deep booms of thunder. Lora joined Eula, and each grasped an armful of laundry and fled into the house while giant drops threatened a downpour. The women dashed to close the windows.

Safe inside the mission house, they listened to the rain pick up a steady rhythm on the roof. Then the heavens opened.

"Where's Paul?" Eula wondered.

A thump at the door brought a sopping man inside. Paul slipped out of wet shoes and went in search of dry clothes.

"Thank the Lord for rain!" Eula breathed a deep sigh as she wiped up puddles.

Lora burst into song and Eula joined in with little Emory singing too.

"We plow the fields, and scatter
The good seed on the land,
But it is fed and watered
By God's almighty hand;
He sends the snow in winter,
The warmth to swell the grain,
The breezes and the sunshine,
And soft refreshing rain." [2]

Paul complimented the singers as he entered the kitchen, his damp hair combed into place.

"I like some of the new songs in the *Church Hymnal*," Lora said as she folded laundry and spread any damp clothing where it could dry. [3]

---

2 "We Plow The Fields," *Church Hymnal*, No. 577
3 *Church Hymnal* was published in 1927.

"You know a lot more of the new songs than I do," Eula replied.

An hour passed and still it rained. Paul's brow furrowed as he peered toward the creek.

"I hope Janie is doing all right," Lora said.

"I hope so too," Paul said.

"We might as well start supper," Eula said. "You never know who might get hung up if the water gets high."

"What are we having?" Lora asked as she lit a lamp.

"Let's do a kettle of vegetable soup." Eula stoked up the fire in the stove.

Lora reached for the kettle, poured in some water, and started to dice onions. Potatoes and a variety of vegetables, including cabbage, followed. Gradually the rain let up as dusk hovered in the hollow. When Paul stepped out on the porch, the familiar song of the creek had swelled to a resounding roar. No question, the creek had risen. Elderly people told about times when the creek became wild and dangerous. The creek could rise suddenly, threatening lives and sweeping homes into the wild, swirling waves. Lora shoved the pot over the heat and breathed a prayer for safety for Janie and everyone else.

Paul slipped over to check on Janie. When he returned, he lingered on the porch, talking to a neighbor about the weather.

The roar of the rushing creek came through the screened windows as they ate supper with gratitude. Fields and gardens would flourish in the next while. Just as supper ended, voices sounded outside the mission house.

"Wonder who's here?" Paul went to the door. "Why, Brother Keener, come in. All of you, come right in!"

"What a surprise!" Lora gasped as H. B. Keener and his daughter, Mary, stepped through the door and pulled off their galoshes. Brother H. B. Keener had served many years in West Virginia missions.

"Come in and dry out," Eula invited as she scrambled for towels.

Young Mary, a woman of about twenty, shivered from head to toe as her father explained, "We had planned to be at Spruce Mountain tonight for a meeting, but the water got so high, we could go no farther."[4]

"Come upstairs and see if we can find you something dry," Lora offered Mary. "I don't know how it will fit though."

"Anything dry will be better than these wet clothes." Mary's teeth chattered as they climbed the stairs.

"Did you find your way here without trouble?" Lora asked as she searched her drawers for clothing.

"It was scary, I tell you. I never saw water that wild and dangerous before. I was terrified when we crossed a foot-bridge." Mary shuddered, her eyes wide. "I prayed hard, too, because one slip of the foot could send you into that rushing water with little chance of coming out alive."

"I'm so glad you made it safely here," Lora comforted.

"Yes. The Lord was with us."

Outside, the creek thrashed and raged out of control. Rain spattered on the windows while the visitors warmed themselves by the fire and ate soup, bread, popcorn, and hot coffee.

"Weather is so unpredictable here," Keener said as he sipped coffee.

---

4 *Gospel Herald*, June 25, 1931, p. 292, Job, WV report: "H.B. Keener and daughter Mary encountered high water on the way to Spruce Mt. They stayed at Roaring Mission Home, returning to Job the next day on foot."

"That's for certain," Paul nibbled at his popcorn. "We face most any kind of weather."

Keener set down his cup, his eyes crinkling at the corners. "When we preachers travel the mountains, we might find ourselves in snow or hail, sleet or rain, or most anything else that comes down from the sky."

Each one agreed, for they had experienced it themselves.

Keener chuckled. "Once L. J. Heatwole was traveling somewhere in these mountains for preaching duties. Had a deacon with him too, and a heavy thunderstorm came up. Then the sky opened and hail pelted him and his horse. That horse got more than a little frantic. They were glad to find a friendly home for the night."[5]

Paul reached to fill his bowl with popcorn. "Well, brother, I doubt this was your first encounter with disagreeable weather."

Keener took another sip from his cup. "Certainly not. But you know, it seems like rain doesn't bother the mountain people much."

"You're right," Paul agreed as the others nodded too.

Keener continued, "A number of years ago I was preaching in an area where people had not heard a preacher for five years. It was a rainy time. The rain poured, the roads were slick and muddy, but the crowds came anyway. Those people were hungry to hear the Gospel. That was a blessing to me."[6]

"Didn't you cross the mountains in snow one time?" Mary asked.

---

5 *The Youth's Christian Companion*, July 6, 1924. L. J. Heatwole tells of a trip on horseback in 1906 when he and a deacon brother traveled the mountains in bad weather.

6 Harry A. Brunk, *History of Mennonites in Virginia 1900-1960*, p. 186.

"Yes. When Mother and I lived at Job, I rode horseback to Harrisonburg for Annual Instruction and Home Mission Board Meetings."[7]

"That's a long trip by horse," Lora remarked.

"Eighty-five miles."

"Didn't you freeze?" Mary asked as she huddled by the stove.

Keener smiled. "I dressed warm, and people were hospitable. They took me into their homes and let me warm up." He grew serious. "The Lord has rescued us many times from danger. How we must thank Him for keeping us safe this evening."

"There's no way you can go home tonight with the water this high. You may stay here for the night," Paul invited.

Brother Keener nodded gratefully. "Looks like we will have to stay."

"It's nice to have a surprise like this." Lora grinned at Mary.

"Well," Eula said as the ladies fixed beds for the visitors, "I guess the dry spell is over."

"Yes," Lora said as she pulled sheets from a drawer. "The garden ought to grow by leaps and bounds."

Aunt Nellie took a set of sheets from Lora. "If the garden hasn't washed away."

The next morning after breakfast, their visitors set off on foot for the nine miles to the Job mission.

---

7 Ibid. This happened on January 4, 1912.

Chapter Twenty-Three

Mountain Schoolhouses

1932

Lora counted out the money from her paycheck. Some for tithe, some for savings, some for spending, and some for her room and board here at home on the farm.

"Here, Papa." Lora placed the money in his large, callused hand.

"I don't know what we would do if it wasn't for the silk mill." Papa smiled. "With several of you girls working at the factory, it helps to make ends meet."

"I'm happy to have a roof over my head, Papa, and I have plenty to appreciate here at home."

Papa put the money in his pocket. "Do you have enough money to meet your needs in West Virginia?" he asked.

"I'll be all right," Lora said. "The small allowance the board gives helps, and I can do without some things. Nobody else has much money either."

"Times are tight," Papa stated, "but remember, the Lord will always provide for our needs."

"I know," Lora said. "Besides, I can wear patched dresses like everyone else does. Like they say: Use it up, wear it out, make it do, or do without."

"I'm glad you know how to be thrifty." Papa smiled.

"Well," Lora said with a grin, "you know who taught me how."

Spring found Lora back at the mission house for another season, but Aunt Nellie didn't come until summer.[1]

"We plan to add another preaching appointment across the mountains," Paul Good announced one day at the dinner table.[2]

Lora took the platter that Eula handed her. "That means another spot to share Jesus Christ."

Eula's eyes shone with interest. "That just encourages me. Even if some have turned away from Jesus, more want to learn of Him."

"Yes," Paul said with a sigh. "No matter where man lives, the heart longs to be filled with spiritual things."

Eula put down her fork. "But Paul, how can you possibly take on another service? You are already preaching at three places."

"And teaching Sunday school too," Lora added with a smile.

Paul grinned with resolve. "I know, but how can we say no when people are requesting the Gospel?"

Eula asked, "When will you start?"

---

1 *Gospel Herald,* May 26, 1932, pp. 164, 165, "Roaring, WV, May 18, 1932," report by Paul Good. In 1932 a new state law allowed only West Virginians to teach in their schools.

2 Ibid. Paul writes that they "added another appointment."

"Soon," Paul responded. "I'm told that large families live there. I'll contact the county school board for permission to use the schoolhouse while school is not in session."

While Paul waited for a response from the board, preaching duties continued at other places. Sunday morning, the loaded auto climbed the steep switchbacks up towering Spruce Mountain. The engine balked as the miles passed. Sometimes they stopped for a radiator check or a tire repair. Then again they moved on.

They bumped along slanted fields and meadows where cattle grazed in shoulder-high grass. The road led in and out of forests where houses perched along the hillsides. About eight large families lived up here in scattered homes.

Paul stopped at the overlook to enjoy the view of mountains stretched to the horizon. Lora touched little Emory's shoulder. "See, Emory, 'As the mountains are round about Jerusalem, so the LORD is round about his people.'[3] Can you imagine God all around you like these mighty mountains?"

Emory nodded as if he understood the deep truth. Perhaps he really did understand, for children can grasp the magnificence of God quicker than many adults.

Lora began to recollect. "Can you imagine those early ministers riding all the way here from home on horseback? How high is this mountain, anyway?"

"It's 4,861 feet." Aunt Nellie raised her brows and a twinkle gleamed in her eye. "It was quite a ride, but for all

3 Psalm 125:2

I know the horseback riders fared better than us modern travelers."

The corners of Paul's eyes crinkled. "You women and children wouldn't be along if we traveled the old way." He eyed the dark clouds that scuttled toward them. "By the looks of things these modern travelers are going to get wet. We'd better go."

As they reached the car, they heard a pounding of hooves and saw a wisp of pink on horseback disappear into the forest. Just then a sudden burst of wind whipped in from the west and rain splattered on the windshield. With a sharp eye, Paul drove on toward the destination in spite of the downpour.

Aunt Nellie leaned toward Lora and asked, "Did you bring your galoshes?"

Lora grinned and playfully pushed Aunt Nellie away from her. "Of course I did. I've lived in these parts enough years to know you never know what to expect with the weather."

Aunt Nellie chuckled. "We learned the hard way, didn't we?"

"Sure enough. We know about slippery roads, ruts, flat tires, getting soaked—and muddy!"

Lora turned from her aunt and spoke to Paul. "You're going to get us there without making us walk, aren't you?"

"Going to try." Paul laughed. "By horseback might be a better option."

The vehicle spun up a slick slope and refused to go farther. Paul backed down the hill and tried again.

"Well, folks, guess we'll wait out the storm." Paul sighed.

A short time later, the shower had lessened to a drizzle.

The group piled out of the car and pulled on galoshes. Lora and Aunt Nellie walked ahead as the Good family followed with Paul holding little Emory's hand and Eula carrying the baby. Inside the forest, the puddles and mud holes would have snagged the vehicle for certain.

"Watch out for the puddles," Lora called back to the rest.

Aunt Nellie pointed to a slippery place and added, "And the muck!"

Rain dripped from the leaves and a few rays of sun stole through the trees. Ahead, the lone schoolhouse sat beneath a clump of trees. People were gathered around the building; a grandmother with a cane, boys and girls, mothers and fathers—all waiting to welcome them.

"I remember you and you and you," Lora said as she greeted the children with a handshake and warm smile. "And you have grown taller since the last time I saw you."

Several children giggled and little eyes shone with joy on this good day when visitors and the minister came to have a Sunday meeting. Lora stepped over to shake the hands of some teens. Shyly the girl in pink reached out to take her hand.

"Did I see you riding horseback?" Lora asked.

The girl only nodded without saying a word.

Lora didn't push for more. "Horseback riding is a lot of fun. I used to ride bareback many times at home on the farm."

The girl's eyes brightened and she nodded again.

Mrs. Kisamore hurried toward them, a baby in her arms and a stair-step line of youngsters skipping ahead of her. A wide grin spread across her face as she reached out to welcome them all. "This is gonna be a plum good day! It always is when you folks come!"

Each one gathered in the building to worship—the work-worn and worried, the weary and the carefree, the wrinkled and the young. Paul stood up to preach the simple message God gave for mankind everywhere.

"My dear people, it is good to worship Almighty God in this place today. We know the times in which we live seem dark and uncertain. We may wonder where the next cent will come from to meet our families' needs. We may be perplexed about the circumstances that surround our nation. The Bible has the answers to our needs no matter what we face. We can turn to the Lord and His Word to sustain us in difficult times. That's what we want to do today."

The listeners hung onto the words, for they faced some of the darkest days of American history. Uncertainty stalked the entire nation. Worry lined the faces of most adults. But Paul plunged on with words of hope.

" 'He that dwelleth in the secret place of the most High shall abide under the shadow of the Almighty . . . He is my refuge and my fortress: my God; in him will I trust.' "[4]

Boys and girls kicked their legs back and forth under the make-do benches while the older ones grasped for the truth set before them. The deep furrows on their brows relaxed a bit.

"To find hope and comfort in hard times, we must come to the Lord, and He will provide a safe retreat, a haven. Whenever you are troubled, take out your Bible and read the words of promise in Psalm 91."

After the service the men set up makeshift tables. While the women spread out a meal, the men's conversation

---

4 *Gospel Herald,* May 26, 1932, pp. 164, 165, "Roaring, WV, May 18, 1932," report by Paul Good.

drifted to the current times. Even though these men lived on a remote mountain, that didn't hinder their interest in what was happening in America.

Jethro's piercing eyes gazed from beneath heavy brows. "Now listen here—didja hear what that Roosevelt said he'd do if they put 'im in the White House? Said he'd help out the 'forgotten man.'"

Another joined in. "They's plen'y of us in them there shoes."

Others nodded and one said, "Yes sir-ree, that man sounds better'n anything I heard yet. Hoover don't do nothin' that amounts to a hill of beans."

Roosevelt's faith in "the forgotten man" brought hope to many, but some doubted that he could carry through with his promises. Others wished to give Hoover's program a chance. All were concerned; what would happen on the national scene?

The children and women sat in the shade eating good food and discussing more pleasant things. A mother smiled with appreciation. "The children 'round here loved Bible school this summer. Them women teachers did a pow'rful job, I tell you."

The children stuffed food into their mouths and talked about the lessons they had heard.

"Did you have Emma Zimmerman or Sadie Hartzler for your teacher?" Aunt Nellie quizzed the children.

A volley of names erupted. "Mine was Emily Kraybill!" "I had Mary Troyer!"[5]

---

5 In the *Gospel Herald Mission Supplement*, July 7, 1932 issue, pp. 294, 298, "Roaring, WV, June 27, 1932" report, Eula Good lists the teachers' names for the Spruce Mountain summer Bible school.

Eula looked at Phoebe, the mother and grandmother of a large family. "Thanks for putting up those teachers in your house."

"Sure thing. We're glad to do it."

Permission was granted to use the schoolhouse across Smith Mountain.[6] Thirteen miles of road meandered uphill and down, around bends, along a wide river, and up a steep trail to a small schoolhouse on a grassy knoll.

An elderly man sat on the rail fence and watched them get out of the car while people climbed the beaten paths to the schoolhouse on the hilltop.

A shy, black-haired teen cocked her head and held out her arms. "May I hold the baby?"

"Sure," Eula responded as she placed her baby into the open arms. A baby always brought opportunities for new contacts.

There came Jason and Mattie Vance, faithful Christians and helpers with the church work. Their children skipped along, excited about the new event. This family had lived on Roaring Creek until Jason had relocated them to this area. He taught school during the fall and winter and farmed in the summer months. Jason and Mattie also taught Sunday school classes and helped with church services in the surrounding communities as needed.

Mattie hurried over to greet them. "It's so good to have you come. Everbody's lookin' forward to this day." She gave

---

6 *Gospel Herald*, May 26, 1932, pp. 164, 165, Roaring, WV, report written May 18, 1932, by Paul Good.

Large families packed into schoolhouses for Bible lessons and preaching, receiving spiritual treasures to savor long after the meetings were over.

Lora and Eula the kiss of charity.

Lora grinned. "It looks like a nice number of folks came."

Mattie rushed on, "We need church for our families. We are so glad you came."

The service began with singing, the older ones carrying the melody while the younger learned the words and joined in the choruses. Brother Paul warmly welcomed them all. He opened his Bible and smoothed the pages.

"It is a joy to bring you the Gospel message of Jesus Christ. Did you know that He is interested in people, especially children? Jesus said about those children who came to hear Him: 'Let them come to me.' Jesus is interested in people; He is interested in each of you here today.

"In the Gospel of John, chapter one, Jesus called some men to come and follow Him. He invited them to 'Come and see.' John 1:39 says they came and saw . . . and stayed with Him that day.

"My friend, come and see what Jesus has to offer. He has said in His Word: 'I am come that they might have life, and that they might have it more abundantly.'[7] Come to Him, and find your life changed and filled with joy."

Seated in the congregation, the girl who had held Eula's baby pushed her short black hair behind her ear and listened intently. The sad eyes caught Lora's gaze, and Lora smiled at her. Who was she, and why was she sad? The young girl barely moved as she listened. Something about her struck Lora's heart. She must make an effort to meet her. After the service, Lora threaded her way toward the girl.

"Hello, my name is Lora." She reached a hand toward the youth.

The girl bit her bottom lip, glanced at Lora, and quickly looked away. "I'm Rosie," the girl whispered.

"I'm glad you have come, Rosie. Did you enjoy the message?"

The violet eyes met Lora's and a smile tugged at the lips. "I wanna come again."

"I hope that you can. Are your parents here? I would like to meet them," Lora said.

Rosie shook her head and her face grew sober. "Nope. I don't live at home anymore. I live with another family now."

"I see." Wisely, Lora decided not to press for more information. "You can think about the message until next time. I hope to see you again."

Lora couldn't forget the people in each community. Many held a treasured spot in her heart, especially the girl with sad violet eyes and black hair who had heard the Gospel message. Would she receive it into her heart? Even in her dreams Lora began to pray for her. *O Lord, please direct Rosie's life.* She would keep contact if she could. *How soon until we return to her area?* she wondered.

Down a different hollow, a matter arose about the schoolhouse there. Summer showers slanted from the heavens and swirled against the school, packed with worshippers.

"Can you move over a bit? Some more people need outta the rain."

"It's rather tight, but we'll make room."

"Something's gotta be done 'bout this meetin' place . . ."

Chapter Twenty-Four

Prospects

1933

Down home in Appalachia, the farmers trimmed their vineyards and orchards. Just maybe that man up at the White House might make a difference in markets for the farmer. Just maybe. Hope gleamed in the farmers' eyes as they talked together. Mothers fried mush and sent their children off to school with a more cheerful voice these days. Since that new man, Franklin Roosevelt, held the reins of the country and promised to take action, maybe things would change. The farmers hoped the man meant what he said.

In the high meadows, lambs nibbled the new grass beside the ewes. In the spiritual flocks, lambs and sheep came to the Great Shepherd for their souls' deepest needs in these dark days. With their coming came a different sort of problem for one community.

"What should we do about the meeting place, fellers?" one man asked. "There ain't 'nough room fer ever'one to sit in this here schoolhouse."

"Yep. The place is packed."

Paul looked at each of the men and smiled. "Building calls for money, and none of us has that," he said. "But I know our heavenly Father knows the answer to our need. So let us all pray about it."

For years the school building at Brushy Run had provided a place for academics and preaching services. Later Bible schools came, youth grew older and married, and families sprouted up and down the hillsides and hollows.

"We gotta have a bigger place," some insisted. "Whatever can we do?"

Others echoed the sentiment, and a volunteer said, "You may have some of my land to build a church. Be glad to help build it too."

"We got the timber to do it," another one said.

"And we'll all help," the others agreed.

In April 1933, the construction project began, and people sometimes came from Virginia to help build the new church. Brawny men shoved the teeth of crosscut saws into the bases of trees. Back and forth, back and forth the saws cut, until a slow groan escaped from within each trunk.

"Timber-r-r-r!"

Leaves crunched beneath the scamper of heavy boots. "Look out!"

The tree swayed and began to fall. Crash! Like industrious ants, each man found his place of duty to dismember the branches and cut up the lumber. Saws hissed, and boys stacked firewood on wagons to haul home to cure for the winter. Darkness settled in that evening upon a stack of boards by the river ready for construction.

One day the mission workers went to help. Mary, a young woman of twenty-seven, stood at the door of the Ketterman home to welcome Lora and Eula. "Mama has her spells and isn't well, you know, so we children tend her garden and do the work."

Lora went inside and set her kettle on the stove. "Good morning, Maud. I know you appreciate all the good help your family gives you."

Maud rocked in her chair and grinned. "Uh-huh. But I don't know what I'd do if ya hadn't come. Don't know how I'd feed all them fellers out there hammerin' away 'thout yer help." Maud coughed into a handkerchief before she continued, "Bless you. A big kettle that size will help out."

Eula nodded and gave the baby to one of the girls. "I have a cake and some pudding to bring inside too."

Lora sat down for a brief visit with Maud and then she stood to her feet. "I came to help. Is there something I can do?"

"Sure," Maud said, "There's taters to peel."

As Maud gave instructions, diligent workers hurried off to the kitchen to carry out her plans. Just as Lora picked up a knife to peel the potatoes, a clatter sounded at the door.

"Why, it's Daisy and Faye! You've come a long way."

Daisy brushed back her short blonde hair that had not yet grown long enough to stay beneath her square-cornered covering.

"Mama sent us 'cause she couldn't come," Faye said. "Here's two pies."

Maud's eyes brightened. "You girls may help Lorie peel taters."

"Get me a knife and I'll get started," Daisy said.

Lora knew these girls. Occasionally Faye and Daisy walked miles down the mountain to hear Bible lessons taught at other locations.

Outside the hammers echoed, and walls and rafters went up under the careful direction of the supervisor. Like bees on a hive, men and boys hovered over the shell of the building. *Tap! Tap! Tap!* Tap! All morning muscles moved and sweat rolled while the men worked.

"Girls, you can run a bucket of fresh water over to the church," Maud said. "Them men will be a-needin' a drink sure nuff, now."

The women set the table and stirred the kettles. They cut the cake and pies and pushed chairs and a bench to the table. A volley of men's voices mingled just outside the door where the men washed their hands in a tub of water. There was a creak on the threshold and a young man stepped inside and sniffed. "Hey, that smells like a mighty good dinner."

"I'm hungry as a bear outta hibernatin'," another joked as he poked the fellow beside him with his elbow.

Lora couldn't help hearing the comments as she set a dish of potatoes on the table. "I know how hungry hard-working boys can get."

"Yeah?" The slim one lifted an eyebrow. "How so?"

"My brothers can put away a heap of food when they've been working hard." Lora grinned and headed to the kitchen, but not before she saw the gaze of the young man drift toward Daisy who was filling the cups with water.

"Oh!" Daisy gasped as she bumped into Lora in her haste to escape to the kitchen.

The girl clasped the empty pitcher tightly in an effort not to let it fall. Then she set the pitcher down and squeezed her hands together while pink stole into her cheeks.

Sitting around the table the men prayed, ate hearty servings of food, and enjoyed friendly banter. The women carried dishes back and forth to the table, making sure that all the men had enough. In the kitchen, Lora smiled at Daisy as she slipped empty serving bowls into the sudsy water and began to wash them.

"I'm glad you've come to help on this busy day."

Daisy grinned shyly, then she picked up a tea towel and wiped the dishes Lora washed.

"Are you enjoying your walk with the Lord?"

Daisy nodded again, her eyes full of joy.

Lora worked quickly while amusing thoughts cuddled in her mind that she dare not speak out loud. In her heart sprung appreciation for this young woman who had made a commitment to Jesus Christ. She may be quiet, but she could work. Besides, some young man had noticed her. Things like this happened over and over everywhere. Perhaps church building provided a good place for love and future homes to bud.

In the meadows and along the roadside, blue chicory swayed in the wind, mingling with tall Queen Anne's lace. Summer gardens thrived in soil made rich from decomposing leaves from the slopes. In the heat of July, mountain farmers eyed the green apples in the orchards and the livestock on the hills. Would the markets be better since Roosevelt had promised farmers better prices? A gleam of hope lodged in the mountain man's heart. Meanwhile, the minister and missionaries nurtured souls as opportunities arose.

Down by the banks of Brushy Run, the new white weatherboard building[1] stood primly like a newcomer, as welcomed by its people as the promise of harvest and the hope of better days. One Sunday when Lora stepped into the new church, she found Avis, a single woman, inside.

"Isn't this place much better than the schoolhouse?" Lora greeted her friend with a holy kiss.

"Oh, it is. My brother can't wait for you to have Sunday school this morning." Avis gazed out the window.

"Good. Now, how are you coming in your walk with the Lord? Do you find that relationship growing in your heart?"

"Oh, yes, Lorie," the young woman responded, eyes bright with knowing a personal experience with the Lord. "It's made a difference."

Lora smiled at the new believer. Kingdom work brought manifold rewards and this was one of them.

Just then young Willie scampered up to Lora, his brown eyes sparkling with life in spite of his mental disabilities.

"Why, Willie, you're all excited now, aren't you?" Lora said as she squeezed his hand in welcome.

"Yeah. It's the bestest day of my life!" Willie exclaimed. "Never been to a new church before."

"Well, it is very special indeed to have a new place to worship," Lora said with a smile.

Outside, the community folks drew near, each face lit with a smile. Let them come, young, middle-aged, and

---

1 Harry A. Brunk, *History of the Mennonites in Virginia, 1900-1960*, pp. 210, 211.

older ones. Even children with limited abilities were lambs as valuable to the Great Shepherd as any other child. Jesus had said to let the little ones come to Him.[2] Let them learn of Jesus and His great plan for all.

On July 20, 1933, the church and community gathered to dedicate the church building. Visitors from other areas came to commemorate this significant event and to encourage the people there.

But more than a new church building inspired the community. Already President Roosevelt had new programs up and running. In the mountain communities, young men packed their bags and headed for the train.

"Imagine that! Thirty dollars a month for working in the Civilian Conservation Corps!"[3]

"Yep. That will help out the folks at home."

So the boys boarded the train. The whistle blew, the engine snorted, and the heavy iron wheels began to turn. Masculine faces smiled through the windows and work-worn hands waved to the tearful crowd along the railroad. The train clattered down the tracks and turned the corner. When, if ever, would the boys return to the quiet communities, the families they had left behind, and the places where they had learned the stories of Jesus?

The heavy rumble grew distant and the whistle faded as their friends and loved ones stood staring down the barren tracks.

---

2 Mark 10:14
3 H. Paul Jeffers, *The Complete Idiot's Guide to the Great Depression*, p. 91.

Chapter Twenty-Five

Lelia

1933

The crow of a rooster filtered through Lora's bedroom window. Lora stretched, rolled out of bed, and began to straighten the covers until she noticed a hump on the other side. The person sleeping there was much smaller than Aunt Nellie, who had slept in the same bed with her for so long. Since Aunt Nellie no longer taught school here, other women came to assist the work.

"Come on, sleepyhead. It's morning!" Lora tugged the sheets off the small woman who still lay in the bed.

"Lora. Stop it." The small form moved and sat up.

Lelia Swope, a young single woman from Harrisonburg, Virginia, sometimes rode the mail truck across the mountains to join the workers at Roaring Mission. She had come to stay the summer.

"Arise, O sleeper," Lora teased. "The day is at hand, and there's work to do."

Lelia leaped off the bed and dressed in a hurry. "I forgot. I'm going berry picking with the community folks! I must hurry!"

"You must watch out for snakes, you know," Lora said. "The folks will tell you about that."

"Snakes?"

"Oh, yes. It's a reality when you pick huckleberries."

"What kind of snakes?" Lelia asked.

"Rattlers, copperheads, and the like." Lora smoothed the sheets and pulled the quilt into place. "They will tell you what to watch for."

"I'm having second thoughts about going," Lelia said as she combed her hair.

"You might fare better than I did," Lora said, taking in the slight figure. "You can probably travel much quicker and with less trouble than me." Lora patted her own waistline.

"I'd better hurry if I'm going," Lelia said, having made up her mind.

"Have a wonderful day," Lora encouraged as Lelia swept down the stairs for a quick breakfast.

Lora grinned. Fresh huckleberries, baked in a pie, and served with whipped cream. Her mouth watered. That was the finest of fixings in the Appalachian Mountains, but let Lelia or others pick the fruit. She would gladly bake pies or can the berries rather than climb three miles up the mountainside and pick buckets of bitsy berries from the low bushes on the high sunny plains.

"Sister Sarah isn't doing very well," Eula remarked one day. The elderly church member suffered with tuberculosis. "She has lots of berries to can."

"Maybe I could help her if you can spare me," Lelia suggested.

"Would you?" Eula asked. "I know she would appreciate help."

When Lelia returned later that evening, Lora looked up from her sewing to see Lelia chewing on something.

"How was your day?" Lora asked.

"Wonderful. Had a big day too. Canned and canned huckleberries." She held up purple-stained hands to prove her industry. "Then Sarah's husband, Wes, gave me maple candy."

Lora turned from the machine and looked at the candy Lelia held.

"Is it any good?"

"Have some and see," Lelia handed her a piece.

Lora took a bite. "Homemade maple candy. It's good."

Lelia inspected a finished dress on the table. "You are such a fast seamstress, Lora. I'm going to watch you and learn some tips. I'm so slow."

"I'll help you," Lora said.

Lelia assisted with many duties in the mission house and with teaching classes.

"What do you suggest I should teach for the next lesson?" she asked Lora.

"You will come up with something," Lora encouraged.

Lelia thumbed through her Bible. "I wonder which Bible theme to use."

"Aunt Nellie and I prayed many times for God's direction. God always placed the message in our hearts. We just knew what He wanted us to teach."

"That's encouraging," Lelia said. "I'm going to pray and ask His direction."

Later, when Lelia joined Lora on the way to church she said, "You know what, Lora?"

"What?"

"God did make the lesson plain. I just know what He wants me to teach today, and I can hardly wait."

"Our God is so faithful," Lora said giving Lelia a warm smile.

One night Lora had just blown out the lamp and rolled into bed when squawks erupted from the henhouse.

Lelia sat up in the darkness and asked, "What's happening?"

"I don't know," Lora answered. "The chickens don't usually raise a ruckus like this. Maybe someone is stealing them."

Lelia inquired, "Shall we go and see?"

"We'd better." Lora lit the lamp. "Let's try not to waken the family."

"All right. Do we have to put on our dresses?"

"No," Lora replied. "It's dark and no one can see us."

Lora picked up the lamp and tiptoed down the stairs with Lelia just behind. The dew moistened their feet as they crept toward the henhouse. For a moment they paused and listened.

"It's quiet now," Lora whispered.

"But the chickens *were* squawking," Lelia whispered back.

Carefully, Lora pulled open the henhouse door and peeked inside. "Looks like they're asleep."

"Good. Everything is all right?"

"Yes," Lora chuckled as the tension ebbed. "Maybe we didn't have a chicken thief after all."

"What would you have done if you had met a thief?" Lelia asked.

Lora gazed at Lelia across the flicker of light. "I think I would have told him to put it back."

Lelia began to snicker and Lora tittered as they headed back to the house.

"Shhh," Lora whispered. "We wouldn't want Paul and Eula to discover we were checking on a thief."

They wiped their feet on the rug and tiptoed upstairs.

When Paul returned from a visit, he shared a concern. "Matilda Hedrick needs someone to help care for her. Her husband Warren and son cannot do it all."

Lora and Lelia listened and looked at each other, wondering who should go.

Paul asked, "Would you like to help, Lelia?"

"Sure. What all would I need to do?"

"Housekeeping and helping at night when she needs you."

"I'll be happy to go," Lelia responded.

"We will pray for you and the Hedrick family," Eula said.

Lora nodded with determination. She would be praying too.

While Lelia worked away, Lora helped with many household duties and sewed.

"I think I'll make Lelia a jacket and dress," Lora said one day.

Eula brightened with an idea. "I'll pay for the material in appreciation for all the help Lelia has been to us."

Several weeks later, when Lelia returned to the mission house, she found a new jacket and dress waiting for her.

"Why, Lora!" Lelia exclaimed with delight.

"Do you like it?"

"Of course. How can I thank you?"

Lora beamed. "Thank Paul and Eula. This is a gift from them as well."

"Thank you," Lelia said as she ran to try on the new clothes.

Lora inspected the fit and found her work satisfactory. Then they sat down to catch up on all that had happened.

"How is Matilda?" Eula asked.

Lelia sighed. "She has miserable nights. I just couldn't get much sleep."

Eula sympathized. "We thought it was time you came back here. I hope she will improve."

Lelia explained more. "The teenaged boy carried water and helped me some. She seems better in the day, but the nights are rather dreadful."

"It's good to have you back," Lora gave Lelia a pat on the back. "After you rest up a bit, maybe we can do some visiting."

The flurry of summer revivals and Bible schools kept Lora and Lelia busy with teaching and summer work.

"Will you help me make some new dresses?" Lora asked as she placed the dress pieces by the sewing machine.

"Sure," Lelia said as she finished pressing a white shirt and hung it on a hanger. "Remember I'm not as fast as you."

"We'll make a good team." Lora sat down and threaded the machine and began to sew. "I'll let you sew and I'll prepare the next seam. I might even cut out another dress."

"All right." Lelia set the iron back on the stove in the kitchen. She sat down and pumped the pedal with her feet. The needle moved up and down. "How nicely you have placed the pieces together already."

The machine hummed and Lora's fingers worked skillfully, fitting each seam together and selecting buttons to finish each dress.

A few hours later, Lora laid the dresses over a chair just as the bishop and Paul arrived from community visitation.

"I learned some new methods," Lelia said as she swept up the threads and scraps. "I think sewing will go easier for me now."

"How about a drink after all your walking?" Lora asked as the men sat down at one end of the table.

"Sure," S. H. Rhodes responded as Paul nodded.

Lora placed water before them and Lelia set out a plate of cookies.

"The response to the Gospel has been encouraging," Brother Rhodes said, a gleam of joy in his eyes.

"Yes, but some are still not saved," Paul responded, his

voice betraying the burden he carried.

"We must labor on regardless of the outcome," Brother Rhodes encouraged, looking from one worker to another. "It is God's work, not our own. Keep up the diligent planting and watering, Brother Paul, and all of you sisters."

Each one nodded consent. Lora paused to take in Brother Rhodes' admonition. She knew the familiar Scripture that he alluded to. The bishop thumbed through his worn Bible to find the verse. He read slowly and deliberately. "Now he that planteth and he that watereth are one . . ."

Lora nodded. She and others had spent untold hours explaining and teaching the Scripture to children and women. The ministers had preached and admonished souls. Planting, watering, nurturing, feeding, training . . . Rhodes read further, his finger moving across the page. "And every man shall receive his own reward according to his own labour."[1]

Lora brightened. She had done her duty and found reward in so many ways. She did not expect acclaim or recognition. Still, the rewards sometimes came in surprising ways. But most rewarding of all was seeing a person changed by the Lord Jesus, indwelt by His person in all of life. That made all the efforts worthwhile. But the work had not been accomplished by human effort alone.

The deep voice read yet another line. "For we are labourers together with God . . ."[2]

"Together with God." Paul repeated the words and his eyes grew moist. "We could not accomplish it in our own strength."

---

1   1 Corinthians 3:8
2   1 Corinthians 3:9

The words channeled into Lora's soul with renewed meaning. She knew the workings of God in her own heart, and she had seen evidence of Christ in people among the hills. Her heart leaped at the very thought of working with the Almighty—a co-laborer with Him, the God of the universe! How unworthy she felt.

The bishop closed the Bible and smiled. "I'm thankful for each of you and your faithful work here in these communities. The Lord has answered so many prayers. He is blessing the work."

"Thank you, Brother Rhodes, for your oversight of the work," Paul said. "May the Lord bless you too."

"My greatest enjoyment is seeing souls get saved and become a part of God's family," Rhodes said. "But my heart aches for those who turn away from the very Source of inner strength. That grieves me deeply."

Each head nodded, for each of them had experienced that grief firsthand. Souls came to the Saviour. Some stayed, others chose to associate with a different congregation, but saddest of all was to see some depart from faith in the living God.

Lora picked up a dress and began to sew on buttons before it was time to fix supper.[3]

---

3 These stories came from interviews and letters with Lelia Swope Hertzler.

Chapter Twenty-Six

The Request

1934

Like a whisper the first drops came—a gentle spritz of raindrops upon the brown hillsides and barren wood-lands. Then the mist came, light and moist, drifting into every nook and cranny of the hollows and leafless forest. Ever so gradually the mist grew heavier until gigantic sheer curtains waved in the hollows and open spaces.

The thirsty land gulped in the moisture and new grass began to creep up the hills and banks. Sap moved up the trunk of each tree to swell the buds high in the treetops. Like the rain brings renewal and growth, so it is with the spiritual life. The Almighty loves to renew souls and desires to make each life "like a watered garden, and like a spring of water, whose waters fail not." [1]

When the sun shone warmly and the ground became tillable, the mountain people ventured out into the gardens and fields. Gleams of hope sparkled in their faces, for

---

1 Isaiah 58:11

spring had come, and with it the hope of the better days that the President had promised.

Again Lora returned to the mission. One afternoon she walked past the henhouse where a new flock of hens scratched in the coop and opened the gate that led into the meadow. The afternoon sun had almost crossed the narrow span of sky, and the coming of evening was much earlier than Lora was accustomed to at home.

Jersey was one of the changes that came to the mission that spring of 1934. Lora buttoned her jacket and quickened her pace. She must find that cow and get the milking done before dark. She dodged the stones in the rocky pasture. Jersey couldn't be seen anywhere. Lousy cow!

Lora hummed a tune as she climbed the steep pasture that disappeared into the forest and kept an eye out for

Lora wrote in her scrapbook: "Did Jersey really know she was playing hide-and-seek in the large, steep, rough, brushy pasture field shortly before milking time?"

Jersey could be a trial for Lora, but as Lora wrote in her scrapbook, "Her milk, cream, and butter were greatly enjoyed."

snakes. It may have been a little early for them to be out, but she dared not leave snakes to chance. She shuddered. They were nasty critters.

Clusters of violets bloomed here and there in clumps beneath the trees. Lora smiled. So many beautiful things abounded in this place. She loved the hills and the people here.

She spied some garlic. So *that* is where Jersey got it. She would have to pen Jersey closer to home lest the milk taste of garlic. Oh, that cow!

Up ahead, Lora saw the cow grazing with apparent contentment. The cow turned and eyed Lora, swishing her tail and stretching her tongue for the last morsels before she must go. Lora followed the fence along the upper boundary.

"Come on, Jersey, get going."

She gave the cow a friendly slap. Slowly the cow ambled down the rough terrain and lolled across the pasture, then stopped to eat garlic.

"Oh, no you don't!" Lora snorted. She swatted the cow soundly on the rump. Jersey jumped and hurried toward the barn. Lora followed, thinking of the changes that had happened in this place over the past years.

She had first come when the Benner family lived here in the 1920s. Then the Good family had shared the work. Now more change had come since the Good family had moved home. James and Vada Shank, from her home community, had moved into the Roaring Mission along with their fourteen-month-old boy.

Lora smiled. She enjoyed working with each one who had come to serve. She must get the milking done and help Vada prepare supper. James would be home by dark.

Jersey ambled into the barn and nibbled hay. Lora squatted by the cow. The rich, warm milk foamed into the bucket, emitting a familiar smell. The soft fur of a cat brushed against her leg. Lora nudged the cat away. No need to get fur in the milk.

Meow! The persistent kitty cocked its head and pled

The James Shank family.

for sympathy. Lora ignored the pleas. By the time the bucket had filled, several more cats licked their whiskers and paced, hopeful for a meal, their tails high in the air. Reluctantly, Lora poured some milk in the empty pan. The grateful kitties lapped up the milk as Lora headed to the house.

Vada looked up from folding clothes. "Does the milk smell like garlic?"

Lora sniffed. "It does. That cow is so ornery." [2]

Vada chuckled. "Really?"

Lora replied, "I wonder what James would say about penning her closer to home."

Vada smiled. "You may ask him."

"Little James won't like garlic in his milk." Lora made a face at the little boy who looked up at her. "It tastes awful. But I'll see what we can do to change that."

Lora poured the milk through cheesecloth. "I don't know if I can stand garlic in the custard or soda cheese."

Vada smiled pleasantly. "I know you, Lora. You will persist until you win."

"I hope so," Lora stated, "but that cow is mighty determined."

"I don't know what we'd do without you or Jersey," Vada said as she picked up a stack of towels.

At supper Vada notified James of the difficulty. "Lora has a little problem with Jersey."

As Lora explained the problem, James began to smile. "Jersey sounds like the children of Israel, hankering after the leeks and garlic."

---

2 A later worker, Mary Huber, writes in her personal scrapbook about Lora's troubles with Jersey, the cow, especially the cow's preference for the "garlic patch."

Lora chuckled. "So what do you think about penning that cow away from the garlic?"

"I think you have a good idea," James said. "Maybe you could keep her in the yard some of the time."

Vada looked surprised. "You mean let her keep the lawn mowed?"

"Why not?" James replied. "It would save us work. Seems there's more than enough other work to do."

Lora nodded. No minister who came to these parts had a chance to be lazy. He had to manage the farm and support a family. In addition, he must conduct church services, encourage the believers, call sinners to the Saviour, and instruct new believers in the Word. The minister must be a loyal father and husband, a friend and good neighbor, and willing to help any in need. Each man that filled this vacancy had more than enough responsibility. To improvise made perfectly good sense.

A knock interrupted supper.

James checked the door. "Why, Abe. Come on in."

"I see it's supper time," Abe stepped in and lifted his hat. "Need a little help, that's all. Just wond'ring iffen you could help round up some cows that got out."

"Of course." James reached for his hat. "I'll get a lantern and be along."

"But, James, you haven't finished supper," Vada objected when Abe had gone.

"I'll eat when I get back."

Vada sighed but didn't complain.

Lora smiled at her across the table. She shoved the ladle toward Vada. "May as well go on and eat."

Vada sighed and dipped stew for herself and the baby.

Later that evening, Lora penned a report to the *Gospel Herald* readers about the changes that had come to the mission. She ended with some Scripture verses that were close to her heart.

"Oh earth, earth, earth, hear the Word of the Lord."
"Call unto me, and I will answer thee, and shew thee great and mighty things, which thou knowest not." Do we believe this wonderful promise? Have we ever tried it?
April 10, 1934 Lora Heatwole [3]

A solemn neighbor brought sad news. "It's Sarah. She's gone on."

"I'm so sorry," Lora said. "She hasn't been well, has she? I'll tell James and Vada." Lora carried the news to the living room where friends of the Shanks, a husband and wife, had just arrived for a visit.

"This means a funeral tomorrow," James said when Lora relayed the message. "There's hay to be harvested tomorrow too."

"I'll help whatever I can," the husband reassured James.

James grinned hopefully. "You may take your pick of jobs. Would you like to preach a sermon or work the hay?"

"I'll do the hay."

"I'd be happy to have you preach," James offered good-naturedly.

---

3 *Gospel Herald*, April 19, 1934, p. 52.

"I'll do hay," the man insisted.

Lora, the guests, and the Shank family walked the short distance to the home of the bereaved. Sister Sarah Vance had raised a large family. She had been a faithful Christian, who had suffered for years with tuberculosis. At last Sarah could rest from her health problems and burdens. But this dear saint would surely be missed.[4]

Lora mingled with the family and whispered to the sorrowing ones. "We will miss her, won't we?"

In hushed tones Lora helped the women prepare the body for burial while hammers rang, nailing together a coffin. When the coffin came, loving hands smoothed white cloth into place and then lifted the body into the box. Friends lingered with the family that evening, consoling as best they could.

The next day while the guest harvested hay, James preached the sermon. Many times Sarah had sung the familiar song "Soon With Angels I'll Be Marching," and now she was doing just that—unhindered by the ailments of this life. How soon would others join her in the Great Beyond where no earthly worries interfered with their bliss?

The family trudged up the hillside to the graveyard. As the wails of the sorrowing hung in the air, Sister Sarah's wearied body was lowered into the ground. But the parting of the faithful sister was not a lost cause, for now the empty seat at church and at home prodded others to consider eternity. Long after her departure, the Spirit worked in the hearts of some who had resisted the call of Christ.

---

4 Sarah Vance died May 3, 1934. She is buried in the Vance Cemetery #12. *Grave Register, Pendleton County, West Virginia, 1977*, p. 64.

Stubbornly, the Chevy cut through the soggy trail. Slowly, the travelers crept toward their destiny until the whine of tires indicated it was no use.

"We're stuck!" James groaned.

"I'll get out and push," Lora said, pulling on her galoshes.

James untied a shovel from the vehicle and dug away the mud. "Vada, you drive. Lora and I will push."

Lora and James shoved the car as Vada accelerated. Thick, wet globs splattered on her good dress and her face. Still she kept pushing. Slowly the car budged and moved out of the mire.

"James," Vada gasped. "Your suit has mud on it!"

"Is it ruined?" James asked.

They crawled down the riverbank and washed away the mud and spot-wiped the smudges as best they could.

"We'll be late," Vada said, a trifle of worry in her voice.

"It can't be helped," James said as he took his son's hand and hurried up the muddy trail.

"The people will sing until we come," Lora consoled.

You never knew just where or when you might be waylaid with trouble on the mountain roads. The people in this photo are unknown, but are thought to be Paul and Eula Good.

The school building resounded with singing as the late-comers stepped inside and removed galoshes. Curious heads turned and smiled as the mission workers found a place on the packed benches.

Then James stood and spoke of hope and of purpose for living. He lifted the Holy Book in his hands and implanted the teaching in the willing hearts of the listeners.

After church, the people spilled out of the muggy building and lingered on the grassy hillside. The chatter of voices mingled with the squeals and laughter of playing children as a group of men approached the minister.

One middle-aged father began with a raised eyebrow and an earnest smile. "We've heard about the summer classes the women have at the other churches. Couldja have Bible school for all our families?"

"Do you think there would be enough interest?" James asked.

Another father stepped forward and gestured toward the crowd of playing children. "Cain't ya see all these here children? I'm one pop that'd be happy fer my younguns t' have such teachin'."

"An' me too," another whiskered father chimed as he hooked his thumbs on his overalls. "Our children jus' love it. Bible school would mean they could larn more lessons."

James grinned. "I'll consider it."

On the way home, James shared the request with the women.

"More Bible school?" Lora quizzed with a hint of enthusiasm. "That would be wonderful. When could we do it?"

"Let's see," James mused. "The other locations have revivals and Bible school earlier in the summer. Maybe we could do it late July or August."

"I see that summer is no time for idleness here in West Virginia," Vada commented.

Lora agreed. "I don't mind. I like to be busy."

"The most important work of all is sharing the Gospel story," James said softly.

Lora mused aloud. "We could repeat the same lessons we give at the other Bible schools."

"It seems to me we should honor the request," James said. "It is an opportunity and the doors are open."[5]

Chapter Twenty-Seven

Sweethearts and Coffins

Up and down the ridges, not far from the scattered cemeteries, pink laurel blossoms peeked from the rich woodland. Here and there fresh-turned clods in the graveyards gradually grew green, even as people bore their grief and attempted to go on with their lives. The memories of the deceased lived on as time moved forward, refusing to stop for the tragic losses that came.

Over the months, young hearts discovered stirrings within such as they had never known. Just like roses, the budding relationships in the hearts of men and maidens gradually unfolded into full bloom. Eyes sparkled as young brides sewed their dresses in anticipation of their wedding days. And grooms and fathers went to search for houses.

The hot sun blazed on Lora as she stood on the brow of the hill and watched the people trudge up to the school.

Her eye fell on Rosie, the girl she had often encouraged. Rosie ran through the tall grass, her covering strings blowing in the breeze, and stopped in front of Lora and grinned.

"How long until the wedding day?" Lora asked with a smile.

"Two weeks. The bishop will marry us when he comes for the meetings."

"Is your dress ready for the special day?" Lora asked.

"Almost! It won't take long to put in the hem."

"I'm so happy you will have a Christian marriage," Lora said with sincerity. "A Christian home is a chance for a successful marriage."

"Thanks, Lorie. I do want that for my life."

Lora's heart glowed with joy for this young woman. Her life could have taken a totally different direction, but she had accepted the Lord and His guidance for her life and future.

Lora spread her hand toward the surrounding peaks. "The Scripture says, 'As the mountains are round about Jerusalem, so the Lord is round about his people.'[1] Will you remember that verse?"

"I will try to, Lorie. I didn't know the Bible had so many verses about mountains."

"Neither did I until I came here," Lora replied. "Mountains are sure and constant. They endure, no matter how dark or stormy the weather. God is like that to us."

Rosie nodded while her gaze drifted to the young man on the edge of the crowd.

"I'll be praying for you and your home," Lora promised.

---

1 Psalm 125:2.

In another community Mary Ketterman swept the floor with extra zest. Then she hurried to put on a clean dress and comb her hair. Someone was coming to her house for a visit! Ever since her trip over the mountains to visit her friend, Lelia, in Virginia, this young man had sent letters and made visits. Ralph Swope would arrive any moment. There he was, coming down the walk toward the door, a smile on his face and a glow in his eyes. The hours passed quickly as the two talked. Before the weekend ended, Ralph had a question to ask.

"Mary, will you be my wife?"

"Oh!" Mary gasped. "I would like that very much, but how would Mama do without me?"

"Well then, you can think about it," Ralph said.

"Yes, Ralph, I will be your wife. Perhaps some of the younger ones could help Mama."

"Wonderful!" Ralph beamed. "I think my papa could help us find a place. Could you be ready to marry in a few weeks?"

"I will try."

Ralph stroked his chin. "We would go to the bishop's house and be married."

Mary gasped. "Oh, this is more than I can hardly believe! To think we will be married!"

On a July day, Ralph and Mary went to Bishop S. H. Rhodes and were united in marriage. Mary happily settled into married life on the Swope farm, but often an uneasy feeling gnawed inside her. How was Mother faring back home? Oh, to be in the woods and by the streams rushing through the hollows. But Mary kept working her garden and keeping house. Sometimes she looked longingly toward the west.

In the West Virginia mountains, affection entwined two more hearts. Daisy's blue eyes sparkled as her groom, Daniel, took her hand and pledged, "till death do us part." Both had become a part of the church and desired to bring up a Christian family.

In a rare moment of solitude, Lora sat in the shade by the creek and watched a dragonfly flit across the water. She held her hand to her chest as if to contain her joy for the new homes that had recently begun. Students who once were children had suddenly grown up, accepted the Christian faith, and took on new responsibilities—the making of a Christian home. Some were able to help in the church work by teaching and guiding the younger.

Lora sighed with deep happiness as she prayed that God would bless each home and multiply His love and grace upon them. The rush of the stream blurred into a distorted maze of water shimmering with specks of sunlight, but her eyes were not seeing. Memories of years gone by occupied her mind.

When she and Aunt Nellie were younger, they had dreamed of marriage. She and Aunt Nellie had both had prospects, but nothing serious had developed for either of them even though the community had speculated about a friendship between Aunt Nellie and the good-natured community bachelor. The Lord had been good and life had been quite fulfilling as single women.

Lora's thoughts drifted to that first summer when Esther Moseman had joined them to teach Bible school. She hadn't thought of Esther's unusual encounter for a long time. It seemed as if she could see and hear everything as clearly as if it were happening now.

"I wonder who this is from?" Esther had mused as she opened the envelope and read the contents. Suddenly her mouth had flown open and she doubled over with laughter.

"Whatever is the matter?" Aunt Nellie had asked when Esther folded into a chair unable to speak for laughing so hard.

Esther stifled laughter and tears. "You won't believe this. This letter is a proposal for marriage and it *isn't* from John!"

Lora pressed the matter. "You're teasing us."

"I am not!" Esther insisted. "A widower has written to ask for my hand and I don't even know the man!"

The women looked at one another. By the accumulation of John's letters, it took no stretching of the imagination to see that Esther was already destined for marriage.

"Whatever will John think? I have no interest whatsoever in this stranger!" Esther seemed on the verge of tears, but she composed herself. "Nellie, will you help me write a courteous reply?"

Lora smiled at the memory. Aunt Nellie most certainly had a way of helping in such an awkward situation. And Esther had married John Mumaw, the man she loved and to whom she had been secretly engaged that summer of 1926.

Lora daydreamed a bit longer. She remembered a rainy evening when an assistant had sloshed to church in galoshes with her. After church the new teacher joined the young people, who quickly accepted her spontaneous interaction. Denny, a community bachelor, had watched the newcomer for some evenings. *This one might be worth a catch,* he thought. He managed to strike up a friendly conversation and at last he approached the opportunity head-on.

"If you like, I'd be happy to carry you home."

The feminine mouth dropped open in utter shock. "No, I think not."

On the way home Lora asked the girl why she had refused the friendly invitation.

"The very idea, Lora. That man asked to *carry* me home. I think that would be entirely out of place, don't you?"

Lora laughed as they splashed home through puddles. "He only meant to drive you home in his car."

"Really?" The voice softened. "I didn't understand what he meant."

"That's an expression here," Lora remarked as the two stepped onto the porch.

The girl moaned with embarrassment. "Oh, that poor man must think me very rude."

Lora couldn't resist some good-natured humor. "You know, you could have had a dry homecoming if you had let that man drive you home."

Lora almost chuckled out loud, then her thoughts returned to the present. A bee hummed past and lit upon a clump of clover. Lora stood and looked up the creek where the ripples splashed down the deep ravine. What good a few moments of solitude were! She must get back to work.

Haystacks dried in the fields and daisies swayed in the sunny meadows when S. H. Rhodes came to officiate Rosie's wedding. The little congregation on the hilltop was holding a series of meetings. J. L. Stauffer spoke to the congregation on courtship and marriage. During the service, S. H. Rhodes married Rosie and the young man. Afterward, the happy couple said good-bye and drove away. Lora clutched her hands together and breathed a prayer as they went. *Lord bless them through whatever they may face in the future.*

She turned to see Jack, a community boy, swing onto his horse. He paraded up and down the schoolyard, his eye turned toward the young girls who chatted together.

"What's with Jack?" the mountain girls asked with disdain as they avoided him.

"Don't pay attention to him."

"Yeah, don't look at him. He just wants a girlfriend too."

"He's so stupid," one girl hissed.

Lora cringed at the words. Poor Jack. All people wanted to be accepted, him included. Yes, she had heard what no one intended for the ears of teachers or leaders. She dare not ignore mistreatment and rude talk about anyone. Carefully she edged toward the girls.

"Good evening, young ladies."

"Good evening, Lora," the girls chirped in response.

"I wonder if any of you remember the Golden Rule. Do you remember what it says?" Lora asked, her gaze scanning each of the faces.

Some fished for the words until one brave girl paraphrased, "As you would that men should do to you, do you to them the same."

"That's right," Lora said. "Now I'd like for you to think about that verse. How do you want others to treat you? Then put yourself in Jack's shoes."

Lora turned toward the church, but already some faces were written with guilt. Perhaps a word of caution would cause some to change their attitudes, but from experience she knew that did not always happen.

Maybe someday someone would find enough heart to be kind to the lonely man. Disappointed, Jack rode home, his head bowed and his heart aching.

Within the hearts of some, faith stretched upward like thickening stems, leaves broadening and tendrils scrambling up the trellis of hope. Lora found her own heart enriched by the effects of the Gospel even as others grew in faith. But with some it was not so.

Lately she had noticed that Avis, a woman in her twenties, had an extra gleam in her eye. Was it any wonder that this young woman absorbed the messages and grew in faith?

A thin, middle-aged man walked into the church with his motherless son beside him. Somehow the grief that once etched his masculine face had softened. Up the hollow a ways, the house seemed vacant without the touch of a woman's hand. A man could warm up beans, fry an egg, and make coffee and such, but it wasn't the same as a woman's fixings. Things didn't seem quite right without a woman around to set down a meal, wash up the clothes, and give a man and boy some affection. Sure, Matilda was missed—missed every day, but Matilda would never come back. The boy needed a mother too.

One day Lora went to visit Avis and found the woman sewing.

"I don't know, Lorie," the lips of the bride-to-be quivered as she added another stitch to her dress. "I don't know if I can handle being the wife of Warren Hedrick and a mother to his half-growed boy."

"God will help you," Lora encouraged as she helped to stitch the hem.

"I hope so." Avis sighed. "Seems like mighty big shoes to fill."

"Whatever God asks of you, He will enable you to do it with His help."

"Thanks, Lorie. I do love the man and want to make him and the boy happy."

In a short while the hands clasped together, masculine fingers entwining with feminine ones, as the man and woman said, "I do." In their hearts, love for God and for one another stirred as they pledged to be true.

The half-grown boy watched, his eyes perplexed and moist. Meanwhile, up the steep hillside in a cemetery shrouded from view, the grass grew thick and green on his mother's grave. ²

---

2 The people and events in this chapter are based on true accounts but some names are changed.

Chapter Twenty-Eight

Conflicts

1934

Lora sat on the porch, her lap filled with a large bowl of apples. She sliced an apple in two, circled her knife around the core, cut the apple into quarters, and dropped the pieces into a kettle beside her.

"We are moving along quite nicely," Vada said as she picked up the full kettle and placed another pan by Lora. "There are twenty-two quarts of applesauce ready to can."

"Good," Lora said. "I enjoy the work, but it sure is nice to see the apples canned up and ready for the snow to fly."

Vada chuckled. "That is so. Well, look who's coming!"

Lora looked up as a familiar woman approached, her covering strings fluttering in the breeze, a note of anxiety in her manner. A boy and a girl skipped along behind her.

"Welcome," Lora greeted as the point of her knife twisted in the center of the apple. She paused just long enough to speak to the children before they ran off to play with the Shanks' little boy.

The visitor had a few polite words, but her eyes watered and her voice seemed strained. Finally the words came, not angry, but short, snappy, and full of emotion. "Well, now, I jus' had to come tell you that we're movin'."

Lora stopped, her knife suspended in midair as she stared at the woman. "You are?"

"Yep. Joe's found a better job. We gotta go, but I can't 'magine livin' anywheres else. This is the only home I knowed my whole life, I tell you!" She hurried on, hardly stopping for breath, "But I knowed it's the best thing fer us. Things should be better fer us over there, maybe a lot better than we ever had before."

"We are going to miss you and the children," Lora lamented.

"Lorie, we're gonna miss all of you—and this place. Don't know how we'll manage, but we gotta go, gotta take care of the family, you know."

"I understand." Lora stood up and dumped apple scraps into a bucket. "Life brings so many changes."

"There's a church there—a good one I hope." The mother sniffled and wiped her nose on the back of her hand. "And schools too."

"How soon will you go?" Vada asked.

"In two weeks iffen I can be ready." She sniffed again.

"How far away?" Lora asked.

"Two hundred mile. I'll have a different house fer sure. Don't know how in the world I'll manage away from these here hills."

"I'm sure you will miss the mountains," Lora said as she scooped more apples into the bowl.

The putter of an engine sounded, and Lora and the women watched as an old car clattered down the hollow toward them, the shriek of laughter and voices drifting through the windows. Several familiar young men and girls occupied the car. Was that Tillie with them? It certainly looked like Tillie.

The visitor squeezed her lips in disgust. "Now I wonder why would Tillie be with them instead of home takin' care of her youngun's and her husband?"

Vada picked up the kettle beside Lora and commented softly, "She hasn't been around to visit much, has she?"

"No, she hasn't," Lora replied, her heart weighted for the sight of the woman among the young.

She knew the young mother was busy with several children now. That responsibility would hinder the once-frequent visits, but there was something more—something she could not put her finger on. The silence lingered as the three stood staring after the dust.

"I always liked it when Tillie stopped in to chat. I wonder what she's up to." Lora sat down and started to cut apples again.

"Probably carousin' off to somewhere, I reckon," the visitor huffed.

"People come and go much more than when I first came," Lora said with regret. "I don't know where all they go since they have faster wheels these days."

The visitor looked Lora in the eye. "You wouldn't wanna know. Well, I gotta git home and start packin'. No time fer gab like this."

Lora worked on, the apple basket almost empty, as her mind recalled the last encounters with Tillie. There was a sense of restlessness in the young woman, even though she was always friendly. Lately she seemed a bit aloof. What could be troubling the young mother, and whatever could she be doing off on a jaunt with frivolous youth? Once outside their remote community, what appealing attractions would lure the seekers of pleasure?

She snatched the last apples out of the bucket. Slice, core, quarter, drop. She worked quickly, but her mind pondered those who had set out to find pleasure. It didn't matter where they lived—here, home, or anywhere. Their experience was common. Too often the naïve intended only to investigate the regions just beyond their boundaries—to see new things beyond their back door. But the bait of sensuous posters or flashy ads tantalized the desires of both young and old. Even when they returned home, the pictures were branded on their memories. What happened in the show? What would it be like to experiment? Just one sip, or one smoke, or . . . ? The inner voice of temptation would whisper, "No one need know. Just try it once, that's all."

All through history, the appeal of pleasure has attracted mankind like a magnet. The tempted ones are left with a choice. Many have reached for the bait without thought of the consequences surely to come. Inward desire quivered with the delight of indulgence, but only for a moment. Afterward, the stone of guilt crushed like dead weight in the soul. The weight seemed unbearable, and for a time the agony of regret lashed at the soul without mercy. The punishment of guilt would subside, but the tempted had been snared, and the heart tainted with sin. The desire would come again, stronger and deeper. Often there was no return from the grasp of carnal desires.

While the last apples plopped into the kettle, the words of Scripture came to Lora. "His own iniquities shall take the wicked himself, and he shall be holden with cords of his sins."[1]

She shuddered and whispered a prayer for the adventurous ones. Surely broken hearts and homes would follow those who experimented with sin. And the way out of Satan's clutches could be very difficult.

There was a better way, a right way. She must tell others of the right way and warn about Satan's snares. The ministers and workers had long been doing this, yet they must keep exposing the truth.

Lora sighed, picked up the kettle, and went inside to help finish the canning. A verse echoed in her mind, "But the path of the just is as the shining light."[2] Oh, that she could help others find that path and to stay on it all the way to Glory.

Another local family sold property. Then they packed up their meager things and left in a truck to some far-off place. Several of the lumber camps had closed, and larger cities and communities elsewhere offered work to men who could no longer support families in the hill country. President Roosevelt's programs attracted men who wanted a better life for their families. Young boys found work in the camps and the faces of home folks brightened with smiles whenever a check came in the mail.

"Another one is going away," Vada said sadly.

"Yes, another one." Lora sighed. "It's so hard to see them go."

1 Proverbs 5:22
2 Proverbs 4:18

"Living off the mountain land is pretty bleak these days," James remarked when he learned the news. "Thankfully Stone Camp still offers some work to the ones who stay."[3]

Lora sang as she walked into the house:

"Work, for the night is coming,
Work through the sunny noon,
Fill brightest hours with labor;
Rest comes sure and soon."[4]

She handed the mail to Vada as she finished her song. "Here are some letters for you and two for me. Wonder how those twins are coming along? It's still hard to believe I have a little niece and nephew—twins born this summer. I wonder what they look like?"

She scanned her letters quickly, savoring the news from home, then went to the kitchen to fry potatoes and slice ham for dinner.

James stepped inside and hung his hat on the hook by the door. Wearily he took his place at the table.

"You look plain tired," Vada said as she dished up the beans.

"I am," James replied in his soft-spoken way, "There hasn't been time to catch a nap with all the work to do."

"You have been working too hard," Vada said gently. "Farming, working at the lumber camp, revivals the last

---

3 Stone Camp, a lumber camp near Roaring, was still operating while James Shank was there, but many of the camps were gradually closing.

4 "Work, for the Night Is Coming," *Life Songs #1,* No. 170, verse 2.

couple of weeks, preaching on Sundays, instruction classes, and visits. Maybe you need to rest up some."

James sighed and stretched his legs full length under the table. "God has given us a great responsibility, but we are young. He will help us."

"Did you know more visitors are coming in two weeks?" Vada handed the recent letter to her husband.

James scanned the letters and brightened. "Good! Maybe I will have a chance to listen to someone else preach that Sunday."

"Most are willing, aren't they?" Lora asked as she flipped the potatoes in the skillet, fried to a perfect golden brown.

"Yes," James agreed, "visitors are such an encouragement."

But Lora remembered frequent visits when the overworked minister would invite the visiting minister to stay for the evening and preach. Often the mission minister craved a break from relentless responsibility.

"Won't you stay and preach tonight?" he would ask.

The guest minister would shake his head. "I really must get over the mountain before dark. It has been wonderful to see the people and what's happening. May God bless you for your faithful service."

With a thank-you for the hospitality, the minister and his travelers would wave and head for the comforts of home. The minister felt he had done his duty by visiting. Meanwhile, the burden of nurturing many souls grew heavier.[5] But visitors also encouraged the workers, leaving

---

5 James Shank told how he often wished for the visiting minister to stay and assist with evening services. He told the author much of what is related here regarding guest speakers.

food, words of cheer, and memories of warm friendship in the days following their time together.

"I don't think visitors know how much they mean to us." Vada scooped up little James and put him in his high chair. Then she turned to her husband and apologized. "I hope you don't mind potatoes again. We are trying to use up the damaged ones before they spoil."

"Dinner looks good," James said. "I don't mind having potatoes every meal."

Lora slipped the platter of potatoes and ham on the table. She wiped her hands on her apron and pretended to be a waitress. "Would you like to place an order for the next meal? How would you like them, sir? Boiled, mashed, baked, or fried?"

James's shoulders shook as he laughed quietly. "I'll take them any way you fix them. I know they will be good."

Lora grinned and Vada chuckled as they sat down and waited for James to lead in prayer. In spite of workloads and full schedules, a good dose of humor added a nice spice to life around these parts.

A chilling breeze swept through the mountain grasses and hollows. Children trudged off to schools while farmers picked fruit from the orchards. Unexpectedly, there came a desperate call.

"Fire! Help!"

The news passed quickly from house to house.

"There's a fire up the mountain."

"Where?"

"Up close to the schoolhouse."

"It's raging and creeping towards the school. C'mon."

"Hurry!"

The fire spread into the surrounding forest. Young forest rangers grabbed shovels. With the grit of determination, the men tore into the work. Muscles rippled under thin shirts. The fire crackled and licked up the mountain growth.

From a distance, elderly men watched the younger ones work. In the homes, mothers and grannies peered from their doors to see if any messenger brought news of the conquered fire. Mothers stilled the whimpers of frightened children and monitored cook stoves where food awaited the return of the firefighters. Those boys would be starving after their hard work.

Hours passed, and a rosy glow mingled with the descent of darkness. Superiors shouted orders and the boys fought on. Ever so gradually the flames sizzled and died. The smell of smoke drifted down the mountainside and settled in the hollows. Weary men breathed a sigh of relief and trudged home to gulp down food and drop into beds, too exhausted to talk.

Up and down the hollows, people sighed in relief. Children and parents slept peacefully while the fire warriors dreamed of a paycheck to put in their pockets.

In the morning, government authorities probed in the ashes as the charred mountain smoked. A man with a badge on his sleeve ventured from home to home to ask questions. Neighbor Abe brought reports to the mission house.

"The authorities think someone set the fire." Abe's eyes flickered with anger.

"Who would set a fire?" Lora asked.

"Don't know, but the officer says someone set that fire."

"Why would anyone set a fire?" James asked.

The brim of Abe's hat quivered as he spoke. "Don't know, but they're plum sure somebody did."

Abe reported back later. An arrest had been made.

"Harry did it," Abe said.

Lora exclaimed, "It's hard to believe Harry would do that."

"Is he one of those boys who comes to services?" James asked.

"Yes," Lora replied. Then she turned back to Abe. "Are they sure it was Harry?"

"Yep. The officer took him riding in his car and the boy got so shook up he 'fessed up. They hauled him off to jail."

"Poor, poor Harry. We must pray for him," Lora moaned. "He was such a sweet boy years ago."[6]

---

6 This is an actual happening, but the name of the perpetrator has been changed.

Chapter Twenty-Nine

Harvest

1934

"*ar and near the fields are teeming,*
F *With the waves of ripened grain;*
Far and near their gold is gleaming,
O'er the sunny slope and plain."[1]

Lora sang about the spiritual harvest while she gathered a bowl of tomatoes. Up on the hillsides, farmers swung their scythes and bundled the grain into shocks. Slim ears fattened in the cornfields. Gardeners served corn on the cob dripping with cow butter, and families munched on the golden kernels. Meanwhile, Bible schools and revivals were held in various churches and brought guest speakers, new faces, new commitments—and change.

"Lorie," a mother approached her, earnest pleading in her voice, "some of my older ones want to come to Bible school, but we're busy in the day."

"I see," Lora replied.

---

1 "The Call for Reapers," *Church and Sunday School Hymnal*, No. 334.

"Even the men want to come. Do you think you could have classes in the evening?"

She smiled at the mother. "I'll talk to James about it. Can you tell me who those young folks are by the tree? I don't think I know them."

Consequently, Bible schools began to be held in the evenings. This made a tight schedule for the minister, who must work to support his family besides carry the responsibilities of several congregations.

One evening, Lora encountered a youth she had seen a few times. She extended her hand to welcome the boy with thick brown hair.

"I'm Earl Champ. I live up on Champ Mountain."

Lora knew about a large family that lived there. She also knew the teacher who had taught the Champ children.

"Did you have Ruth Garber for your schoolteacher?" she asked.

Earl's eyes glowed. "Yes. She was a good teacher. Made us do a leaf project."

Lora nodded. She noted that this young man was respectful and confident. She moved on to welcome others to the service and give encouragement. What would become of these youth in future years?

As the service began, her strong soprano blended with the volume of voices. Her heart felt uplifted and encouraged with the zesty singing, the deep men's voices in unison with the women and children. How she loved these dear people who wanted to hear the stories of Jesus and pled for Bible teaching, not just for their children, but also for themselves. The minister stood to speak, and she turned the pages of her worn Bible to follow the message.

Throughout her busy days, Lora communed often with the Lord. More people had come to the Saviour while others drifted away, wanting freedom to pursue their own interests. Would the weary and sinful come as the Lord Jesus whispered their names?

Many messages had been preached and many souls invited to Jesus. Many had taken the invitation seriously, but some had found the cost too great, the sacrifice of discipleship too difficult. Some remained faithful. Others listened and wanted to come—someday. Lora sang softly,

"Why will you longer doubt Him? Come, sinner, come!
What will you do without Him? Come, sinner, come!
For you His heart is yearning, Come, sinner, come!
Why not to Him be turning? Come, sinner, come!"[2]

She thought of Gracie, that spunky young girl who had all these years been so curious about the believer's faith. Why did she refuse to accept the call of the Shepherd? Why did she linger outside the fold and promise again and again to someday come in? She must find time to speak to Gracie again. The girl was nearing adulthood, and the soul that refused the Saviour's gentle call would become calloused and hardened. She must speak to her—now, before it was too late. Not long afterward, Lora had another chance.

"Gracie," Lora called as the teen stepped outside the church.

"Yes?"

---

2 "While Jesus Whispers to You," *Church Hymnal*, No. 569.

Lora smiled at the spirited blonde girl as she approached her. "How has your summer been?"

"Busy. Been helpin' out the Wise family. Makin' a little money, you know."

Lora noticed that the slim face had filled out. Gracie appeared to have gained a bit of weight over the summer. "I see," she said. "I imagine you are good help too."

"Hope so."

"Glad to see you coming to the services. Are you able to understand the lessons and sermons?"

"I understand. Makes sense."

"Good. But we must do more than hear the message. We need to respond to the Lord's call. Does He call your name, Gracie?"

She looked away and wrinkled her nose, grinning shyly. "I don't know."

"Do you understand that all people are sinners? All have come short of God's desires?"

"Yes."

"The Lord Jesus wants to do a miracle in your life if you will let Him into your heart."

Gracie looked at the ground and shifted her weight from one foot to the other. She clasped her hands together then unclasped them.

Lovingly Lora pled, "If He is prodding your heart, please listen to His voice. Harden not your heart, but open it wide so He can come in and live there. He wants you to be His child too."

"I know," Gracie whispered.

"It is a dangerous thing to put off the Lord's call," Lora warned softly. "The Scripture urges us to respond today, when we first hear the call. I hope you will say yes to Jesus."

A nervous smile tugged at the girl's mouth. "Sometime, Lorie."

Gracie turned to go, and Lora watched her walk away. Sadness crept into her heart for the girl who would not receive light and truth, peace and inner joy. Then she saw movement in the shadows of the forest, and a young man stepped forward to walk Gracie home. A stab of grief pierced Lora's heart with pain that made her wince. This man was not a Christian. Did it matter that the missionaries sacrificed comfort and money to bring the richest treasure to the mountain people? Did it amount to anything? Was all the effort a lost cause? She trudged home with a heavy heart and dropped to her knees beside her bed. Her anguished soul poured out to God.

Lord, touch the hearts of the willful and wayward and draw them unto Yourself. I know You are ready to shine Your light into the hearts of anyone willing to receive salvation. You long to remove the sinful nature, to cleanse the inner soul, to heal sad hearts, and to give peace and joy for empty longings. You want to guide hearts through life and share heavenly wisdom. You bring Heaven itself into the human heart and create new life, new desires! Encourage the discouraged. Lift up the fallen. Convict the sinner.

O Lord, show Yourself strong to these people. The tempter convinces people that living for God cannot equal the fascinating party he offers. Lift the blinders from their eyes, that they may see truth. Help them to know that You are the way, the truth, and the life.[3] Help them to realize that they might have life, and that they might have it more

---

3 John 14:6

abundantly.[4] *Turn hearts away from the tempter and the glamorous things he flaunts. Lord, we seek men to follow You. Why do they reject the best that Heaven can offer?*

In the solemn silence, the Lord whispered to her heart. *I know the hearts of mankind everywhere.* "Men loved darkness rather than light, because their deeds were evil. For every one that doeth evil hateth the light, neither cometh to the light, lest his deeds should be reproved. But he that doeth truth cometh to the light."[5]

Lora's knees grew numb as her weight pressed them into the ridges of the rug beneath her. Still she agonized in prayer for lost souls. *Lord, I know You care about Gracie and Tillie and . . .* She had a long list of concerns. *Soften their hearts, O God, and make them weary of the darkness. Cause them to long for light and life and love. Show us how to lead them into the right way and send more workers to help us teach the Word.*

Finally she rose from her knees and read her Bible. "For the LORD hath heard the voice of my weeping. The LORD hath heard my supplication; the LORD will receive my prayer."[6] Her heart lightened and a familiar song sprang to her lips as she went about her work.

"Teach me the wayward feet to stay,
  And guide them in the homeward way."[7]

Her lips quivered as she finished the words, but a gentle peace filled her soul.

---

4 John 10:10.
5 John 3:19-21
6 Psalm 6:8, 9
7 "O Master, Let Me Walk With Thee," *Church Hymnal,* No. 441.

Outside the church, Lora clutched her lesson supplies as she started up the steps. She heard her name and turned to see Daisy, the young married woman, coming toward her, a twinkle in her eye. What special news would she have to tell?

"Guess what?" Daisy's sky-blue eyes danced as she whispered in Lora's ear.

"What?"

"My man has been asked to help with Sunday school work."

"Well, I know Daniel will do a good job. I'm so happy for you."

Daisy leaned over to whisper more. "We've been asked to help with other churches too."

Lora's lips curved with a wide smile. "We need you younger ones in God's work. You will find that God gives fulfillment in it."

Just then Mary Ketterman Swope ventured over to shake hands with Lora.

"So you moved back home?" Lora asked.

"Yes. Mama has spells and needs help, so my husband and I decided to move here. I missed West Virginia so much. It's good to be home again."

Lora smiled. "I know we could use your teaching skills in the Sunday school."

Before long, several young couples became loyal helpers in the Sunday school work. Lora thanked God for answered prayers.

Dusk lingered outside the windows as the minister ended his message and the congregation sang an invitation song. From the corner of her eye, Lora saw someone respond. Across the room young Earl Champ, the teen with thick brown hair, stood with bowed head. Lora's heart leaped with joy. *Thank You, God, for this young man.* Lora prayed while others responded to the message. *Thanks for choosing individuals to be a part of Your family. Some do want the Light of Life.*

Several weeks later, S. H. Rhodes arrived for a baptism at the schoolhouse. He spoke privately with the ones who had made new commitments.

"Earl, I understand you were a Christian before you made this recent commitment," S. H. Rhodes said.

"Yes, I was saved and became a member of another church."

"Why do you want to be a part of this church?"

Earl explained, "I have listened to the Bible teaching and am convinced that your leaders are teaching what is true and right. I want to be a part of this church."

"Your decision is encouraging," Brother Rhodes commented as they shared in depth. Then the bishop asked, "Do you wish to be baptized, or would you like to be received on confession of faith?"

"I want to be baptized," Earl replied.[8]

"That is what we will do then," Brother Rhodes responded. "May the Lord bless you abundantly."

---

8 This information was given to the author by Earl Champ with confidence that he had made the right choice for his life.

On a summer day in August, 1934, S. H. Rhodes received Earl into church fellowship along with others.[9] Lora swallowed the lump that formed in her throat. God was indeed working in people's hearts.

Earl grew in his experience with the Lord.

Earl became a faithful leader in the church. After his first wife died, he married Elva, daughter of Rhine and Anna Benner.

"Earl, would you teach the boys' Sunday school class?" Lora asked one day. "The lesson is on Daniel, and I think you will do a good job."

"I'll try," Earl said, taking the Sunday school book.[10]

Only God knew the plan He had for this faithful man to build His church.

Meanwhile, the mountain farmers worked hard to harvest the golden sheaves and store them in the barns. Yellow

---

9 *Leaders and Institutions of the Southeastern Mennonite Conference,* Earl and Elva Champ. Earl Champ also gave this information during interviews.
10 Earl remembered that Lora asked him to teach his first Sunday school class on Daniel.

stubble lay across the steep hillsides, waiting for the planting of the next crop.

Chapter Thirty

Camp Cooks

1935

I n the summer of 1935, Mary Huber, a single woman from Rockingham County, Virginia, joined the Roaring Mission work. Together, the thirty-something-year-old maidens trudged up mountain trails bringing

In Lora's scrapbook, she wrote under this picture:
"The Roaring Mission and its family in the spring of thirty-five.
This was some team. We had many enjoyable experiences together."

encouragement and friendship to women and children. They sewed together, taught Bible lessons, and sang together.[1]

One day Lora and Mary helped Vada clean the house. Lora removed the patched cushion from a cane-bottom chair. Then she dusted the chair and inspected the holes in the seat.

Lora wrote in her scrapbook: "A ball of binder twine, patience, will power, elbow grease and some paint made fine chairs about as good as new . . ."

"Chair bottoms that let in fresh air are not very practical," Lora said.

Vada inspected several more chairs. "Something ought be done for these; there's no money to buy new chairs."

"There is some baler twine in the barn," James said. "I wonder if we could weave some twine around the seats like people cane chair bottoms."

1 Lora Heatwole, *Gospel Herald*, August 29, 1935, p. 468, Roaring, WV, report, August 20, 1935.

Lack of money called for creativity. A fresh coat of paint and bailer twine woven across the seats made the chairs look like new furniture.

"Who would have guessed we could come up with such good results?" Lora grinned as she placed the painted chairs in the sun to dry.

"It's amazing!" Mary agreed.

"We won't need to be ashamed when we have company now," Vada said with pleasure.

"It didn't take much money either," James added in his soft-spoken manner.

Coolness still lingered in the mountain mornings, though spring had come. Lora no longer needed her heavy winter coat but still wanted something a little heavier than a sweater.

One afternoon she took out some buttons and supplies she had brought from home and spread a piece of fabric on the table.

"What are you making?" Mary asked.

"Jackets. I think if I'm very careful how I cut, I can make one for each of us."

Mary watched Lora skillfully place and cut the pieces. Lora spent hours sewing the jackets, complete with buttons and a belt. Each one tried on her jacket, and Lora made the needed adjustments.

"Triplets, huh?" Vada said as she admired her new garment.

Mary read the words on the buttons. "Strictly the best."

"Too bad the words don't show very well," Vada commented, "because these jackets are made strictly by the best seamstress."

Lora grinned as she hung her new jacket on a hanger and set to work cleaning up the sewing clutter.

An unexpected adventure greeted Lora and Mary. The lumber camp a mile up the hollow needed cooks for one week while the usual cook was absent.

"Cooks?" Mary asked, looking at Lora in wonder.

"Yes," Lora answered with a grin. "Do you think we could cook for all those hungry men?"

"We know how to fix meals," Mary said, "but cooking for men in a lumber camp isn't exactly what I had in mind when I came to serve on the mission field."

"Me neither," Lora responded with amusement. "But it's only for one week, and Vada says she can spare us."

Some extra money would be welcome. Lora never knew when her shoes would need repairs.

Early Monday morning, a lantern lighted their way to Stony

Three mission women dressed in new look-alike jackets made by Lora. From left to right are Mary, Vada, and Lora.

Lumber Camp. At last Lora and Mary neared the dark cook shack.

"We must not wake up the men," Lora whispered in the quietness.

From the nearby shack, snores rumbled through the thin walls. Something furry rubbed against Lora's leg. What was that? Lora shrieked and leaped away. In the glow of the lantern a skinny cat peered up at her.

Meow-w-w.

Mary snickered while Lora glowered at the cat. Suddenly a dozen cats surrounded them. Mary rocked with stifled laughter while Lora plunged toward the cookhouse, unsympathetic of the feline pleas.

"Cats!" Lora said disgustedly, gently shoving them out of her way with her foot as she stepped into the cook shack.

Inside, she and Mary lit the lamps and started a fire in the cook stove. Then they prepared a hearty breakfast. The cats loitered in the kitchen waiting for a morsel to eat. Lora ladled another dip of pancake batter on the hot skillet. Then she went in search of a broom.

"What are you doing?" Mary asked.

"Getting rid of cats," Lora hissed through her teeth. She found a broom behind the kitchen door. "These cats have got to go if I'm the cook." She shooed them through the door. "Scat! Scat! Scat!" She swished her broom at the dozen furry creatures lingering on the steps.

The cats leaped out of danger's way and crouched a short distance away. Mary clapped her hand over her mouth and shook with quiet laughter.

Lora pretended to scowl. "Can't cook with cats in the kitchen, now can you?"

"I guess not." Mary tittered as she stirred gravy.

Suddenly the sound of men's voices floated through the walls. They heard the thud of men's shoes, speech broken by yawns, and the clomping of feet. Lora wiped the table clean and scrubbed a crusty spot, and the two set coffee mugs, plates, and eating utensils.

Coffee steamed in the pot and pancakes lay waiting on the warm stove. The men shuffled slowly into the room, bleary-eyed and unshaven, their eyes searching the stove for the source of the good smell. At the sight of women in the kitchen, some combed their hair and guarded their language.

"So we have a new cookie and cook today?" The man plopped into a seat at the table and grinned as Mary poured hot coffee.

"Huh?" Mary paused with the pot held in the air.

"A cook and cookie. You know—that's what we call the kitchen help."

"Oh!" Lora set the pancakes and gravy on the table. "Which one are you, Mary?"

Mary laughed. "Don't know. I just came to cook."

In a matter of moments, the breakfast vanished.

The blue-eyed man leaned back and rubbed his stomach. "Mighty fine fixin's, mighty fine."

Another brushed back shaggy hair and spit on the floor. "Yep, mighty good grub."

Others nodded or grunted their agreement.

"I hope it gives you a good start on your day," Lora commented kindly. "Would you like another cup of coffee?"

"Yes'm. That's mighty good coffee."

Lora tipped the pot. As the black liquid filled the cups, steam curled into the air and left a pleasant aroma around the table. The men took their hats from hooks on the wall and left the shack. As the clunk of men's shoes faded, the ladies sat down to enjoy breakfast.

"Ugh!" Mary grimaced, looking at the chairs and floor. "This place hasn't seen the sight of a woman in a long time!"

"Maybe never," Lora retorted. "Looks like we have some hard cleaning ahead of us this week."

After breakfast, she put soap in the wash pan and dipped hot water from the water tank in the stove. Hot suds foamed as she poured the water over the soap, and before long the dishes had been washed and put into the cupboard. Then she filled a bucket with hot soapy water.

Both women scrubbed the chairs, and black water appeared beneath the suds. They dumped dirty water again and again, each time threading their way between the cats outside the door. Last of all, they scrubbed the floor with a brush.

"Well, that looks better," Lora said, surveying the clean kitchen.

"It surely does, but there's more cleaning to do," Mary said.

"Each day we can do a little more. There are beds to make and dinner to fix."

"We can make beds while the floor dries," Mary suggested.

In the bunkhouse they encountered a problem.

"Ouch!" Mary exclaimed. "Lora, the bedbugs are terrible. I don't see how any man can sleep in those beds." Mary pulled her skirt away from her leg to find red bites.

"Hum-m-m," Lora mused. "We'll have to work on them through the week."

The cookshack where Lora and Mary "gained experiences which were not available elsewhere."

"What do you do about bedbugs?"

"Kill them. I think we'll have a busy week," Lora said. "We had better start dinner. Wonder how many potatoes it takes to feed those men?"

"Probably a bushel," Mary exaggerated. "Those men work hard."

"We'd better get going. We'll peel potatoes together and then you can fry some of that cured meat."

"Sure, Lora." Mary reached for a knife and a big pan. "Loggers eat a-plenty. I hope we have enough."

The men sighed with contentment after another good meal. One wiped his whiskers while the corners of his blue eyes crinkled.

"You're good cooks! Just like Mom."

"Thank you," the women replied. "West Virginia women are very good cooks."

After the dinner dishes had been washed and put away, Lora and Mary stirred up a batch of cookies—several eggs, a hunk of lard, scoops of sugar, and other ingredients.

"How much flour, Lora?" Mary held a handful of flour above the huge bowl.

"Another one, I think." Lora paused from stirring the mass of dough. "The dough is getting closer to what it should be."

"How long will it take to bake all these cookies?" Mary asked.

"We'll find out," Lora said. "I hope we can go home before too late this evening."

The two spooned cookie dough onto cookie sheets and baked them in the oven. Pan after pan of cookies cooled on the table under a cloth. The clock ticked on and suppertime neared.

"Guess I should get the macaroni cooking," Lora mentioned after a brief spell of propping up her feet.

She set a large kettle filled with water on the stove and allowed it to boil. Then she measured large amounts of macaroni into the boiling water along with a scant handful of salt.

The cook and cookie on duty at the sawmill.

By evening a pile of cookies awaited the sweaty men's return to the cookshack. The men gobbled macaroni and cheese, beans, and cookies with appreciation for the good cooks on the job. After supper and cleanup, the women walked home, ready to drop into bed.

Every morning for a week, Lora and Mary walked up to the camp. Faithfully they cooked, scrubbed, and tried to exterminate bedbugs. At the end of the week the men wished the women could stay on, but the "cookie" had returned. Lora and Mary took their pay and headed toward the mission home where they preferred to be, and where they could focus on a different type of nourishment.

"Now that was an interesting, educational experience," Mary said as the mission house came into view.

"It most certainly was," Lora agreed.

"I think we should have a diploma for all that."

Lora looked at Mary with surprise. "A diploma?"

"Sure. We worked hard for that degree as camp cooks and managers."

Lora laughed. "We certainly know how to do it now."[2]

---

2 Mary Huber's West Virginia scrapbook. "Our work at the mill was both interesting as well as educational: making biscuits, spilling buttermilk, killing and catching bedbugs, and last but not least the spitting of snuff on our clean scrubbed floor all went together to help make the week what it was. When Saturday noon drew near, we decided we were ready to graduate with a diploma." Lora Heatwole says in her own West Virginia scrapbook: "One week at the sawmill was plenty for me. Although the cook and cookie gained experiences which were not available elsewhere. The cook did the cooking and the cookie carried water, scrubbed, made beds, swept, and attempted a battle with the bedbugs, but was defeated."

Chapter Thirty-One

Fire!

"**T**here's been another fire up thar on th' mountain." Neighbor Abe wrung his hands and wiped sweat from his brow when he brought the news to the mission workers on Roaring Creek.

"Oh, no! What happened?" James asked as Vada and Lora crowded to the screen door.

"Ike's barn burnt down. His boy got mad at him and set the barn on fire, then sat back and watched it burn."

"No!" Lora stood horrified as Abe went on.

"Yep."

Lora asked, "Which boy?" Mentally she ran down the list of Ike's boys. Not one of them could be bad enough to burn down a barn—or could they?

The mission workers held their breath, waiting for the answer.

Abe licked his lips and answered, "Buddy."

Lora gasped. "Not Buddy!"

"Yes, Buddy. When the police came to check it out, Buddy came up to the officer and said, 'You lookin' fer who did that there fire?' And the officer said, 'Yes. Do you know who did it?' Buddy said, 'It was me.' "

Lora stared dumbfounded as Abe told more.

"The police asked Buddy, 'You sure you did it?' He said, 'Yep.' The police asked, 'What did you do?'

" 'Went to the house.'

" 'Then what?'

" 'Got a match.'

" 'Then what?'

" 'Went to the barn.'

" 'Then what?'

" 'Got some straw.'

" 'Then what?'

" 'Struck a match.'

" 'Then what?'

" 'Started fire.'

" 'Then what?'

" 'Sat back and watched.' "

Mouths gaped open and eyebrows lifted in wonder at the brazen actions of a silly boy.

Abe continued. "The police said, 'I'll have to put you in jail.' Buddy just laughed and said, 'It'll be a good place to be.' "

Lora's brow knit with perplexity. "Why would Buddy say a thing like that?"

"Buddy wanted to get into jail with his friend Harry who's in jail for starting another fire."

Lora's heart sank. Not another person in jail. Hadn't those boys learned any moral values in church services and Bible school classes? Workers had labored earnestly to reach souls and point them to Biblical principles. Was it all for no purpose?

Lora shook her head as tears gathered in her eyes. "Poor Buddy. We can pray for him and his friend in jail," she whispered.

"I guess two mothers' hearts are broken." Vada wiped her eyes with the corner of her apron.

Abe took out his hanky and blew his nose. "Ike's mad, and you can't blame him."

James didn't say anything for a while. Then he added, "We must pray for those boys and their families. God can speak to their hearts."

The new blackened area on the mountains reminded the community of the results of fire and anger out of control. Saddened by the report, Christians prayed for those in jail and for their families. Slowly the blackened slopes greened again, and the community built a new barn over the ashes of the old one.

Buddy's wish to join his friend in jail, however, had not turned out as planned. The police took Buddy to another jail in another town. Poor Buddy had some hard lessons ahead.[1]

Fires broke out repeatedly, and the Department of Forestry directed the control efforts. Young men and boys flocked to the fire to participate.

Someone voiced a concern. "I wonder if someone is setting those fires."

The opposing opinion was doubtful. "Now why would anyone want to start fires?"

---

1 A true account with names changed.

"Well, times are hard, and people need money. If there's a fire, the men get paid to fight it."

"Well, maybe so."

But a firm conclusion could not be made. All the while, Buddy and Harry stayed behind bars. But Lora and the mission workers could not imagine how God would work to bring about change in another sinner's life.

Fires of a different sort burned in people's souls as the Gospel was taught in the churches and schools. The long years of praying for Noah's conversion paid off. Perhaps Noah's nearly-fatal accident years ago and the gift of a prosthesis from Christian brethren, coupled with Bible exposure and earnest concern for his soul, had budged the unresponsive heart.

Sis Polly beamed as she shook Lora's hand before every service. Lora understood the woman's deep joy. She had seen Noah struggle to his feet, head bowed and tears rolling down his cheeks. Sis Polly had gasped and squeezed her handkerchief as she saw her repentant husband standing there. Then she smiled through her tears and helped the congregation sing:

"And that thou bidst me come to thee,
  O Lamb of God, I come, I come."[2]

At last, Noah had received salvation, and his sins were cleansed by the blood of Jesus Christ. He would encounter spiritual struggles like all Christians, but he had made a start.

---

2 "Just As I Am, Without One Plea," *Church and Sunday School Hymnal,* No. 213.

Others had also felt the flame of conviction as the minister spoke forthrightly of Christ, who forgave those who falsely accused Him, spit on Him, and abused Him. He took those insults without retaliation. He treated His tormentors as if they had never done Him wrong. The Christians could forgive those who had wronged them because the power of Christ within enabled them to do likewise.

Ruby squirmed with discomfort. She knew she had sin within her heart. For years she had refused to speak to her sister. Her heart had become as hard as iron with bitter hatred for her sister. The words of Scripture cut like a knife in her heart. "For if ye forgive men their trespasses, your heavenly Father will also forgive you: but if ye forgive not men their trespasses, neither will your Father forgive your trespasses."[3]

"Come to the Saviour," the minister encouraged the audience. "Christ will make a difference in your life. Like Christ forgave, forgive those who have wronged you. When you forgive others, then God will forgive your sins."

Tears spilled down Ruby's cheeks. Meekly she stood to acknowledge her need. After the service, Lora prayed privately with Ruby.

"Oh, Lorie, I feel so clean and peaceful," Ruby said. "Now I must go home and speak to my sister. I can't wait to make things right with her."

"That is the power of Christ in your life," Lora rejoiced. "May the Lord go with you and help you clear all the trouble."

The community watched with amazement as the broken relationship mended.

---

3 Matthew 6:14, 15.

"Did you know that Ruby and Lilly are talking to each other? Haven't uttered a word to each other fer years. Now look at 'em. It's sumthin', I tell you. Never seen anything like it in all my life."[4]

While Ruby and her family encountered a flood of Heaven in their home, believers praised God for the power of Jesus' blood. But some still held back, even though conviction burned in their souls. Over and over they heard, "Ye must be born again."[5] But what did it mean to be born again? How would it change your life? They were sinners, no question about that.

Other verses left little doubt about the meaning. "He that believeth on the Son hath everlasting life: and he that believeth not the Son shall not see life; but the wrath of God abideth on him."[6] To miss Heaven would be horrible, but to give up worldly pleasures was too much. Someday, they thought, they would make that decision, but not now.

Gracie watched friends and family choose to accept Jesus as Saviour. She repeatedly heard the Scripture, "That if thou shalt confess with thy mouth the Lord Jesus, and shalt believe in thine heart that God hath raised him from the dead, thou shalt be saved."[7]

The girl mused on the invitation. *Just maybe I, too, should make that decision—the next time.* But the meetings passed, and the convicting words of the sermons and lessons seemed to dissipate into thin air. Somehow it didn't seem so urgent to make a decision just now. *Someday I will,* she thought, *for it would never do to miss Heaven.*

---

4 A true account with names changed.
5 John 3:7
6 John 3:36
7 Romans 10:9

For all, time was running short. Sinners could not enter Heaven. Oh, that every soul would be prepared and ready for eternity when they drew their last breath!

Chapter Thirty-Two

Choices

1935

Lora said good-bye to Mary Huber, who returned home before the summer ended. To replace Mary, another young woman came from Harrisonburg, Virginia, having just graduated from nurses' training.[1] The lean, dark-haired woman filled the empty drawers in the upstairs bedroom with her clothing.

"I won't need a uniform here," Ida Eshleman said as she closed the last drawer.

"No uniform and very little silver and gold, either," Lora remarked. "I know you gave up a good-paying job, but the rewards for working here are much richer than money."

"I know." Ida snapped the suitcase shut and shoved it under the bed. "My friends at school could not believe I would give up a good paycheck to come here to work. But I told the Lord I didn't want money. I wanted to go where He

---

1 *Gospel Herald,* August 29, 1935, p. 468, Roaring, WV, report written August 20, 1935 by Lora Heatwole.

wanted me to go and here I am, Lora. [2] You'll have to put up with me, somehow."

Lora thumbed through her stack of Bible lessons and gave Ida a sideways glance. "I think you will be a fine roommate, but I hope you know that opportunities are often disguised as hard work."

"I'm young and energetic, you know, even if I'm 'green.' You tell me what to do, and I'll do it." Ida lifted her chin and gave a determined nod. "They say you can tell a person's character by what he turns up when offered a job—his nose or his sleeves."

Lora chuckled. "I think you'll do, young lady."

Fresh out of nursing school, Ida Eshleman came to help with medical needs and teaching classes.

Ida raised her eyebrows and grinned at Lora. "I don't think you know what you are in for."

"I suppose you don't know either," Lora teased, "but I don't believe it will be your nose that gets turned up." Then she turned serious. "The Lord has been doing wonderful things in people's hearts. A good number have come to the Lord lately."

"The Lord's work is thrilling, Lora. Even at home, being

---

2 From Ida Eshleman interviews.

in God's work just lifts you. There's nothing compared to it."

Lora grinned at her comrade. "God brings us blessings galore, doesn't He?"

Ida nodded and picked up her Bible. "I can't wait to get started. Sowing the Seed is absolutely delightful!"

Each evening, Lora and Ida and the Shanks attended Bible school after their busy day of work. And every evening, Jack galloped up the hillside to the school and scooted off his horse. He tied the horse to a tree and milled around among the people. Mothers and dads ushered in troops of children while grannies hobbled into the building with anticipation. The evening air grew cool as the congregation sang heartily.

> *"The B-I-B-L-E,*
> *Yes, that's the book for me.*
> *I stand alone on the Word of God,*
> *The B-I-B-L-E."*

The children divided into classes and James opened his Bible to teach the adults.

One afternoon after Bible school ended, Lora lined up the jars of pickles and beans on the shelf in the basement while Ida added more from her armload.

"This place is busy," Ida said.

"Sure is," Lora said. "I'm glad Bible school and revivals were held earlier. With canning in season now we can concentrate on that."

One day James asked Lora, "It's time to report the summer activities. Would you mind to write the *Gospel Herald* report?"

"Sure," Lora replied. "I'm ready to sit down and rest a while."

She took a sheet of paper and a pen and went to her room.

> Dear Herald readers,
> "God is love, I see it in the world about me, God is love, I see it in the world above me: God is love, all nature doth agree, but the greatest proof of His love to me is Calvary."[3]

She reported on the various Bible schools and individuals who participated in teaching.

> These Bible schools were all conducted after night so as to accommodate the most people. It was for every one both old and young. The interest was good . . .

She must write about the huckleberries currently in season, and the good price people were getting for them. She wrote the lines and sat back to think how to end the report. Ah, yes, she must entice the readers out there to want to come to this lovely place. She set the point of the pen on the paper and scrawled:

> If you enjoy being in the heart of nature, a hard climb, pure fresh air, raw sunshine, stones, rocks, brush, pine trees, and a grand scenery, come to this wonderful place, for God's handiwork is facing you on every side.
> Aug. 20, 1935 Lora Heatwole[4]

---

3   Lora began her report by quoting this paragraph, but its source is unknown.
4   Ibid.

*In spite of hard labor and disappointment at times, the scenery
provided relaxation and serenity for the mission workers.*

A young man stood at the door of the mission and spoke
to James. Lora paused from setting the table as she recognized the familiar voice of the boy who had stumbled into
class some years ago. Jerry, son of the moonshiner, had
almost reached manhood.

James gestured for the visitor to enter. "Won't you have
supper with us?"

"Nope. I can't stay."

Lora smiled as she recalled the bashful boy who had
grown accustomed to regularly attending church. "Hello,
Jerry."

Jerry smiled back, but rushed on to state his reason for
coming. "Jest came to tell you I'm leavin' fer Pennsylvania."

"You are?"

"I got a job." Jerry described his work and where he was
going.

Lora lingered at the door. Over the years she had seen
this student grow in spiritual interests. "We will miss you
at church," she said sincerely.

"I'll miss it too," Jerry said, shyly stuffing his hands in his pockets.

This youth, barely into manhood, was leaving the mountains for another life in a different community. Would he find spiritual nurture there, or would he be lured into ungodly attractions in societies beyond the mountains?

"Well, I gotta go."

James reached out and shook his hand. "Keep reading the Word. It will guide your life."

The young man nodded, a smile on his lips. "There's a church there I want to attend."

"We will pray for you," Lora said. "We can't forget you even if you are miles away."

Jerry grinned. "I won't ferget you, neither. Well, goodbye."

He waved as the car puttered down the hollow. Lora stared at the lingering dust. What would become of that young man? With a silent prayer, Lora returned to the kitchen and soberly dished up the meal.

Lora poured the dishwater out the back door and hurried inside to answer the phone.

"Hello. Yes, this is Lora." She recognized the voice of Rosie, the young bride.

Rosie burst into sobs as she brokenly gave the news. "Lora—somethin' terrible's happened. I don't—know how—I can stand this."

"What is it, Rosie?"

"It's Jack."

Lora recollected. Jack often rode horse to church and longed for female friendship. "What about him?"

Rosie momentarily gained some control over her emotions. "He wanted a girl s'bad, but she turned him down."

Lora listened. What could be so awful to affect Rosie this way? Rosie had lived with Jack's family before her marriage. Jack was like one of her family.

Brokenly, the girl found words. "He told his mother—good-bye. He said—he said—he's gonna die."

"Oh, no!" Lora exclaimed. "He couldn't have been serious!"

Rosie sniffled and continued, "He most definitely was serious! Oh, Lorie—I ran after him—I tried to stop him." Rosie sobbed again. Then she went on, "But I couldn't—catch him."

Lora waited, breathless for the outcome. "What happened?"

"Jack jumped into the river—and drowned!" Rosie wailed.[5]

"Oh, no! I'm so sorry." Lora searched for words of comfort. "This saddens our hearts too."

Gently, words of Scripture came to Lora. "Rosie, Jesus promised to be with us no matter what we face. He said, 'Lo, I am with you alway,'[6] that means even for difficult times like this. May you find the hand of Jesus to help you."

The girl sniffled. "I know He will."

Lora continued, "His presence helps us in troubled times. The Bible says, 'My flesh and my heart faileth: but God is the strength of my heart.'"[7]

---

5 This is a true incident with names changed.
6 Matthew 28:20
7 Psalm 73:26

"Yes," Rosie whispered, "He will help me."

"Please tell the family we are praying for all of you," Lora consoled.

Rosie continued tearfully, "The funeral will be tomorrow."

"I will let the Shanks know."

Lora hung up the phone and stared at the wall.

"Whatever happened?" Vada asked.

Softly, Lora broke the news. The grim reality brought a sober mood to the mission house and the community. Another soul had entered eternity. Would the next death be one of joyful homecoming? Or would it be otherwise?

Lora shuddered. There were still souls to tell of the blessed hope—if only they would accept it.

The knock at the mission door sounded urgent. Vada opened the screen door. Lora recognized Tillie's husband.

"Hello, Bill."

Bill didn't have time for greetings. "Have ya seen Tillie?"

"No, haven't seen her for a few days."

"Where can she be? She's been missin' all night."

"Maybe she went to her mother's," Lora suggested.

"Nope. She's not there. She's gone somewhere. The younguns are at her mother's."

"Could she have gone visiting up the mountain?" Vada asked.

Bill shook his head, and the ladies silently contemplated where Tillie might be.

"She hasn't been stopping to visit us like she used to," Lora ventured.

"I know," Bill said. "She hasn't been herself the last while."

"We'll pray," Vada said. "Surely God knows her whereabouts."

Sadly, Bill left while the women paused to pray. Uneasiness wrestled in Lora's heart. For some reason Tillie had become dissatisfied with her life and responsibilities. Lora's heart ached as she prayed earnestly.

Eventually, the shocking news spread through the community that Tillie had forsaken her husband and found another man. Oh, Tillie! Would she not come home and love her husband and children?

"Poor Bill and the children," Vada lamented.

"People are usually loyal to their marriages around here," Lora explained to James and Vada.

Silently, the community mourned for the broken home, and Christians prayed for Tillie's repentance. The neglected husband and children waited for the return of their loved one, but Tillie refused to return.

Lora knelt by her bed in prayer. Her heart felt like lead. This young mother was her friend. Perhaps she should have encouraged Tillie more or helped her with her work. Sometimes the spiritual battles seemed impossible for some, but God was still the victor. She must be thankful for the faithful ones who still clung to the Lord.

The young preacher hung his hat on the hook and drooped into a chair.

"Are you all right?" Vada asked her husband.

"Just weary. That's all. Abe and I got the hay in. A good night of sleep is all I need before I head back to the lumber camp."

The young couple pressed on in the duties at hand with a faith that carried them through the hardships. But weeks later, it became evident that the relentless responsibilities and burden of souls had taken their toll on James. Even though the countryside held lovely places of quiet solitude, there was no time to indulge in such luxury on the mission field. Perhaps a rest at home would be good for the minister.

"We hope to return soon," Vada said.

"We will miss you and pray for you," Ida said.

Lora nodded and said, "I'm glad Ida is here to keep me company."

Surely, it wouldn't be long until the Shanks returned.[8]

---

8 James Shank told the author that he needed to return home for a while. Ida Eshleman Horst tells in *Ida's Path From Buggy to Jet Ski,* page 35, that the Shanks returned home.

Chapter Thirty-Three

Mountain Strangers

1935

O
ne day, a persistent noise from the neighbors aroused Ida's curiosity. *Thunk!* What was that? *Thunk!* Lora agreed to investigate with her new chum. Before they had gone far, a lone horse galloped full-speed toward them. Lora and Ida veered off the road lest the horse trample them.

Lora mused, "That horse seemed frightened."

Thunk! The women ventured toward the noise at the neighbor's barn.

"Well, I never saw such a thing in my whole life!" Ida stood with hands on her hips, flabbergasted at the sight.

"Well, now you have seen how mountain farmers harvest corn." Lora chuckled. "That's what I thought you would find."

The women watched as corn shocks swept down the steep hillside on a cable and landed against the side of the barn.

"Smart men, I'd say," Ida ventured.

"Exactly. They find ways without a lot of cost. Besides, hauling crops to the barn on tractors and wagons could be hazardous."

A spry young man in overalls and straw hat raced toward them. "Hey, Lorie! Seen any horse 'round here?"

"Yes, we just met one."

"It's our horse. Got skeered t'death and run off." The fellow lifted his hat and scratched his sweaty hair. "Dad thought them shocks bangin' on the barn wouldn't skeer that horse, but he's dead wrong."

"Looked terrified to me," Ida quipped. "Poor ol' horse."

"I'll catch him. He'll quit running sometime. See ya later."

While the two strolled back to the mission house, Lora brought up a different subject.

"We'd better take Sunday school supplies over to Jason Vance's today so they have them for Sunday. We should leave this afternoon."

"Are we going to take the car?" Ida motioned toward the hunk of metal that the mission board had provided for transportation since the James Shank family had not returned.

"I don't trust it to get us there and back," Lora stated. "That car has seen its best days."

Ida nodded consent. "So how do we get to Jason's?"

"We walk."

"How far is it?" Ida asked.

"Three miles."

"Couldn't Denny run us in his car? He offered to take us wherever we need to go."

"I know, but I think we can walk. Let's pack our night-gowns and Bibles and stay for the night. Mattie always welcomes friends. She won't mind."

Lora filled two tote bags with supplies. Then they set out for the mountain. Leaving the road, Lora used her stick to scramble up the steep terrain.

"Where's a path?" Ida asked.

"Isn't any."

"Are you sure you know the way?" Ida teased.

"Yes, I know that the Vances live just across this mountain. I'd like to arrive before dark because there are bears on this mountain." Lora hid a mischievous grin from Ida.

"Bears?" Ida looked around suddenly.

"Yes. Brother Benner encountered wild beasts when he traveled in the mountains." Lora paused to check on her young traveler. "The Lord always took care of him."

Ida nodded as Lora shoved her stick against the sharp incline and pushed higher. She followed Lora's experienced steps.

"And watch out for snakes," Lora warned. "They can be anywhere in these mountains."

Ida stiffened, her glance darting in all directions. "You let me know if any are around. I surely would not enjoy meeting one."

"No need to be afraid," Lora assured her. "It's only sensible to respect wildlife. Usually they won't bother us if we don't aggravate them."

Ida shuddered and stayed as close behind Lora as she could. For some time they ascended, stopping now and then to catch a breath. Birds hopped through the undergrowth in search of grubs and worms in the damp soil. The swish of a bushy tail and the scolding of a squirrel overhead broke the concentrated climb for a moment, and they paused to enjoy the wildlife.

Gray shadows crept beneath the forest canopy as the afternoon wore on. Both women panted with fatigue as the weight of books cut into their shoulders. At last they reached the crest.

"Whew!" Ida exclaimed as she allowed her bag to slide to the ground while she sat on a fallen log to rest. "I'm so tired."

Lora took a seat by Ida. "Now, take a look out across the valley." Lora gestured toward the open view.

Ida gasped. "It's beautiful. So beautiful."

The mountainside swept downward with a hint of fall colors on the tops of trees. In the gathering dusk, smoke rose from houses scattered among the trees and cleared spaces.

Lora scanned the valley for the right house. "There it is." She pointed to a house among the forest trees below. "That's where Jason and Mattie Vance live. We'll keep our eye on the house or we may lose the way."

"Sure," Ida agreed. "It's getting dark. We'd better go."

Lora agreed. "When we get there, Mattie will have us a good supper."

"I hope so," Ida said, "because I'm hungry, and I hope there are no starving bears on this mountain."

Down the sharp decline they plunged, with eyes ever on their destination. Even as dusk gathered about them, the light in the windows shone brighter as they neared the home. Like a starving, sin-sick soul keeps his eye on Jesus, the women made their way toward warmth, comfort, and well-being.

Darkness had deepened by the time they had crossed the field. Shoulders pled for relief, and muscles groaned for rest.

At last they stood before the two-story house and knocked.

The door swung open, and the silhouette of a woman loomed in the lighted doorway.

"Howdy, Lorie! Come go in!" Mattie Vance exclaimed, stepping back for them to enter. "Why, if I'd a know'd you'd be comin' I'd a cooked you a cake."

Ida looked at Lora with perplexity while Lora beamed back an unspoken comment that said, "It's customary mountain speech."

"No need to make us cake." Lora grinned, stepping through the door. "Most anything else will do."

Lora introduced Ida and said, "We brought you Sunday school materials." She unloaded the books and plopped into a chair near Ida.

"Thanks," Jason said, paging through the new pupil's book. "This will make teaching easy."

"I know you're weary," said Mattie. "Let me cook you some supper. What would you like? I have chicken, beef, pork, rabbit, squirrel, deer, and bear."

"Bear meat?" Ida questioned with upraised eyebrows.

"Yeah." Mattie grinned. "Have you ever eaten bear?"

"No," replied Ida.

"Would you like to try it?"

"Yes, if Lora wants to."

"Sure," said Lora good-naturedly. "It will be good if Mattie is the cook."

Mattie asked, "Bear then?"

The girls looked at each other and nodded in agreement. They offered to help, but Mattie refused.

"Nope. You sit yourselves down and rest while I get you somethin'."

Later, surrounded by the warmth of Christian friends, Lora and Ida ate Mattie's fluffy biscuits, potatoes, beans, and bear meat.

Ida spooned a bite of bear meat into her mouth. "Um-m," she said, closing her eyes in enjoyment.

"Is it good?" the children asked, watching by the table.

"Delicious!" Ida said. Lora nodded in agreement.

The next morning Ida moaned as she sat up in bed.

"My aching legs and back!"

"Climbing pains," Lora teased her friend in the dim light of day.

"Don't you ache too?"

"No, but I used to years ago. You will toughen up eventually."

"It's raining, Lora. How are we to get home?"

Lora flung her calloused feet over the edge of the bed. "Maybe the rain will let up after breakfast."

Ida stood up and stretched. "I haven't slept this good in weeks. Must have something to do with fresh air." Ida grimaced.

"And mountain climbing," Lora added with a teasing grin.

The smell of bacon and coffee drifted upstairs as the girls combed and dressed.

After a good breakfast, Lora and Ida washed dishes and kept an eye on the weather. By mid morning, the rain still had not subsided.

Lora considered the situation. "We'll have to go home in the rain, Ida. We have to be back to teach Sunday school in the morning at Roaring."

Mattie offered, "I'll get you something to keep you dry."

Draping a large coat over Lora's shoulders and one over

Ida's small frame, Mattie stood back and surveyed them with satisfaction. The large coats engulfed the women and hung below their knees. The two women looked at each other and chuckled.

"And put this over your heads." Mattie gave them colored flannel pieces.

Ida laughed and spun around, flaunting her apparel.

Lora grinned at Ida's girlishness. "This should help. Well, pal, shall we start on our way?"

"Might as well," Ida replied with a teasing note. "I don't want to meet up with hungry bears in the dark."

Lora reached for her tote bag and slipped it under her coat. "Thank you, Mattie, for all your kindness."

Ida echoed the sentiment. "Thanks for putting up with us and putting us up," she joked good-naturedly. "Everything was good."

Chuckling, Mattie saw them to the door. "Come anytime. Anytime at all."

Over the field they trudged, letting the flannel soak up the cold rain that fell. In the woods, the canopy of trees protected them as they climbed the mountain and started the sharp descent. The way became easier. Still, they must dodge rocks and use careful footing lest they tumble. Before they knew it, they had reached the bottom and strolled down the road past houses. By now the damp coats hung to their ankles and the wet flannel clung to their heads as they trooped on toward the mission house.

"I wonder what we look like?" Ida giggled.

"Your friends would never recognize you." Lora laughed. "I'm glad we're about home. Dry clothes and a good dinner will be welcome."

"I'm hungry, and my feet are killing me."

"It's no wonder," said Lora. "We've walked six miles since yesterday."

"Six miles?" Ida questioned. "I'll have to take a look at this shoe. I think I have a loose sole."

Lora pushed open the door and hung up her wet clothes to dry. Then she pulled off her shoes and inspected the ragged places. "These shoes have to go for repair again, Ida. We'll have to box up our shoes and send them with the minister who comes to preach."

Ida stooped down and examined her sore feet. "Does it ever feel good to stop walking!" she said.

While they dried themselves and prepared lunch, the telephone jingled several times but the ring was not for them.

"I wonder what's so important that everybody's talking on the line," Ida said as she wrapped her hair in a towel. "I'm going to listen and see what they are saying."

While Lora stirred some soup on the stove, Ida listened on the phone. Suddenly, Ida clamped a hand over her mouth and doubled over with silent laughter.

Lora mouthed to Ida. "What's going on?"

Ida slipped the phone back into place and guffawed. "It's the neighbors calling to see who those strange people were who came through the hollow a while ago."

"They didn't recognize us?" Lora questioned with amusement.

The phone rang again.

"Shh," said Ida. "I'm going to listen to what they're saying."

Lora slipped silently over to Ida's side and pressed her

ear close to Ida's. She heard the neighbor's voice questioning another.

"Do you know who they were?"

"No."

"They looked awful! Nobody seems to know."

"Must be some strangers coming through here."

Lora and Ida held back the laughter until the phone had been hung up. Then they held their sides, unable to stop their laughter.

"They didn't even recognize us." Ida laughed.

"Why should they, as drenched as we were and with Mattie's coats and flannels?"

Ida wiped away her tears and looked straight at Lora. "I always have believed that 'all work and no play makes Jill a dull girl.' A good laugh after a six-mile journey is good for us."

"I agree." Lora smiled as she dipped soup into bowls. "How about some dinner, young Jill? I'm hungry."

They laughed again and bowed their heads to thank the Lord for dinner and a safe trip home.[1]

---

1 Ida recounted this story to the author and also tells about it in *Ida's Path From Buggy to Jet Ski.*

Chapter Thirty-Three

Apple Trees

1935

T he gnarled limbs arched with the weight of ripened apples.

"Looks like work ahead," Lora said as she set the ladder against the tree. Ida climbed up and began to pick apples while Lora gathered the ones on the ground and stretched for those she could reach on the stooped branches.

Rarely had she stayed this late in the year, but due to the Shanks' temporary departure, the two women remained to continue the harvesting and Sunday school work.

"Maybe James and Vada will be back in time to enjoy some fresh apple pies or cider," Ida said as she climbed down the ladder with a loaded basket.

"I hope so," Lora agreed. "Sometimes a minister needs a change from all the responsibility."

"Folks keep asking when they will return," Ida said as she grabbed another bucket and moved the ladder.

Later that day, processed applesauce cooled in the cellar, but it was during the night that apples from a different tree brought troubles to the weary workers. *Plop! Ploppity-plop!*

Lora jerked awake. In the darkness she heard apples dropping and rolling down the roof outside the window. *Plop! Plop!*

Ida rolled over and grumbled. "I can't sleep with all those apples falling on the roof, Lora."

"Can't either," Lora mumbled. "Haven't had a good night of sleep for a long time because of those apples."

"That apple tree is disgusting!" Ida's impatience showed. "I'll tell you what. I'm going to do something about that tree."

"What can you do?" Lora asked in the darkness.

"I'll think of something."

After a restless night, Ida ventured outside into the crisp morning. She stood with her hands on her hips, watching the knobby fruit fall. Lora came outdoors to see what Ida was up to. She found Ida dragging a crosscut saw from the shop.

Ida's eyes crinkled as she smiled. "Come on, Lora, let's cut down this apple tree."

Lora looked at her. "Are you serious?"

"Indeed I am. Lora, you said the fruit is no good, and it certainly is a nuisance dropping apples at all hours of the night."

"Well," Lora stalled for time, "we can't do that. This tree is mission property."

"The apples cannot be canned," Ida persisted.

"That's right," Lora agreed.

"Can't sleep, neither," said Ida, setting the saw to the base of the trunk. "Well, are you going to help me or not?"

Lora thought about the sleepless nights and the no-good fruit that had to be picked up. She wished James were here to give advice. But that tree had been so bothersome lately. "Yes, I'll help."

Ida suggested, "Let's do it close to the ground so you can't tell the tree was there. Maybe James and Vada will never notice it's gone." She dropped to her knees and shoved the saw toward Lora.

Lora bent over and tried to shove the saw. That didn't work, so she sat down. Back and forth they sawed, giggling like little girls at their preposterous attempt.

"Wait," Lora stopped sawing and looked at Ida with perplexity. "What will happen if this tree falls on the roof and breaks down the porch?"

Ida shrugged. "When we get it almost cut through, we will push it where we want it to go."

Lora eyed the younger with doubt, but the suggestion sounded reasonable. They returned to the job.

"Now!" said Ida, jumping up and bracing against the tree. "You help me push as hard as you can so the tree falls between that tree and the shed." She pointed.

The two pushed with all their strength, and the trunk began to move.

"Push, Lora. Now jump out of the way!"

Lora leaped backward and watched the tree crash to the ground exactly where they had targeted. Right or wrong, the deed had been done. The two worked up a sweat cutting up branches and stacking them in the woodshed.

"I'm getting tired," Lora huffed after some hours.

"Me too," said Ida, "and we still have that big trunk to cut up."

Ida brightened with another idea. She looked at the worn car that sat unused, even though it was their only transportation. Somehow, the two women never cared to use that car. They would sooner walk any day than use an unreliable car on rough, winding roads.

Ida's eyes sparkled. "I'm told there is a way to rig up a belt on the wheel of a car to run a saw," she said.

Lora caught sight of Denny passing by. "Hey!" she called, "can you give us a hand?"

Denny wandered into the yard, his eyebrows raised with curiosity. "What in th' world are you two doin'?"

"Just cutting down the apple tree." Lora gestured toward the freshly stacked wood.

Denny shook his head. "Now if you two don't beat all." His eyes twinkled with amusement. "That looks like a right good size trunk, though. I'll help you cut it up."

The women agreed, and the work moved along swiftly once Denny helped rig a makeshift power saw using the wheel of the car jacked off the ground.

Under the song of a saw, slabs of tree trunk became wood for the stove. By evening, the woodshed stood stuffed full and the makeshift saw had been disconnected and put away. Every twig had been scoured from the yard and burned. With an ax, they chopped out the stump and filled the hole with sod.

Ida followed Lora into the house and plopped down to rest. "I wonder how long it will take the mission folks to notice that the old apple tree is gone?"

"I don't know," Lora said, "but I'm tired enough to sleep tonight even if the apples were dropping."

A few weeks later, James and Vada returned to take

more of their things back home.

"It looks so different," James said, trying to figure out what had changed.

"We've dug the potatoes and got a good many," Lora tried to distract his attention. "Would you like to take some home?"

"Sure." James smiled.

Not another word was said about the apple tree or the wood stored in the woodshed. But Lora and Ida slept soundly—something they had been able to do since the day they cut down the apple tree.[1]

---

1 Ida gave these true incidents to the author and also tells them in *Ida's Path From Buggy to Jet Ski*.

Chapter Thirty-Five

Nurse and Assistant

1935

Gardeners picked their pumpkin patches clean and prepared to make pies and spiced baked goods. Ever so gradually, the lavish fall colors dulled to curry, cinnamon, clove, paprika, and nutmeg.

One by one, leaves floated to the ground and crunched beneath the feet of hunters. Still, the Shanks had not returned. The cow had been sold to another farmer, so Lora and Ida connived new ways to meet their needs.

Ida stirred the grapenuts on the baking sheet in the oven. "I wonder what is keeping the Shanks? It seems like a gigantic hole left without the minister here. We all need him."

"I know," Lora answered, as she opened a can of store milk and added water to stretch the commodity as far as possible. "I'm glad a minister is coming Sunday. We'll have to prepare a meal for him and his family. We don't have plenty of cream and milk to do pudding like we used to."

"We have pumpkin and apples and spice in the cupboard," Ida commented as she removed the grapenuts from the oven. "This should last us for a little while, don't you think, Lora?"

"Yes, but I sure miss Jersey's good milk and soda cheese."

Just then a knock sounded at the door. Lora answered. There stood a neighbor with a gun across his shoulder and a bunch of squirrel carcasses. "Have some fresh squirrel for dinner. I've got a-plenty."

"Thank you." Lora took two skinned carcasses. "That should make a wonderful dinner."

"How will you fix it?" Ida asked as Lora closed the door and placed the meat in a bowl of water.

Lora sprinkled salt over the contents. "Well now, squirrel is mighty good fried golden brown. I'm thankful the Lord provided meat for dinner."

"If you're the cook, I just might even like squirrel," Ida said.

One Sunday morning while Ida and Lora taught Sunday school, the church door burst open and a nervous father searched the congregation.

"Where's the nurse?" His eyes were wide in his whiskered face.

Ida paused from her teaching. "I'm here. What's wrong?"

"You gotta come. My girl's hurt bad."

Ida handed her teacher's book to another adult and hurried after the man.

Outside the church the desperate man explained, "My girl fell and cut her lip and is bleedin' awful."

"I have to get my black bag," Ida said. "I'll run to the mission house quick and get it."

"Certainly," the man replied gratefully.

Ida returned and hurried up the slope behind the man.

The screams had subsided to whimpers by the time Ida arrived. She approached gently as the mother held a bloody cloth over the girl's lip. Gently Ida pulled away the rag and inspected the injury.

"That's a nasty cut," Ida said, opening her bag and cleansing the cut.

The girl squirmed and hid her face against her mother.

"The nurse will help you," the mother assured her child. "Be a good girl."

"I think I can butterfly the gash." Ida cut the tape with scissors and carefully placed it on the gaping wound. "There now, I really think that lip should be stitched," Ida advised. "The saliva will ooze into the sore and prevent proper healing. How far is it to a doctor?"

The father answered. "Thirty miles."

Gratefully, the parents took Ida's advice and found a driver to take them for medical assistance. Some hours later they returned to the mission house. Ida ran out to see what the doctor had done.

"Doctor didn't do nothin'." The mother grinned.

"Nothing?" Ida shrieked, staring at the swollen lip of the sleeping child.

"That's right," the daddy said with a grin, his blue eyes sparkling. "Doc said whoever taped that cut done a purty good job. Said nothin' more needed done."

Lora ventured up beside Ida and peered into the car to see the child.

"But I sent you to him to have it stitched," the young nurse sputtered with indignation. "It would heal much better."

Lora patted Ida on the back. "You must have done a good job to pass the inspection of a doctor."

Ida shook her head in disagreement. "I'll be up the trail to check on it over the next couple of days."

The parents nodded their appreciation and headed up the hollow. Lora and Ida watched until the vehicle disappeared. Then slowly they turned and walked to the mission house.

"I think it's good to have nurse expertise here," Lora said.

But Ida didn't seem to hear. "That doctor should have stitched that lip," she muttered.

For several days, Ida climbed the trails to dress the injury and watch for infection. To her amazement, the cut healed completely. Meanwhile, the community began to appreciate the presence of a nurse among them.

"Look, Ida," Lora opened the box the minister handed to her. "Our shoes have returned."

"Good!" Ida exclaimed. "I was hoping they would come before my last pair fell apart."

Lora handed Ida the shiny shoes. "See how nice they are? Lovett's is the best place to send them."

"Why's that?" Ida asked.

"They always come back with a free shoe shine. And look, here's a big bottle of shoe polish too. Lovett's will have my business."

Ida echoed, "Mine too."

The visiting minister had been smiling all the while. "You know the Home Mission Board covers the cost of shoe repairs?"

"They do?" Ida asked.

"I think the Lord has been good to us, don't you think?" Lora asked Ida, and the younger one nodded in agreement.

"I have a message from the shoe repairman." The minister's eyes twinkled.

"What would that be?" Lora asked.

"The repairman says to tell you, 'Lord needs a new pair of shoes'."

"What?" Lora stared at him perplexed.

"Well, the repairman couldn't quite read your name on the inside of your shoe. He thought it read 'Lord' rather than 'Lora'."

Lora chuckled, picked up her shoes and examined them. "Well, there are quite a few patches. Maybe I do need new shoes. I've gone through a few pairs in these mountains."

A hunter brought a wild turkey for the women to enjoy. The aroma of roast turkey drifted from the oven as the women finished the morning work. Just then the telephone broke the stillness of the morning.

"Hello?" Lora answered. "But we have a turkey in the oven." She paused. "Yes, well maybe we can come. See you after while." Lora hung up the phone.

Ida waited to hear what Lora had to say.

"That was an invitation from Sis Polly. She said for us to come for dinner."

"But we have dinner baking in the oven," Ida responded.

"I told her, but she insisted quite strongly that we come."

"We could use some fellowship," Ida added. "Well, why don't we go?"

Lora shoved the burning wood apart in the stove, went for her coat and scarf, and followed Ida out of the house. An hour later they had climbed to Noah and Sis Polly's house where a dog straddled the path and barked, his eyes watching them each step they took. Lora led the way toward the door.

"Wait." Ida scrambled up close to Lora in alarm. "I don't want you to get bit by the dog."

"He won't bite me. He goes for the last one." Lora grinned mischievously.

"Why, Lora Heatwole. So that's why you always go first?"

"Sure. Now you can try that trick when someone else is with you."

"I wouldn't be that mean," Ida retorted.

"Just teasing," Lora said with a grin.

But they need not have worried; Noah called the dog off. Sister Polly stood at the door, her brow etched with worry.

The woman pulled them inside the door. "I'm so glad you came." Her eyes searched theirs, pleading for help. "My girl's time is here."

Ida gasped and put her hand to her opened mouth. Lora stared at Sister Polly. They had known a girl in the household was expecting a baby. The time was now? Lora looked from Ida to Sister Polly to the children playing on the floor. What would they do now?

"Why didn't you tell me?" Ida questioned. "I didn't bring my supplies."

"I was afraid you wouldn't come," Sis Polly explained as she wrung her hands. "You've got to help," she urged, pulling Ida after her.

Ida stopped Sis Polly. "Wait. I'm a nurse, and I don't even

have a license to practice childbirth. It would be illegal for me to deliver a child."

"Please, Ida. You must help." Sister Polly looked wearied.

Lora looked at Ida and prayed silently for an answer.

Ida stared into space and muttered, "Yes, the doctor I worked for told me that if this should happen, try to get a doctor."

"What doctor would come forty miles out to these mountains?" Sister Polly seemed desperate. "Besides, she's going to have it soon. Please, Ida."

Ida considered. The doctor had also told her that if she could not get a trained professional, to just do the best she could. However, there was a midwife in the community with considerable experience.

Ida asked, "Have you contacted the midwife?"

"No. You are a nurse," Sister Polly insisted.

"You must get the midwife and I'll help her." Ida took Sister Polly's arm and squeezed it. "Listen, you must not let that midwife know I'm a nurse. You hear? Just act like I'm with Lora." She turned to Lora. "Lora, you pray hard."

Lora nodded solemnly as she eyed the 21-year-old nurse and silently prayed that God would lead and protect them all. Meanwhile, Noah went to call the midwife. A short while later, the gallop of a horse announced the midwife's arrival. The hours ticked past. Lora set the table and fed the family. Then came the cry of a newborn. Lora's heart fluttered. A tiny, new soul had come into the world in such an untimely way.

"Is everyone all right?" Lora searched Sister Polly's tearful eyes.

Sis Polly blinked back tears. "Yes. It's over. It's a little boy."

Lora sighed with relief. But one of the children whispered to the midwife and pointed toward Ida. "That one is a nurse."

Lora tried to still the words, but it was too late. The midwife spun on her heels and thrust the bundle into Ida's arms.

"Here, you know more than I do." The midwife snatched up her supplies and disappeared down the stairs.

Ida stared at the empty doorway, her mouth gaped open wide.

"Wait!" Ida tried to stop the midwife.

But the midwife could not be persuaded to stay. "I'm goin'. You know what to do."

"You might as well check the baby," Lora said, peeking at the tiny face in the blanket. "What a sweet little one." She squeezed the mother's hand and said a few comforting words.

Ida's professional skills kicked into gear. She checked the baby thoroughly. Then, wrapping the blanket snugly around the little one, she placed him into his mother's arms.

Some hours later, Lora and Ida ventured down the trails.

Ida lamented, "Oh, if I only would have had my black bag. I could hardly stand it, Lora. I wished for more sanitary conditions. I'm so afraid that baby will get an infection."

Lora reasoned, "The midwife has delivered many a baby on these mountains and they turn out healthy."

"I hope I never have another experience like that again!"

"I know," Lora sighed, her heart heavy with the situation. "We've prayed long and hard, but some things stubbornly continue."

"I'm going to keep praying," Ida said as they reached home. "I must remember that some have embraced Christian teaching."

When they arrived home, the smell of turkey still lingered in the kitchen.

"It seems so lonely without the minister and his family here," Ida said as they took off their coats and hung them up. "I hope James and Vada can return after the season."

"I hope so too," Lora agreed.

For ten days, Ida climbed the trail to check on the patients and teach the new mother how to care for the child. The tiny one grew robust, and to Ida's amazement, infection was kept at bay.

The sky spit snow and spread a white covering over the mountains. However, the minister and his wife did not return as the days crept toward Christmas.[1]

---

1 The nurse stories were told to the author by Ida. Some are written in her book *Ida's Path From Buggy to Jet Ski.*

Chapter Thirty-Six

Tracks in the Snow

1935

Snow fluttered down through the darkness onto the mission home snuggled in the narrow valley between two mountains, down on the barns, schoolhouses, and churches tucked in the hills and hollows. Unseen to the sleeping folks of the hill country, the flakes silently filled the crevices and banks along the mountainsides. By morning, every branch and twig displayed an outline of delicate white. Out across the blanket of snow, hidden fences hinted at the boundaries of gardens and pastureland.

Lora crept down the stairs, her sweater pulled tight around her. She stoked up the fires while Ida ventured to the window.

"What do you know, Lora? It snowed last night."

Lora peered across Ida's shoulder at the white world outside. For a while she studied the scene and mused on the handiwork of the Almighty. She searched for words to express her deep inspiration. "Even nature is glorifying the Lord in all this royal beauty. No man-decked Christmas tree is adorned any more richly than this. How I wish all people could glorify God more! We could each think less of self and earthly affairs and allow the meek and quiet spirit of a Christian life to shine pure and clean in our lives—just like this pristine picture before us." [1]

Ida touched Lora's arm. "What words of eloquence."

By now the fire crackled in the stove. Lora set the skillet on the hottest spot on the stove and cracked eggs into the frying pan. "You know, Ida, our time here is almost gone. I think we should make at least one more visit up the mountain. We should go today."

"Do you mean it?" Ida turned from the window and faced Lora.

"Why not?"

"Because it's cold and snowy."

Lora didn't look up from the frying eggs. "The snow isn't very deep, and you do have boots, don't you?"

"Yes."

"Well, whatever do you have them for?" The corners of Lora's lips threatened to curve upward.

"You are something else, Lora." Ida chuckled. "You don't let the weather stop you from anything."

After breakfast, the two tramped up the mountainside, leaving footprints along the way. They skirted massive boulders with dark crevices that surely sheltered wild beasts.

"You know that wolves followed Brother Benner one time long ago, don't you?" Lora asked. Slyly, Lora left out the reminder that most animals had hibernated for the winter, sleeping safe and sound in the dark hollows beneath the snow.

---

1   Lora had written words like this in a winter report for *Gospel Herald*.

"I've heard those stories, Lora. I don't think you need to recall them now. Besides, the Lord protected Brother Benner, you know."

"I know. I shouldn't tease you, should I?"

Still, Ida's eyes darted here and there, making sure no threatening creature followed. It would not do to be the dinner of any wild animal.[2]

Just ahead, a cottage sat on the hillside with smoke curling from the chimney. A short, plump woman opened the door and peered at them with unseeing eyes.

"Good morning, Elsie." Lora leaned forward and clasped the woman's hand. "It's Lora and Ida. We've come to visit you. May we come in?"

"Oh yes, yes, yes. Do come in." Elsie's cheeks glowed like red apples as she opened the door wider and beckoned for them to come inside. Then her voice turned to a singsong. "It is so-o-o special to have you tramp all the way up here to see me."

Lora stomped the snow from her boots and eased inside with Ida just behind her. "We haven't been to see you in a while, and we thought we'd better come because we are going home soon."

"Now, Lorie, I know you'll be back again. Others come and go, but you always come back. You belong here."

Lora's heart stirred with the words of friendship. "This is a wonderful place to live and enjoy God's creation. Such lovely scenes we saw on the way to your house."

"How I wish to see the snow again." Elsie held her hands together in a wistful way, her eyes staring vacantly.

---

2 In *Ida's Path From Buggy to Jet Ski*, Ida tells how Lora teased her about wild animals on the way up the mountain.

"I wish too you could." Lora sat down in a chair by the stove. "Can you remember what it looked like?"

"Almost. Yes, I remember. It turned cold, didn't it? Poor ol' Larkins is gonna freeze from the holes in his overalls."

Elsie spoke of her husband, who was likely in some out-building, waiting for the visit to end.

"Let me have a look at them," Lora offered.

From another worn pair, Lora cut a patch from the back of the leg where the material was not as worn. She placed the stronger piece beneath the tear. Then she turned under the ragged edges and stitched them into place. Elsie's teen-aged daughter watched Lora work, taking note of the steps to follow for future mending.

The stove burned warmly as Lora mended and talked of God's goodness and the promise of eternity in Heaven for those who accept Jesus in their hearts. In and out the needle flicked until the hole was repaired.

The daughter inspected Lora's work. "Now Papa will have a warmer pair of overalls this winter."

Elsie sighed. "Larkins would've froze the rest of the winter iff'n you hadn't come."

"I'm so glad to help," Lora replied as she placed the finished overalls in Elsie's arms.

After the visit, Lora suggested they go down the other side of the mountain. Then they would follow the road until they came to the store.

"We can stop and buy a few things we need," she explained. "We need milk."

Two large workhorses stood at the store when the weary walkers arrived.

"Hey," Neighbor Abe hollered. "Could you girls ride my

horses up home fer me? I gotta go somewhere and don't got a way of gettin' 'em home."

"Sure," Lora agreed. "We can do it."

The two purchased items at the store and stuffed them into their coat pockets.

Ida sized up the massive hunks of horse muscle with apprehension. "I've never ridden a horse."

"You can do it," Lora said. "It's not far to home, about a mile. Anyway, we could use a ride after all that walking."

One horse stood calmly while the other pranced impatiently.

"I'll take the frisky one," Lora said. "You take the other one."

"But there's no saddle. How do I get on?"

Abe offered, "I'll take the horses to the porch. Then you can hop on and go."

Lora climbed the porch and slipped onto the horse's bare back. She had ridden horseback for many years. She took the reins in her hand and clicked her tongue in a language that horses know. The horse stepped forward and Lora turned him around to wait on Ida. Ida hesitated.

"Go on," Lora encouraged.

"I never did this before." Ida slid her leg across the horse and settled into the bowed back.

"Take the reins," Lora instructed. "Hold on tight and make him go where you want him to."

Ida did. They trotted up the road, leaving hoof prints in the fresh snow. Lora rode with a song on her lips. Behind her, Ida bounced along, her bulging, grocery-filled pockets flopping.

Crisp air stung their cheeks, and their breath rose in misty vapor as they talked. Along the frosty creek, a melody of ripples dodged the clutches of solid ice ledges. Through the hollow came the shout of a neighbor and the boisterous barking of dogs as the horses plodded up the valley. The smell of wood smoke hung heavy in the air. Lora's toes and nose tingled from the cold. Soon they would be home.

Lora sighed with happiness at the whole world about her, yet nagging thoughts probed her mind. How could she leave this place again when she would be so happy to stay here always? These folks lay on her heart. She knew their heartaches and joys from living among them for ten summers. She loved their eagerness to learn the Bible lessons and their quest to pursue the Christian life. So many longed to serve God faithfully, yet new ways and uncharted paths brought unforeseen challenges. Some were faithful even though they sometimes floundered. She would happily live for years among these people and encourage them in the footprints of Jesus.

A weathered footbridge spanned the creek to a cottage just on the other side. Out on the porch a mother gathered an armload of wood to add to the fire. Lora called and waved. The neighbor waved and smiled in return. The horses clopped forward, slower now. Lora allowed her mind to drift back to her questions again. What did God have in mind for her life? When would the minister return to nurture the flock? More souls still needed to find the way.

Ida jolted her from her musing. "Look, Lora, there's a dog by the mill."

Lora saw the frisky pet. "Yes, I hope he won't spook our horses."

Ida became alarmed. "I don't want this horse to take off in a panic! Don't know if I can handle him."

"Hold the reins firmly and don't let him get away," Lora advised.

Just ahead was the mill, pretty as a picture with snow drooping from its roof and a horse and wagon stacked with sacks of flour waiting at the hitching post. Ever so gently the giant waterwheel beside the mill began to turn. The gears groaned and water began to spill from the top of the wheel. Lora's horse shook his mane and kicked up his heels.

"Here now!" Lora warned.

But the frightened horse galloped back the way they had come. Ida's horse followed. Lora pulled the reigns tight and gave her horse a loud smack on the rump. With a neigh of rebellion and a toss of his mane against Lora's fingers, the horse reluctantly shuffled a circle of prints in the snow.

Lora gave another sound whack and said, "Let's go!" The horse swished his mane and paced toward home. Cautiously, Ida's horse followed. A neighbor observed the happenings and laughed and laughed.

The steady clopping of hooves brought them to the ford. Lora's horse splashed through the water, but Ida's horse had another idea.

"Lora!" Ida yelled. "My horse wants a drink. I'm afraid I'll fall in the creek when he bends over."

"Hold the reins tight," Lora replied. "Don't let him get his head down."

"But he's slobbering," Ida wailed.

"Let him slobber!"

At last the riders arrived, the hoofprints leaving a trail where they had been.

"How do I get off?" Ida asked.

"Just lie forward, put your arms around the horse's neck, and slide off."

Ida followed her advice and landed safely on the ground.

"Lora Heatwole, don't you ever ask me to get on a horse again," Ida exclaimed. "That was just too scary!"

"It was?" Lora laughed. "You made it just fine and you even got to hug a horse."

"Lora!"

"Well, didn't you?"

Whenever Lora had a chance to tell what happened on that day, she loved to tell how Ida had hugged a horse. [3]

The sky stayed gray for a few days. A chill wind whipped around the corners of buildings and rumbled the roof of the mission house. Saturday night more snow fell, and on Sunday morning, fresh new snow covered the white-packed roads and foot-tracked pathways. Behind the barn and along the forest a gray haze hung in the shadows. Softly the snowflakes fell.

Ida added water to the canned milk. "No one will come to church today, Lora."

"Some will," Lora replied as she poured homemade grape-nuts into her bowl. "We need to be there for those that come."

The crystal flakes lingered on their hair and melted on their faces as they walked to church. Behind them a jingle of bells grew louder, and the heavy clomp of hooves drew nearer. Lora and Ida stepped aside.

3 *Ida's Path From Buggy to Jet Ski*

"Good morning." The sleigh swished past full of bundled children and parents.

Lora waved and stepped onto the new-cut tracks of the sleigh. In spite of the joy of new snow, something weighed on her heart.

"I wish the minister was here," Lora said softly.

"The people need him," Ida added. "There must be some reason he hasn't returned."

"I'm glad for your help with teaching Sunday school and for good superintendents too."

Ida kicked at a clump of snow. "I'm glad to do my share. Maybe after Christmas James and Vada will return."

Lora stomped the snow from her boots, opened the door, and hung up her wraps. The children trooped inside, shivering and chattering as they removed coats and caps.

"Do you like the snow?" Lora asked brightly as she reached out to shake hands.

"Yeah. You should see our snowman!" The girl clung to Lora's hand and tipped her head back to see Lora's face.

"I'd like to," Lora replied.

"You should come sledding with us."

"Maybe I will," Lora responded. "Do you know who makes the snow?"

"God does."

"It's mighty pretty too," Lora whispered. "Now let's find our seats."

In the haze of dawn, a horse trotted down the mountain. The rider was a woman, her shoulders slumped and her head hung low. Usually the midwife returned from her duties with the good news that a little one had joined a happy family. The midwife spotted Lora returning from the henhouse. A whistle shrilled from the rider's lips. Lora hustled over to the gate where the horse pranced in place.

"Is it good news?" Lora asked hopefully.

The midwife pressed her lips together and shook her head. "'Fraid not. We fought long and hard. Gracie didn't make it. Neither did the baby."

Lora gasped. "Really? Gracie is gone?"

The midwife nodded, her face grim.

Lora's hand flew to her mouth as reality struck her. Where was Gracie now? The girl had never come to the Lord, but always thought she would sometime.

The horse snorted and strained at the bit as the midwife looked at Lora and said, "Couldn't get the baby either. But I tried."

Lora sucked in her breath and stared at the midwife. "Oh!" she muttered. "And there's no minister for the burying."

"That doesn't stop people from dying." The midwife's words seemed harsh, but facts were facts.

"Thanks for stopping to tell us," Lora said, numbness creeping into her heart.

The midwife trotted off, her job completed. New babies usually came with lusty lungs and robust health. But once in a while things turned out differently. Friends and neighbors gathered to make a coffin, comfort the family, and say good-byes.

Lora and Ida dressed warmly for the trek up the mountainside to the graveyard. The wind snarled and tore brutally at Lora's coat. The crunch of boots in the snow mingled with the sobs and sniffs of family members who followed the men carrying the coffin up the mountain. Ida nudged Lora's elbow and pointed to the ground where drops of blood had leaked from the coffin, leaving a red trail mingled with the multiple footprints. Lora and Ida shifted to the side of the trail. Just ahead, the family approached the graveyard where a minister from another community waited to give the final words. Nothing could have changed this circumstance, even if James and Vada were here, except that James would have given the last words. Even so, Gracie was gone.

Lora swallowed the knot in her throat as the men lowered the coffin into the hole. The family grieved. Here lay a mother and child, gone forever into eternity. Lora stared as if in a daze. She had so hoped to direct Gracie and all the local girls down a different path. Did their efforts to teach Bible principles and guide the seekers make any difference at all?

The words of the minister droned in her ears, "We commit the body to the ground—earth to earth, dust to dust—and commit the spirit to God who gave it."

The sound of dirt against metal spades seemed amplified in the solemn moment. *Thud!* Raw dirt fell upon the box that held a young girl once full of life and fun. *Thud!* More dirt. Silently the group watched, unable to shake off the reality of death.

Lora's thoughts roamed. Why had Gracie refused to accept the Lord as Saviour? Was it because she thought she had plenty of time? Countless times Gracie had been invited to come to the cross. Often she had been warned of the danger of putting off the invitation, "To day if ye will hear his voice, harden not your hearts."[4]

The dirt piled faster. Lora's thoughts raced on with the warnings of Scripture. "So we see that they could not enter in because of unbelief. Let us therefore fear, lest, a promise being left us of entering into his rest, any of you should seem to come short of it. For unto us was the gospel preached, as well as unto them: but the word preached did not profit them, not being mixed with faith in them that heard it."[5]

Another familiar Scripture scrolled through her memory. "He that believeth on the Son hath everlasting life: and he that believeth not the Son shall not see life; but the wrath of God abideth on him."[6]

Oh, Gracie! Lora caught her breath. Perhaps Gracie did come to the Lord in her last moments, but that rarely happened. But Gracie had heard the Good News. She had listened to the words of hope and eternal life.

If only souls could understand the reality of rich life in Christ. Jesus said, "I am come that they might have life"—new life, abundant life, a life free from sin and con-demnation![7] "And this is life eternal, that they might know thee the only true God, and Jesus Christ, whom thou hast sent."[8] Why would anyone refuse?

Bit by bit the grave was filled. Lora squeezed her lips together. She must pray more for the unsaved. Other lives hung in the balance. Would they also wait too long? Softly, she whispered words of comfort to the family.

---

4   Hebrews 3:15
5   Hebrew 3:19—4:2
6   John 3:36
7   John 10:10
8   John 17:3

"It's over," Ida whispered, biting her lip to still its quiver, her eyes moist with tears. "Let's go home."

Silently Lora turned away from the mourners. It had begun to sleet. The bits of ice stabbed at her face. She followed the tracks back down the mountain, carefully dodging the red trail that marked the way. Questions tumbled inside her mind. She longed for changes that would better the lives of these people she loved.

"We try, but it seems we often fail to reach them," Lora groaned.

"It's God's work, Lora. He has saved some of them." Ida brightened.

A sudden glimmer of hope penetrated Lora's sorrow. "That's right." She nodded in agreement. "There's Avis, a single mother of two who married a widower; that's a faithful family."

"And what about Daisy and her husband?" Ida reminded her.

"Of course. They are faithful and even help with some responsibilities." Lora's voice had become moderate. "And Mary is a teacher of the Word, a good Sunday school teacher. Thanks, Ida, for the reminder of the faithful ones. But Gracie is gone—gone forever with never an opportunity to speak to her again."

Hoofbeats approached behind them, and Lora turned and recognized the rider.

"Lora, wait a minute," Jason Vance called.

Lora and Ida stopped and watched the horse trot up to them. Stopping with a snort, the steam puffed from his bridled mouth.

"What's up?" Lora asked.

"I wanted to tell you about Buddy."

Lora's heart sank. Could anything worse be added to the morbid story of Buddy? Buddy had been in jail for starting forest fires. Then he had been released for good behavior. One night he was found frozen in the river, a result of being drunk. The only hope had been to amputate both legs. What more could Jason add to that already sad account?

"Just had to tell you," Jason paused and grinned. "Buddy has been listening to some of us talk to him about the Lord."

"Really?" Lora's solemn face brightened.

"Uh-huh." Jason went on, "But it's more than that. Buddy has received Christ into his heart and wants to serve Him."

"What good news!" Ida exclaimed.

"Wonderful!" Lora added.

Jason continued, "You know, Buddy's life looked pretty hopeless after the amputations, but it brought him to the Lord. Says it won't stop him from walking either." Jason chuckled. "Someone is rigging up padding for his stumps for after they're healed. At least he's determined about worthwhile things."[9]

"Thanks for telling us the good news," Lora spoke with genuine interest. "We will be praying for Buddy. May the Lord bless you and those who minister to him."

"Thanks." Jason swatted the horse. "I hope the Shanks will be back the first of the year. We really need them around here."

"I know." Lora lifted her gloved hand to wave good-bye as the horse started to move. "Good-bye. Tell Mattie hello for us."

---

9 This is a true account with names changed.

Ida nodded in agreement and waved too. The two walked down the hillside to the road and turned home.

"I tell you, Lora, the time I've spent here this year has been the most rewarding experience of my life—much more than the big paycheck I would have received."

"That's how it goes when you serve God," Lora stated as she trudged homeward. "I've never been sorry to live here among these people. There have been disappointments and sorrows. But then there are the Buddys that have been rescued and brought into God's family."

Ida threw back her head and tried to catch a snowflake in her mouth. "Got one."

Lora whistled a tune. Then she glanced at Ida. "You know, it's almost time to go home—to Virginia."

Ida gazed at Lora with serious eyes. "I almost don't want to go home. There are so many spiritual needs here."

"I feel the same, but a letter says the mission board is sending someone to get us."

"How soon?"

"Friday. We have to start packing."

Ida mimicked a sob. "And say our good-byes."

Chapter Thirty-Seven

Good-bye

1935

"All packed?" Ida asked as she shoved the last drawer shut and deposited her clothing into her luggage.

Lora snapped her suitcase shut. "Yes, I'm finished."

Outside, the truck motor churned, warming up for the long journey home. Lora carried her luggage downstairs and put it by the door. She pulled on her boots and put on a heavy scarf and coat. Then she opened the stove door and pried the wood apart so the fire would die.

"I'm taking the ashes out and then checking the shop," Lora said as Ida scurried to open the door for her.

"I'm coming too. The cats can have the last of our dinner. It wouldn't do to let it grow moss while we're gone."

The glare of sun on the snow hurt her eyes. Lora squinted as she paced to the snow-covered garden to spread the ashes. The ashes lay gray and ugly on the snow. Her mind raced. Who would tend the garden next year and in the years to come? Would the Shank family return, or would someone else occupy the mission house and lead the work here?

She set the ash bucket on the porch and stepped over to the shop. She opened the door and checked inside. Yes, everything seemed okay. She locked the door and started back to the house.

Meow! Ida scraped leftovers into a bowl while the purring cats lapped up the contents.

"Poor things," Ida cooed. "You'll have to fend for yourselves while we are gone."

Lora occupied herself by checking windows and locking up the mission property. "They will be fine without us," Lora stated matter-of-factly.

Ida petted the cats. "You don't have any sympathy for them at all, now, do you?"

Lora picked up the ash bucket. "Nope. Cats fare just fine in the barn, where they belong, with a banquet of mice to keep them fed."

"Lora!" Ida scolded as she reluctantly followed Lora inside the house. "I'm glad the sweet things had a decent meal before we go."

Lora put the ash bucket into the stove and glanced over the house. The rug needed straightening. With her foot she shoved it into place and straightened a chair. The sink had been scrubbed clean and the dishpan hung on a nail on the wall.

Lora looked at Ida. "I'm ready to go."

"Me too," Ida said.

Lora ventured to the front door. She had said so many good-byes during the last days. Now she would go home and spend happy days with her family. All of her brothers and sisters and nieces and nephews would soon gather for Christmas around a table loaded with farm-grown vegetables, baked and cooked to perfection. At home she would not need to skimp on milk or ration food in quite the same way as she had for the last months. Once again she would ride to town with a carload of single women who worked at the silk mill.

She pushed her luggage toward the driver, who loaded it on the truck. Lora followed Ida outside into the cold and hesitated, reluctant to fit the key into the lock. While Ida walked through the snow to the truck, Lora gazed toward the little church up the way. A yearning stirred in her soul as memories descended—memories of twelve confessions just this past summer—some here and some in other congregations. Who would carry on the work and nurture the new Christians? What about those who had given up their Christian faith? Who would encourage them to return and find the joy of living for Jesus? And who would disciple the faithful ones?

She must hurry. It wasn't like her to waste time or keep people waiting. She turned the key in the lock, then, with a determined stride, she headed for the truck. She heard voices—children's squeals and laughter along with the slicing of metal against snow. She stopped in her tracks as a sled piled with children whizzed past, snow spraying into the air.

A familiar voice, one she had not heard for some time, called to her. "Wait, Lora!"

Tillie! She had not seen her for some time. The memory of seeing that girl for the first time flashed into her mind. Tillie was just a teen then, sweet and innocent, a mother with a toddler, married with adult responsibilities at such a young age.

Lora waved. The woman broke into a run and panted up to Lora.

"You goin' home?"

"Yes. It's Christmastime." Lora looked into the eyes that had grown slightly older. "Were those your children?" Lora asked with a smile.

Tillie pulled the muffler away from her face. "Yeah, they're full of energy."

Lora chuckled. "That's the way God made them, you know. I love children."

"I know."

"You could bring them down to the church to learn Bible stories," Lora encouraged. "It would be wonderful to have you come again."

"I know, but things have changed. It wouldn't be the same."

"God is still the same," Lora replied. "He is always faithful."

"I know." Tillie's eyes searched the ground.

Lora studied the young face. In some ways the woman had matured, yet she was still young, with the hope of many years ahead. Perhaps she felt she had plenty of time to take that needed step to assure her place in Heaven.

The rhythmic turning of the motor reminded Lora she must go. She had lingered much too long. There was so much more she wanted to say, but time had run out.

Lora grabbed the door handle. "I must go." The door swung open. She pulled herself up and slipped onto the seat.

"Bye, Lorie. Come back again!"

Lora searched Tillie's face, her own heart as weighted as if a heavy stone lodged there. If only there was more time to persuade Tillie to make the right choice. Some, like

Gracie, had entered eternity unexpectedly. Their opportunity to choose Christ was over and gone forever. She must say at least a few words, but which ones?

The gears shifted. Lora slammed the door and rolled down the window as the truck backed onto the road not far from where the woman stood. There wasn't much time. The truck was moving forward now. She leaned through the opening, the cold slicing into her face.

"You still have opportunity, you know."

She tried to smile, but it felt forced. She would rather cry than leave this woman unprepared for eternity. The words seemed so trite and incomplete, yet it was the best she could do for the moment. She watched for any response from the woman.

Tillie nodded and squeezed her lips as if in thought. Then she threw up her hand in a warm farewell and beamed a smile.

As the gears shifted and the truck picked up speed, Lora glanced back at the mission home. The unlit windows stared back, dark and foreboding. There was no sign of the life that had once teemed within it: visitors, meals, work, lesson plans, prayers, praise, and encouragement. Lora faced the road with a deep sigh.

Ida looked at her. "It's hard to leave, isn't it?"

Lora nodded. "I hope somebody will be back soon."

Ida wiggled over to make more room for Lora. "The months I spent here have been good for me, Lora. How must you feel leaving after ten summers?"

Lora sighed again. "The same way I feel every time I leave. I would like to stay, but I must go home and work to keep my job."

She didn't feel like verbalizing what she had known for the last while. Next summer she would not be returning, perhaps never. How could she bear to miss the joy of presenting precious Seed to eager children and adults? How could she abandon those students who had floundered through youth and had entered adulthood, still in need of wisdom and teaching? Certainly, ministers could preach and guide, but women missionaries filled a great need by helping women and children apply the Bible in practical ways at home.

The facts were plain. She could no longer meet her financial needs while giving her heart and life in the mountains, even with her small allowance from the mission board. The mission board had expressed appreciation for her years of selfless service, but they could no longer appoint her to the work nor expect her to subsist on hardship. They had commended her for her sacrificial gift of ten summers, which sometimes stretched beyond the season because someone was needed to fill the vacancies. She had served longer than any other missionary woman, and the Home Mission Board appreciated her efforts. In a nutshell, she had been advised to go home and work at the mill.

"I think I could come again," Ida ventured with a cheerful tone, unaware of the thoughts in Lora's mind. "I can see why you love these people and this place."

"God has been so good to me. My life has been blessed beyond measure," Lora said with sincerity.

The truck lumbered along the snow-covered, winding roads. Already, the faint flutter of nausea stirred in her stomach and the fingers of a headache stole around her head and tightened their grip.

Yes, God could send other people to do the work she loved, perhaps even younger people with energy like she had when she first came. He could provide ministers, teachers, and helpers to nurture the hearts of those who remained. Thankfully, some of the faithful already were helping with the church services and sharing their faith with family.

Oh, to be home! Miles of travel, multitudes of curves, more mountains, and more shifting of gears increased her misery. And then the truck rolled down the last curves through the woodlands, past ice-lined streams, and along the familiar road that led to home. Dusk gathered as the travelers jostled past rolling fields and farms. Lights gleamed from the cracks in weatherboarded barns and from windows of houses where women cooked to feed hungry farmers after their chores.

Lora watched the dark, familiar road lit by the two head-lights. That helped to keep the nausea somewhat subdued until she could set foot on solid ground.

The twinkle of a lone star gleamed in the evening. Other stars began to show, faintly at first, growing brighter until the night sky revealed a multitude of silver specks. The moon rose huge and white above the farms and towns of her region, high above the isolated communities hidden in the folds of the Appalachian Range, shedding beams down on the eastern seaboard, on the towns and cities and communities where many mountain people had scattered like seeds on the wind.

Those who had heard the stories and the words of God carried a priceless treasure within their hearts. Where had they gone, and what would they do with the treasure given to them? Would they allow it to die, or would it bear fruit in their lives and be passed on? The moon shone brightly on all those who had received and those who had shared this treasure and on those who had yet to hear the message.

The truck rumbled up to Lora's home where the porch light fanned onto the dark lawn. The truck rolled to a stop.

"Good-bye, pal." Lora patted Ida's knee.

"Good-bye, Lora. I won't forget our time together."

Lora climbed down from the high step and took the luggage the driver handed to her. "Thanks for the ride."

"You are welcome. Glad to do it."

Taking deep breaths helped the nausea to subside. Before long it would be gone. She waved as the truck moved on, then grabbed her suitcases and scurried up the steps and flung open the door.

"Anybody home? Is there anything to do around here?"

Epilogue

L ora had just experienced ten summers of indescribable fulfillment! Then came disappointment and change. How could Lora turn away from the people, churches, and duties that had become so much a part of her life? In spite of sacrifice, hardship, and uncertainty, God had given grace.

Harry Brunk states in *History of Mennonites in Virginia, 1900-1960*: ". . . Lora worked a large part of ten years with no remuneration except that her board was paid. Lora sacrificed more in time and money than any other person. The board realized that and at the end of the ten years, it could not ask her to go back again."

In spite of her disappointment, Lora accepted the verdict. She encouraged the younger workers who went in her place, willingly making dress patterns for Ida Eshleman, who served on the field the following year. Occasionally she visited the familiar mountain missions.

With the passing of time, lumber camps closed, further complicating the existence of folks in the mountains. Gradually the mountain communities dwindled as people left their homes and ventured beyond the isolated hollows into metropolitan areas and new communities. In their hearts, they carried with them the treasure of the Gospel. Wherever they lived, the Scriptural truths they had been taught could be passed on like seeds dropped into the soil.

Following the Shanks' absence in 1935, the Home Mission Board sought to fill the ministry vacancy. Other ministers were appointed to fill the position for a period of time. In 1941 Earl Hartzler was ordained minister, and his family lived in a new mission house built near the original one. Eventually other ministers were ordained and lived in the communities they served. New congregations sprang up in other communities in the region, creating the need for new workers. Some of Lora's relatives settled into the areas where Lora had worked and stayed permanently as pastors or participants in the church.

Although Lora never became wealthy, she worked cheerfully throughout her lifetime. She was a faithful worker, teacher, singer, seamstress, and aunt. After retirement she sewed hundreds of dresses each year for the Valley Sewing Circle. The dresses were sent to the needy around the globe.

The local Harrisonburg, Virginia, newspaper, *Daily News-Record,* printed an article about Lora and her sewing hobby on September 13, 1997. "I've been doing this for over ten years," Lora said. "I make around 300 dresses a year. I love to do it."

In the article, Lora's sisters described her frugality, skill, and ambition. They told of her carefulness in her dressmaking hobby; every piece of fabric was used without waste. "She watches her pennies," Nancy said. "But she has to . . . she has more ambition than money."

*In her later years, Lora made many dresses
for girls around the globe. This labor
of love brought her much fulfillment.*

From the scraps left over from cutting out dresses, Lora and her sisters pieced comforter tops which they gave to a West Virginia sewing circle to be made into blankets and distributed among needy families.

In addition to sewing dresses, Lora made aprons and sunbonnets to sell in local shops. She also liked to crochet tablecloths of intricate detail.

On July 10, 2007, Lora passed from this life at the age of 103. After years of faithful service, she entered into eternal rest from her labors. She is buried at the Bank Mennonite Church in Dayton, Virginia.

Author's Note

How do you begin a story you know little about or find all the puzzle pieces to complete the picture? In amazing ways, the Lord brought this story into existence.

The story search began with Lora and her sister Nancy telling facts of Lora's ten summers in West Virginia. Nancy often furnished names and phone numbers of others who knew more details. A piece here and there and the puzzle began to take shape.

In the process difficult issues surfaced, delaying my writing progress. Time and again I placed the entire work and myself on the altar, seeking divine guidance on how to handle the material. Several church leaders expressed interest in the story—particularly Lloyd Horst, Chester Heatwole, Charles Heatwole, Larry Showalter, and Kenneth Martin—some reading early versions of the book. I'm grateful for writer friends, reviewers, and interested persons who critiqued and encouraged over the years. Thanks to all of you.

As the story emerged, I stepped into Lora's ragged shoes and looked from her perspective. Poring over *Gospel*

Herald issues, old letters, and Lora's West Virginia scrapbook of pictures and comments, I sensed hard times and felt her heartaches. No matter how hard or disappointing the work, I could hear Lora singing, and see her cheerful endurance through it all. Such an example would lift any of God's workers!

It made sense to generalize many details that would have made the story monotonous, such as revival speakers, guests, and communions. The characters Tillie, Gracie, Daisy, Faye and others demonstrate people and real happenings as people remembered them. Many details are actual happenings.

I wish to recognize and thank those who helped make this book reality. My family: husband J. P. (John Paul), Annette, Shana, Sherwin, and Amber filled in responsibilities when I was scavenging for facts or recuperating from surgeries. The family encouraged me to go to Florida with my parents, Howard and Esther Good, while writing the early version. However, the majority of the writing and interviews happened right at home. My husband took extra measures to protect the manuscript after a computer crash and sometimes traveled with me to get material.

I am indebted to various people and resources for details in the story. The historical library at Eastern Mennonite University provided mission records, minutes of ministers' meetings, *Gospel Herald* reports, and other material. Thank you, James Lehman and Lois Bowman, for your assistance and patience.

Nelson and Florence Heatwole took me to visit people and places where Lora had been. (Nelson was a cousin to Lora.) Connecting with real people helped me see enthused students clasping treasured lessons and prizes. Eyes sparkled from wrinkled faces as they recalled memories. "I still have that dollar from Nellie Coffman," or "I have those lessons Lora copied by hand."

Rhoda Benner Hertzler told vivid details about the Benner family's years at Roaring Creek. Helen Mumaw Peachey permitted me to copy her mother's (Esther Moseman Mumaw) lengthy love letters. Written in July 1927, these letters gave insight into mission life and the origin of vacation Bible schools in the Mennonite church. Earl and Elva Champ answered scores of questions and told many stories with such intensity and expression that events came alive. Interviews with James Shank revealed the tremendous responsibilities mountain ministers carried during those economic hard times. James and Vada found Lora's cheerfulness, faith, and loyalty an inspiration when added demands came.

Phone calls to Kansas introduced me to Ida Eshleman Horst, bringing her personality and laughter into the account. Visits or calls to Gae Arbogast *always* produced vivid stories of mountain events and culture. Lora's hand-drawn Bible lessons were a window into Lora's creativity and her burden for the students she taught. Mabel Knicely kindly permitted the reproduction of original lessons in this book.

And Christian Light Publications has been an encouragement, assisting in multiple ways to bring this book into existence. Thank you, Leon Yoder, Caleb Crider, David Miller, Jotham Yoder, Ruth Schrock, and many of you I never saw as you brought this book into being. Thank you also to editors Brian Yoder and Diane Freed.

The Bible schools Lora and Aunt Nellie began far exceeded their expectations. Their initial goal was to reach children, but during the 1930s, evening classes accommodated the whole family. By then the minister was involved with teaching. Bible schools eventually spread into surrounding communities, becoming an important outreach in Mennonite communities to this day.

Like Lora, kingdom workers rarely see the fruit of their work, yet they labor faithfully. While researching for this book, I was privileged to see some results of the mission work. Some retained their faith even through difficulty and hardships. One person told me her grandfather became a Christian in his later years. "Jerry," the son of a moonshiner, married a Christian girl and later became a minister of the Gospel. "Buddy," the boy who lost his legs and walked on padded stumps, remained a Christian until he succumbed to infection a few years later and died. While some renounced faith, others carried the Gospel within their hearts, passing the faith on to others. Only Heaven will reveal the results of sharing the Gospel in the region where Lora worked.

Today these mountain churches are small, but still active. Some of the schools are obsolete or in disrepair. Eventually, the original mission house where Lora lived was sold and is privately owned. Though years have gone by, a minister still lives in Roaring Hollow. Roaring Creek church no longer holds weekly meetings, but a service is held periodically.

If you were to step into the small white church along Roaring Creek today, you might notice a musty smell, for floods and destruction have threatened the building. If you were to sit on a bench and recall the activity that once occurred there, you might hear the faint chatter of children on the mountain trails, and the patter of feet coming down the aisle. You might catch the sound of fervent preaching, hear the repentant sobs of sinners, or glimpse the baptism of new Christians on the front row.

Now the building is silent, only a memory of the active role it played in the mountain community long ago. Years ago, I had seen that lonely church building by Roaring Creek and I wondered about its past. I had no idea that someday I would discover the people who had entered its doors. I would travel up those rugged trails in Lora's ragged shoes and imagine meeting the people. I would sit as an invisible guest at the table and listen to conversations or hear the hum of Lora's machine as she sewed. I would agonize with her over the burdens, sorrows, lessons, coffins, and setbacks. I would rejoice with her over new Christians, friendships, answered prayer, and victories won.

Writing this book brought dimensions to my life that I didn't expect. I now know Lora better than I ever knew her when she sat on the front bench of my church when I was growing up. Her example of faithful, cheerful, sacrificial service inspires me to do the same—no matter where I am called.

Janis Good
2014

Appendix A: Recipes

Wild Huckleberry Pie

Crust:
  Flour
  Pig short'nin'
  Milk
  Salt

Roll dough and put in tin pie plates. Wash berries and put in crust. Sprinkle with a little sugar. Top with dough rolled thin or make strips and weave across the pie. Crimp the edges. Heat wood oven to hot. Put pie in and bake till done.

Wild Huckleberry Pie

Modern Translation

Crust:

- 2 cups flour
- ²/₃ cup lard or Crisco
- 3-4 T cold milk or water
- 1 tsp. salt

Measure the dry ingredients in a bowl. Mix well. Using your fingers, mix the lard into the flour until the shortening is about the size of peas. Mix in the milk and stir only until the dough forms into a ball. Divide the dough in half. Roll out and place into a pie pan.

Filling:

- 3 cups of berries
- ³/₄ cup sugar
- 3 T cornstarch, slightly rounded

Mix the cornstarch and sugar, then stir in berries. Fill the pie shell then roll out the rest of the dough and place on top the pie. Crimp the edges. Make slits over the top crust. using a knife to vent steam. Bake at 375° for 10 minutes. Reduce heat to 275° and bake for 50 minutes. Remove and cool. Serve plain or with whipped cream.

Lora's Soda Cheese

1 gallon thick sour milk*
½ tsp. baking soda
3 tbsp. margarine
1 cup rich milk
1 tsp. salt
1 egg, beaten
Several drops yellow food coloring

Heat the sour milk to 115°. Cut through milk in both directions with knife while heating to separate the curds. Drain overnight in cloth bag. Crumble when dry.

Mix in the baking soda and let stand 4 or 5 hours.

Melt the margarine in a heavy skillet and add curds. Heat on low, stirring constantly until curds are melted. Add the milk, stirring until smooth. Stir in the salt, egg, and coloring, and heat to boiling again. Remove from heat. Pour in dish to cool. Chill. Yield: approximately 1 quart of cheese.

* To obtain thick sour milk, stir 1 or 2 tbsp. of sour milk starter into it. Let stand at room temperature approximately 24 hours or more until it thickens or clabbers. In the summertime it may thicken in 14-16 hours. Store tightly covered in the refrigerator when thickened. (If you don't have starter, use purchased buttermilk or 1 cup of sweet milk with 1 tbsp. vinegar or lemon juice added.)

Appendix B:
Lora's Lessons

ANTS

Go to the ant thou slugard
consider her ways and be wise
Pro. 6:16

Busy - not idle
     Idleness - the devils workshop
       you suffer
       others suffer

Ants provide
    and so should we
       for winter
       for spiritual things
       for eternity

Thy WORD IS

a mirror	strength
a light	comfort
a guide	everlasting
a sword	inspiring
food	unchangeable
drink	satisfying

easily understood

THE LAW OF THE LORD IS PERFECT

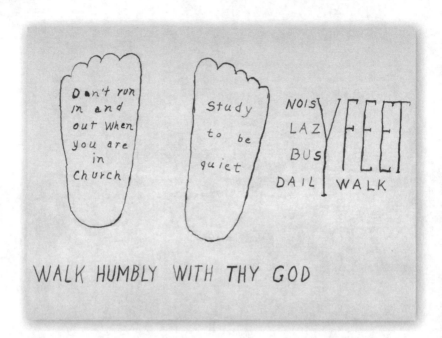

WALK HUMBLY WITH THY GOD

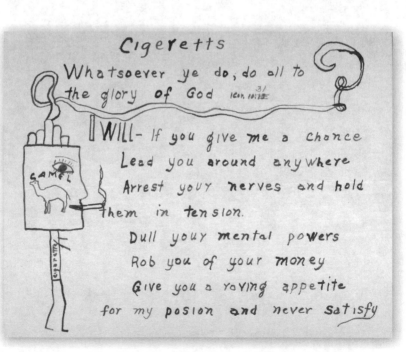

one little tongue his praise to tell,
one little voice a song to swell.

A little member
Unruley in church
Angry words
Kind words
Praising God

TONGUE

KEEP THY TONGUE FROM EVIL

MULE

A mule is quick, stuborn, tricky
and strongheaded
So is human nature
We need to be controled
Jesus is waiting to master our lives

THE WAY OF TRANSGRESSORS
IS HARD   Proverbs 13:15

Wheelborrow Churchmembers

Must be pushed

Easily upset

Can't get back up again

    Wake up

Don't ask your minister to carry your load

Help to lighten his burden

Incourage him and others.

WHAT MEANEST THOU, O SLEEPER? ARISE

SPIDER

Be not Decieved.
Col. 6:7

A spider is
    every
       where
         is cunning
is deceptive
        a traper
is a murder

And so is satan
SO BEWARE

Bibliography

BOOKS

Ambler, Charles H. and Summers, Festus, *West Virginia, The Mountain State,* 2nd Edition, West Virginia University, Prentice Hall, Inc., 1958.

Badger, Anthony J., *FDR: The First Hundred Days,* Hill and Wang, A division of Farrar, Straus, and Giroux, NY, 10011.

Brogan, Denis W., *The Era of Franklin D. Roosevelt: A Chronicle of the New Deal and Global War,* New Haven: Yale University Press, 1950.

Brunk, Harry Anthony, *History of Mennonites in Virginia, 1900-1960,* McClure Printing Company, Inc., Verona, VA, 1972. The Home Mission Board, Benners—1922-1929, Other East Side Leaders, Missionary Sisters, Summer Bible School, Roaring, Brushy Run, North Fork, Spruce Mountain.

Brunk, J. D., *Church and Sunday School Hymnal,* Mennonite Publishing House, Scottdale, PA, 1902.

Brunk, J. D. and Coffman, S. F., *Church Hymnal,* Mennonite Publishing House, Scottdale, PA, 1927.

Brunk, John D. and Coffman, S. F., *Life Songs,* Mennonite Publishing House, Scottdale, PA, 1916.

Clark, Jim, *West Virginia, The Allegheny Highlands,* Westcliffe Publishers, Englewood, CO, 1998.

Cohen, Adam, *Nothing to Fear: FDR's Inner Circle and the Hundred Days That Created Modern America,* The Penguin Press, 2009.

Fausold, Martin L., *The Presidency of Herbert C. Hoover,* University Press of Kansas, Lawrence, KS, 1985.

Femon, David, K., *The Great Depression in American History,* Enslow Publishers, Inc., Springfield, NJ, 1997.

Graebner, Fite, White, *A History of the American People, Volume II,* McGraw Hill Book Company, 1971.

Hertzler, Patricia Heatwole, *The Story of Melvin Jasper Heatwole and Mollie Grace Coffman,* 1983.

Horst, Ida Eshelman, *Ida's Path From Buggy to Jet Ski,* 2nd edition, edited by Ruby Horst Sawin, 2004.

Jeffers, H. Paul, *The Complete Idiot's Guide to the Great Depression,* Alpha Books, Indianapolis, IN, 2002.

McElvaine, Robert, *The Great Depression, America, 1929-1941,* Time Books, New York City, NY, 1984.

Naardo, David L., Book Editor, *The Great Depression,* Greenhaven Press, Inc., San Diego, California, 2000.

Reiman, Roy, *We Had Everything But Money,* Reminisce Books, Reiman Publications L.P., Greendale, WI, 1992.

Stephenson, Steven, *Upland Forests of West Virginia,* McClain Printing Co., Parson, West Virginia, 1933.

_____ *Leaders and Institutions of the Southeastern Mennonite Conference,* Southeastern Mennonite Conference, Rhine and Anna Benner, Earl and Elva Champ, Earl and Eunice Hartzler, James and Vada Shank, Brushy Run Mennonite Church, North Fork Mennonite Church, Roaring Mennonite Church.

_____ *Holding Forth the Word of Life 1919-1969,* 50th Anniversary/Virginia Mennonite Board of Missions, no copyright.

_____ *Inaugural Addresses of the Presidents of the United States: Volume 2,* Applewood Books, Carlisle, MA, 2001

ARTICLES

Carr, Minnie R., " 'Potter' John Heatwole," *Valley Mennonite Messenger,* Vol. 5, Nos. 27, 28, 29 (January 5, 12, 19, 1967).

Hoffman, Robin, editor, "Good Old Dirt Roads," *Farm and Ranch Living,* Greendale, WI 53129, 2010.

Miller, Fred, "Sewing for the Master," *Valley Mennonite Messenger,* September 9, 1965.

Prey, Hal, "Readers Recall Being 'Bogged Down' By Muddy Roads," *Reminisce,* March/April 1993, pp. 31-33, Reiman Publications, Greendale, WI 53129.

Puckett, Bettina, "So Much Sewing," *Daily News-Record,* September 13, 1997.

These *Gospel Herald* and *The Youth's Christian Companion* articles are given in order of date published.

"Fifty Years of Missionary Effort in the Two Virginias," L. J. Heatwole, *The Youth's Christian Companion,* Scottdale, PA, June 1, 1924 and June 8, 1924.

"A Missionary Trip to the Mountains of Virginia and West Virginia," A. D. Wenger, *The Youth's Christian Companion,* June 15, 1924, and June 22, 1924.

"Notes and Incidents of a Trip to West Virginia," L. J. Heatwole, *The Youth's Christian Companion,* July 6, 1924 and July 13, 1924.

"Report of Rural and City Mission Activities of the Mennonite Church: Rural Mission Opportunities of the Mennonite Church," S. C. Yoder, Secretary, Mennonite Board of Missions and Charities, *Gospel Herald Mission Supplement,* August 1925.

"Evangelism Among the Mountaineers of the Allegheny Highlands," C. Z. Yoder, *Gospel Herald Mission Supplement,* August 1925.

"Opportunities for Service Among Our Mountain People," Lelia Heatwole, *Gospel Herald Mission Supplement,* August 1925.

"Cheerful People," author unknown, *Gospel Herald,* June 17, 1926.

"Report of Rural and City Mission Activities of the Mennonite Church: Rural Work as the Approach to the South for the Mennonite Church," Selina G. Jennings, *Gospel Herald Mission Supplement,* July 1926.

"How Can the Sunday School Stimulate Interest in Mission Work?" Blanche Warner, *Gospel Herald,* July 15, 1926.

"Women's Part in Missionary Work," Lina Z. Ressler, *Gospel Herald Mission Supplement,* December 2, 1926.

"Sisters' Activities in Foreign Fields," Florence B. Lauver, *Gospel Herald,* January 6, 1927.

Gospel Herald written reports for Roaring:

Written January 7, 1927 by Benner; published January 20, 1927, p. 901

Written February 28, 1927 by Benner; published March 10, 1927, p. 1060

Written September 2, 1927 by Nellie Coffman; published September 15, 1927, p. 532

Written January 16, 1928 by Benner; published January 26, 1928, p. 932

Written January 21, 1928 by Benner; published January 31, 1929, p. 916

Written July 20, 1928 by Nellie Coffman; published August 2, 1928, p. 396

Written May 26, 1930 by Lora Heatwole; published June 5, 1930, pp. 220-221

Written August 22, 1930 by Nellie Coffman; published September 4, 1930, p. 507

Written November 18, 1930 by Paul Good; published November 27, 1930, p. 740

Written May 18, 1932 by Paul Good; published May 26, 1932, pp. 164-165

Written December 5, 1932 by Nellie Coffman; published December 15, 1932, p. 788

Written September 6, 1933 by Lelia Swope; published September 21, 1933, p. 532

Written April 10, 1934 by Lora Heatwole; published April 19, 1934, p. 52

Written July 24, 1934 by Lora Heatwole; published August 9, 1934, p. 408

Written January 29, 1935 by Lora Heatwole; published February 7, 1935, p. 974-975

Written August 20, 1935 by Lora Heatwole; published August 29, 1935, p. 468

HISTORICAL RESOURCES

Virginia Mennonite Conference Assembly Minutes, Virginia Mennonite Conference Archives, Harrisonburg, Virginia

Virginia Mennonite Board of Missions, Virginia Mennonite Conference Archives, Harrisonburg, Virginia

Middle District Minutes, Home Mission Board, Virginia Mennonite Conference Archives, Harrisonburg, Virginia. Collection I-K-1, Boxes 1 & 2

Gospel Herald, Menno Simons Historical Library, Harrisonburg, Virginia

Roaring Sunday school attendance records, Fred Miller

Brushy Run Sunday school attendance records, Fred Miller

Harry Brunk Collection, Virginia Mennonite Conference Archives, Harrisonburg, Virginia

Middle District Ministerial Meetings Minutes, Virginia Mennonite Conference Archives, Harrisonburg, Virginia, Collection I-K-1, Boxes 3 & 4

Lora's picture books and memory book from EMS Bible School

Lora Heatwole's original Bible lessons

Lora Heatwole's scrapbook: "Lora's Life in West Virginia"

Mary Huber's West Virginia scrapbook

Rhoda Benner Hertzler's picture books

Lora Heatwole's speech: "The Mountain Work and People," (thought to have been given in 1936). This document is found in the Harry Brunk Collection, Box 1, File 12, Virginia Mennonite Conference Archives, Harrisonburg, Virginia.

Aunt Nellie: December 23, 1896-October 26, 1986 (a compilation of Nellie's original written articles and stories, some pictures, and her commencement program of 1925), printed by Linda Swartz, Grottoes, VA.

Grave Register II, Pendleton County, West Virginia, 1977

Pendleton County Historic Society: family records, pictures, and information

Hanlon, Howard A. *The Ball-Hooter, From the Forests They Felled—Cities Grew,* Prospect Books, Prospect, N.Y., 1960, Appalachian Collection, Appalachian State University Library, Boone, North Carolina.

OTHER RESOURCES

Wonderful West Virginia magazines—assorted articles and pictures

Assorted pictures from books, magazines, and clippings of the 1920's and 1930's

INTERVIEWS

Lora Heatwole

Rhoda Benner Hertzler

Nancy Heatwole

Ida Eshelman Horst

Earl and Elva Champ

Virgie Torkleson

Gae Arbogast

James T. Shank

Thelma Brunk

Eunice Hartzler

Lois Risser

Emory Good

Nelson and Florence Heatwole

Ralph Swope

Lelia Swope Hertzler

Josie Trumbo

Fae Rawlings

Hansel Ketterman

Janet Vance

LETTERS

Esther Moseman letters to fiancé John R. Mumaw: July 4, 1927, July 8, 1927, July 12, 1927, July 15, 1927, July 18, 1927 (she wrote 1926 but it had to be 1927 because she writes about the death of Russell that they heard about that evening), courtesy of Helen Mumaw Peachey and her husband Laban Peachey.

Esther Moseman letter to friend Russel Mumaw, July 14, 1927, courtesy of Helen Mumaw Peachey and her husband Laban Peachey.

Nellie Coffman letter to Mrs. Glenn Shank, August 15, 1926.

ENCYCLOPEDIAS

America, International Edition, Scholastic Library Publishing, Inc. Danbury, Connecticut: lumber.

Encyclopedia of American Forests and Conservation History, Volume II, Davis, Richard, C., Macmillan Publishing Company, New York, 1983: West Virginia forests, Civilian Conservation Corps, Conservation under New Deal, National Industrial Recovery Act.

The New Encyclopedia Britannica, Chicago, 2003: Great Depression, New Deal, Civilian Conservation Corps (CCC)

World Book, Chicago, IL, 2008: United States History, U.S. in the Great Depression, The Roaring Twenties.

Photo Credits

Lora Heatwole: frontispiece, pp. 38, 86, 89, 113, 140, 141, 207, 214, 261

Mary Huber's West Virginia scrapbook: pp. 4, 6, 16, 24, 25, 53, 85, 230, 254, 255, 256, 295, 296, 298, 302, 303, 317

Mr. and Mrs. Laban Peachy (Helen Mumaw): pp. 27, 100, 109, 145

Mr. and Mrs. Stanley Champ: p. 293

Janet Vance: p. 26

Eldwin Showalter: p. 31

Ruby Sawin: p. 314

Nancy Heatwole: p. 375

Christian Light Publications is a nonprofit, conservative Mennonite publishing company providing Christ-centered, Biblical literature including books, Gospel tracts, Sunday school materials, summer Bible school materials, and a full curriculum for Christian day schools and homeschools. Though produced primarily in English, some books, tracts, and school materials are also available in Spanish.

For more information about the ministry of CLP or its publications, or for spiritual help, please contact us at:

Christian Light Publications
P.O. Box 1212
Harrisonburg, VA 22803-1212

Telephone – 540-434-0768
Fax – 540-433-8896
E-mail – info@clp.org
www.clp.org